BEYOND
the
DEAL

BEYOND

—— *the* ——

DEAL

{ Mergers & Acquisitions
that Achieve Breakthrough
Performance Gains }

HUBERT SAINT-ONGE
JAY CHATZKEL

New York   Chicago   San Francisco   Lisbon   London   Madrid   Mexico City
Milan   New Delhi   San Juan   Seoul   Singapore   Sydney   Toronto

1 2 3 4 5 6 7 8 9 0   DOC/DOC   0 1 0 9 8

ISBN: 978-0-07-155010-9
MHID: 0-07-155010-0

This publication is designed to provide accurate and authoritative information in regard to the subject matter covered. It is sold with the understanding that the publisher is not engaged in rendering legal, accounting, or other professional service. If legal advice or other expert assistance is required, the services of a competent professional person should be sought.

> —*From a declaration of principles jointly adopted by a committee of the American Bar Association and a committee of publishers*

McGraw-Hill books are available at special quantity discounts to use as premiums and sales promotions, or for use in corporate training programs. To contact a representative, please visit the Contact Us pages at www.mhprofessional.com.

Contents

Acknowledgments

We are indebted to the executives who participated in our research. They spent extensive time with us sharing their approaches and insights from their mergers and acquisitions. They were more than generous in giving us a remarkable window into their acquisition and integration efforts. Our conversations were marked by exceptional candor, which allowed us to delve in great detail into their experiences and lessons learned. Our contributors fleshed out the stories of what happened in their large-scale acquisitions. These are some of the most accomplished people in their fields. The richness of their perceptions gave invaluable input into the writing of this book. Each contributed a major piece of the picture of how organizations take on the challenge of a major acquisition and make it into a positive outcome for an organization. We wish to thank:

- Melinda Bickerstaff, formerly vice president and chief knowledge officer, the Bristol-Myers Squibb Company
- Ron Bowbridge, formerly director of project management office for mergers and acquisitions for Alcatel, currently vice president for research and development for Copiprak

- Randy Croyle, director of the Dow Chemical's Mergers and Acquisitions Expertise Center
- Kent Greenes, formerly chief knowledge officer of Science Applications International Corporation (SAIC) and currently president of Greenes Consulting, and his colleagues Kevin E. (Ed) Murphy, senior vice president, director of mergers & acquisitions at SAIC, and Kevin Werner, formerly senior vice president of strategic initiatives at SAIC
- Anthony E. Kuhel, formerly core member of BP's Group Knowledge Management Team, program manager for The Olympus Initiative (the US KM Initiative), and BP's chief process engineer and currently managing director with Escalys
- Dirk Ramhorst, vice president, Siemens Business Services

Writing a book that covers new ground took considerably longer and was a far more involved project than we expected. We wish to thank our spouses for putting up with the considerable time devoted to hashing out the issues, writing, and editing this book. We cannot overstate the ongoing support, patience, and tolerance of our spouses, Barbara Chatzkel and Norma Weiner, for this project, which can only be called an act of love.

We extend our appreciation to Shannon Malolepzy, Hubert Saint-Onge's administrator, who helped us in a multitude of ways, including making sure that we set aside the time to meet despite hectic schedules.

We have to express our sincere gratitude to Ruth Mills, who worked extensively with us to make this book a rich, usable resource, written with clarity and precision. Finally, we would like to give special credit to Leah Spiro, our editor at McGraw-Hill, for seeing the promise and value of this book, for providing insights and support, and for working tirelessly with us to bring *Beyond the Deal* to final form.

Hubert Saint-Onge
Waterloo, Ontario, Canada

Jay Chatzkel
New River, Arizona

Introduction:
Beyond the Mirage

Beyond the Deal offers a strategic approach to leveraging mergers and acquisitions to achieve extraordinary performance and create unprecedented value. The stakes in major acquisitions are high, both for the acquirers and for the targeted acquirees. The companies that are going to acquire other companies successfully are those that have cultivated the best capabilities for effecting the right acquisition and that can best integrate the new company. This may sound quite simple, but achieving quantum leap outcomes from an acquisition requires a disciplined, comprehensive, and highly proactive effort.

Because of changing economic conditions, record numbers of companies are becoming involved in sizable strategic acquisitions. However, mergers and acquisitions are often not structured in a way that will create greater value from these potentially high-risk undertakings.

Although making a good "deal" and achieving extensive expense savings are very important, they can also be a mirage. Both may be necessary for mergers and acquisitions (M&As) success, but they are only the start of that successful journey, not the end point. In fact, many acquisitions *lose* value, typically for any or all of the following reasons:

- Inadequate readiness to undertake an acquisition
- A poorly thought-out approach to acquiring another company
- A lack of ability to integrate the newly acquired company effectively

Companies and managers who target the "deal" and focus on eliminating expenses often give short shrift to the issues involved in integrating another company and to how the newly combined company functions *after* the integration gets under way. Yet the data show that most acquisitions either succeed or fail during the critical integration phases.

That's why we wrote this book.

Beyond the Deal focuses on significant (i.e., large-scale) acquisitions that require major realignments both inside and outside a company. It takes into account the intangible assets, as well as all the tangible assets, of both companies involved in order to make an acquisition an opportunity for true transformation. The intangible assets are what enable breakthrough leaps in performance and strategic outcomes. We explore the role of capabilities in every interrelated phase of the predeal acquisition process, and we strongly emphasize the critical integration phases. We look at what is needed to engage in a quantum leap process and the things that block most companies from making that leap effectively. We illustrate how *your* company can make major gains by using the real-life experiences of people who played key roles in *their* company's acquisitions and in integrating the acquiree into a stronger company.

This book emphasizes larger acquisitions, those that are 15 percent or more of the acquirer's value. We deliberately focused on larger acquisitions because they have far greater requirements and ramifications. Because of their size and complexity, they demand that companies rethink their strategic intent, recalibrate the products and/or services they offer to their customers, and reevaluate their relationships (with customers, suppliers, and other stakeholders) to make this decision:

Will we seize the opportunity to stage a quantum leap transformation into a new entity? Or will we simply mutate into a larger version of what we already were?

In particular, this book focuses on preparing for the integration phase of these larger acquisitions and implementing the integration effectively. These are the least extensively examined and yet the most crucial phases of a successful acquisition. Much has been written about "the art of the deal," but far less about what is necessary to make that deal pay off for all key stakeholders.

Although our focus is on larger acquisitions, many of the principles and practices discussed are highly applicable to more limited and smaller acquisition pursuits. Smaller acquisitions are primarily add-ons; they are simpler and usually can take place without major changes in the nature of the acquiring organization. Although smaller acquisitions may be significant over time, they do not offer the full set of challenges or possibilities, either in the acquisition process or in the integration process, that larger acquisitions do. A company can, however, use the lessons from its smaller acquisitions to develop a quantum leap perspective that will enable it to stay ahead of its competition and carve out new markets. For example, Cisco had a very successful strategy of making a series of smaller acquisitions that worked very well for it for over a decade. The quantum leap challenge came when Cisco made major acquisitions and found that the requirements and capabilities were on a considerably different scale. Acting as if larger-scale acquisitions such as Dow Chemical's acquisition of Union Carbide or Daimler-Benz's acquisition of Chrysler have the same dynamics and requirements as smaller acquisitions is a costly mistake.

A breakthrough approach first requires establishing acquisition "readiness" by developing a core set of capabilities. When capabilities readiness is applied to opportunities, the result is exceptional returns. Second, our methodology focuses on *creating value* in the newly combined company. It links the two traditional approaches to M&As—cutting costs (the expense synergy approach) and increasing capabilities (the growth synergy approach)—in order to raise the performance of the newly combined company to new levels and separate it from the rest of its field of competitors. The outcome of a successful integration is the emergence of a new, transformed company. Hubert Saint-Onge draws extensively from his experience as senior vice president at Clarica (one of the largest Canadian life insurance companies), where he was directly involved in its acquisitions and integrations, and subsequently in the integration of Clarica into Sun Life of Canada after the acquisition took place.

Who Can Use This Book

This book is for everyone who is in the crosshairs of an acquisition and its integration, either as an acquirer or as an acquiree. This includes senior executives, middle managers, and practitioners responsible for integration, as well as members of acquisition teams who

- Are currently engaged in an acquisition.
- Are considering an acquisition.
- Are at the integration stage of an acquisition.
- May be an acquisition target.

The ability to conceive, plan, and carry out strategic acquisitions needs to be part of the repertoire of business leaders. If you want to achieve quantum gains in your company's performance, you need to cultivate a set of skills, values, perspectives, and relationships that together will enhance the value of both the acquiring and the acquired companies. Here's what each level of management needs to do:

- *Senior leaders.* You need to appreciate how the value proposition of your business must keep changing as a result of market shifts, and you must formulate your business logic for combining the capabilities of two companies. Will your company be better able to achieve your growth objectives organically, or do market conditions require you to grow by acquiring another company? The siren attraction of "trophy acquisitions" may be enormously appealing to you, but such targets should have a strategic fit with your company, and you should be able to integrate them effectively without losing momentum in your marketplace. With the enormous growth in the value of intangible assets (which we'll describe in Chapter 2), you need to reconsider the old yardsticks that focus solely on the final *financial outcomes* of an acquisition, and you need to take into account the increasingly important impact of *intangible assets* as precursors to your company's sustainable performance. Senior leaders must make high-quality decisions quickly, in order to maintain both momentum and a positive climate during the integration. The framework and principles we outline will provide you with useful reference points for making these decisions.

If you're a senior leader in the target company, you also have a key role in the success of an acquisition. Once you've carried out your duties to optimize value for your company's shareholders, you must decide whether you can focus your effort on giving shape to the newly combined company with an equal level of commitment. Most often, you can make an invaluable contribution to the success of the integration.

- *Midlevel managers.* You carry on your shoulders the day-to-day responsibilities for making the new organization work. You will participate in the due diligence investigations to gather, distill, and analyze the data that will determine whether or not to proceed further, and to validate whether the combined companies will be able to realize the anticipated expense and capability synergies.

  Then, whether you are part of the acquiring company or the acquiree, you are likely to be on integration teams to facilitate the integration of the two companies. Eventually, you will become the backbone of the emerging company and will be intimately involved in achieving your new company's high levels of performance.

Both senior and midlevel leaders need to communicate clearly, both internally to employees and externally to shareholders, investors, regulators, and the community at large, about the plans for integrating the two companies. Everyone will have some degree of uncertainty about the future when the news of an acquisition becomes public. Some people will have their lives disrupted by reorganization and relocations, and some will lose their jobs. Short- and long-term communications initiatives provide information on the change, the beginning of the new operating model for those who will be remaining with the new company, and, where necessary, exit plans for those who will be discharged.

Individuals who are prepared for the tumult and the challenges involved will be in the best position to navigate these rough waters. The framework established in this book will enable these different players to deal with the challenging tasks they will face and equip them to be proactive actors who can make quantum leap gains.

How This Book Is Organized

Beyond the Deal is organized into two parts:

1. *Part I* focuses on what happens *before* you make a deal to acquire or merge with another company. This is the predeal phase. Chapters 1 through 4 cover the critical issues you need to attend to during this time period:

   • *Chapter 1* presents a new approach to acquisitions, one that goes beyond the traditional approaches of either cutting costs or increasing company capabilities, and instead truly *creates value* in the newly combined company. Chapter 1 then describes how to determine whether your company is ready to acquire another company and how you can prepare to acquire another company that will catapult your company to breakthrough, quantum leap performance. To illustrate these points, the chapter includes a number of case studies: Hewlett-Packard's acquisition of Compaq Computer, Dow Chemical's approach to acquisitions, as well as examples from Clarica, Boeing, and Siemens.

   • *Chapter 2* provides deep background for the ideas in the book. (We think this background information is critical to understanding the rest of the book, but if you're in a hurry to "cut to the chase," you may want to skip to Chapter 3.

Still, if you skip this chapter now, you may find that you want to come back to it later.) Chapter 2 begins by describing why M&As are more important now than ever before—and one of the reasons is that companies are no longer measured solely in terms of their *tangible* assets, but also by the growth of their *intangible* assets. The chapter then describes three types of intangible assets—human capital, structural capital, and customer capital—that are key to implementing the value-creating approach to acquisitions that is described in Chapter 1. Finally, the chapter clarifies the difference between a company's *stock* (or inventory) of knowledge and its *flow* of knowledge—and how both relate to a successful acquisition.

- *Chapter 3* focuses on what your company needs to do *before* you should even *think* about acquiring another company: set your overall strategy and determine what you want to achieve, as well as recognize and compensate for risk factors. Once you know that, you can consider how acquiring another company—and what type of company or even what specific company—will help you achieve those goals. Chapter 3 identifies and develops ways to respond to *risk management* issues. It also describes four different acquisition strategy scenarios and four different ways to combine companies. To illustrate these points, this chapter includes examples from a broad variety of companies and industries, including Dow Chemical, a U.K. equipment company, a midsized pump company, Symantec (software), SAIC (technology consulting), Siemens, Elan (pharmaceuticals), and Clarica (insurance).

- *Chapter 4* reviews the first four steps involved in acquiring another company:

  1. Targeting a company (or companies)
  2. Doing due diligence to ensure that you're making the right decision and that the targeted company is worth acquiring and will be a good fit

3. Negotiating the deal
4. Getting approval for the deal

To illustrate these points, this chapter includes examples from General Electric's attempt to acquire Honeywell, Washington Mutual bank, Cisco, Dow Chemical, SAIC, and Clarica. That might seem like a lot of information to cover in one chapter, but the focus of this book is not on these four steps, so this chapter is intended to be only a brief review. Unfortunately, too many companies think that these four steps are all that they need to do, but we've seen too many M&As fail, and we know better: the real work of making an acquisition successful is in the *integration*— which is why we've titled our book *Beyond the Deal*. What comes *after* you've acquired another company is what will determine whether you can achieve a quantum leap in performance. So let's move on to Part II of the book.

2. *Part II* focuses on what you need to do *after* you make the deal, to ensure that your acquisition goes smoothly. This is the postdeal integration phase, and *Beyond the Deal* focuses on effective integration planning and integration; everything that goes before is a prelude to carrying out a successful integration.

- *Chapter 5* addresses the first challenge to successfully integrating a newly acquired company: *planning* how you will integrate the new company into your existing company. A successful plan outlines how you will handle the following activities:
  1. Developing an *integration playbook*, which serves as a comprehensive guidebook for integration planning
  2. Exploring your newly combined company's *new markets* and *new customer requirements*
  3. Auditing all the *capabilities* of your newly combined company

4. Determining the *governance* of your new company in terms of leadership, values, behaviors, and overall identity

5. Deciding how you will handle all the *people issues* involved in an acquisition

This chapter has examples from Pfizer, Cisco, Bristol-Myers Squibb, Clarica, and Alcatel.

- *Chapter 6* examines the development of an integration framework that ensures the continuity of the core businesses of the new company and supports the extensive reorganizations and continuing change that will produce a quantum leap company. This involves

   1. Creating the *operating structure* of your new company
   2. Developing an *accountability structure* that ensures employees' accountability for the goals that are set for the acquisition
   3. Establishing *metrics* to gauge how the company is performing and maintaining continuity of operations
   4. Making sure that the integration planning makes it a priority that the *continuity* of the company's core business is maintained during the integration, providing seamless service to customers

   To illustrate these points, this chapter includes examples from Sun Life-Clarica and Dow Chemical.

- *Chapter 7* describes six springboards that jump-start your integration to achieve quantum leap performance. These six springboards are

   1. Customer strategy and branding
   2. Company strategy
   3. Culture and leadership principles
   4. Knowledge inventory and business logic
   5. People strategy (especially for recruiting)
   6. Information technology and systems

If you don't align these six key areas, your acquisition won't really succeed. To illustrate these points, this chapter includes examples from HP, Best Buy, NationsBank, Norwest, Clarica, Newell Rubbermaid, Dow Chemical, and BP's acquisition of Amoco.

- *Chapter* 8 examines the set of critical success factors that, when taken together, form a guidance system for the integration—specifically:

  1. Focus on the primacy of your *customers.*
  2. Create a strong—but flexible—*business plan.*
  3. Keep in mind that *speed* is critical to successfully combining two companies.
  4. *Partner* with the company you're acquiring.
  5. Establish clear *accountabilities* for every task involved in the integration.

  This chapter then describes the four critical actions that your company needs to take:

  1. Set time, cost, and performance targets.
  2. Select the leaders who will run the new company.
  3. Manage people.
  4. Manage change.

  To illustrate these points, this chapter includes examples from Sprint Nextel, Dow Chemical, Siemens, Sun Life-Clarica, and BP.

- *Chapter* 9 explores how the leadership and transition teams for the postdeal integration implementation take over from the predeal acquisition team to make the transition from the two existing businesses to one ultimate business. This involves how to

  1. Cull, transfer, and combine capabilities from the acquired company to create the new company.

2. Allocate the necessary resources of time, people, and finances.

3. Make the integration plan broadly available to everyone involved in implementing the integration.

4. Carry out a comprehensive communications strategy.

5. Engage the leadership steering committee in ongoing strategy decisions.

6. Maintain the flow of knowledge and information to keep all parties to the integration in synchrony.

The chapter illustrates these points with an example from Sun Life Financial-Clarica.

- *Chapter 10* describes the engines of breakthrough that you need to employ to mobilize your new company to achieve unprecedented levels of performance and value creation:

  1. Focus on renewal strategies that leverage the core capabilities of the two legacy companies.

  2. Enlist employees' commitment by creating a vision and engaging them in realizing that vision.

  3. Create a cohesive culture in which people are driven to collaborate in order to succeed.

  Examples from Bristol-Myers Squibb, Sprint Nextel, and Clarica show the benefits of using these engines to produce remarkable outcomes as well as the costs incurred by an acquisition when these engines are not brought into play.

- Finally, the *Epilogue* shows how the number of major acquisitions will continue to grow. The companies initiating those acquisitions will be coming not only from North America and Europe, but increasingly from Asia and the oil-producing countries as well. What the successful acquirers among these companies will have in common is that they will implement the integrated capabilities perspective we put forward in this book. These companies will focus on building the dual priorities of your company's acquisition readiness and its need to have the ability to create remarkable value and unprecedented high performance. By subscribing to the principles and practices outlined here, these companies will become quantum leap companies that make their own future.

Special Features in the Book

Throughout this book, we've shaded all the examples so that you can easily find them and learn from what other companies have done during acquisitions. In addition, we've included questions for you to consider at each stage of your acquisition to help you move it forward smoothly. Finally, each chapter concludes with a list of "success factors" and "derailing factors" for each stage of the acquisition, and another set of questions to help you think through the critical issues you're likely to encounter during each phase. These questions are derived from a questionnaire used in our case study research on acquisition readiness and effectiveness; use them as a checklist to see how well your company has taken key issues into account.

In addition, *Beyond the Deal* includes three appendixes:

- Appendix A provides a brief recap of three other ways (in addition to M&As) in which a company can partner with other companies: it describes licensing arrangements, strategic alliances and partnerships, and joint ventures.
- Appendix B is a recap of all the end-of-chapter questions. Feel free to copy this checklist and use it for all acquisitions you're considering or embarking on. You can also use it as a starting point for conversation on what is necessary to prepare your company for quantum leap performance through acquisitions.
- Finally, Appendix C is an exercise for auditing your company's strategic capabilities.

The Journey

This book is the culmination of a continuing reexamination of direct experience, research, and theory. New tools were developed, particularly the questionnaire that was used in company research to cull the essentials of the acquisition experience. The work that companies do to enhance the way they acquire and integrate companies has largely remained hidden. Most companies that make an acquisition soon discover that more traditional approaches did not adequately reveal, capture, or leverage the value embedded in the company they acquired. As companies start carrying out a large integration project, many discover that their processes are inadequate. This is what we set out to do in this book: to provide more effective approaches and custodial frameworks.

At the same time, very few companies have mastered all the dimensions of the acquisition process. Several are very skilled, and there is much that can be learned from them. Yet these experiences and sets of practices came out of particular companies with very specific conditions. The general principles can be identified, but it is up to the leadership and practitioners of each individual company to take these frameworks and lessons, try them out, and make whatever changes are necessary to have them work better. Quantum gains in both value and performance through acquisitions are very possible. With the perspectives developed in this book, there is no need to leave value on the table. At the same time, the most significant gain is to cultivate the capability for mapping and carrying out effective acquisitions as part of a continuing strategy for enhancing performance and creating the future company. That will be your ultimate competitive advantage!

BEYOND
the
DEAL

PART I

THE PREDEAL PHASE

A New Approach to Acquisitions: Creating Value in Combined Companies

How many dollars, euros, and yen are left on the table when approximately two out of three of current acquisitions do not reach their goals?[1] This is an enormous and often preventable waste. The reality is that the collective common wisdom on mergers and acquisitions (M&As) is not on the mark, especially in the knowledge era we are operating in. The question is: *what can be done differently?*

The high failure rate of mergers and acquisitions is the result of serious limitations in how companies approach M&As and carry them out. In too many cases, a company is unprepared when an acquisition opportunity arises. Not being ready leads to all of the following problems:

- A limited skill base to execute the acquisition
- A one-sided focus on financial synergies that underpins a limited view of the strategic gains from an acquisition
- Poor due diligence
- A weaker position in negotiating the deal

- Unrealistic expectations about getting regulatory approval
- A slow and ineffective integration of the acquirer and the acquiree into a newly combined company

This creates a situation of unwarranted high risks and low success rates.

For many companies, acquisitions are unique opportunities to make a *quantum leap* in performance. However, that quantum leap requires

- Building the capabilities to be ready for making an acquisition
- An approach that *creates value* and fully realizes both the financial *and* growth advantages that can occur when the resources of two companies are integrated to form an entirely new company

There is some evidence that the more frequently a company acquires other companies, the greater its success. Although this is true, companies that go through the acquisition process *mechanistically* are not necessarily incorporating the lessons they learned during earlier acquisitions, nor are they using their experience to transform their processes as they integrate. Instead, they are simply *repeating* the same process over and over, without taking their acquisitions to the next level and seeking the quantum leap gains that may well be possible.

For example, one North American bank carries out five acquisitions a year, each in very much the same manner, and it is efficient at getting the job done. The problem is that the bank is primarily having the same experience five times in the course of each year, instead of incorporating *new knowledge* and taking its acquisition process to *new levels*. The bank's leaders are seeking sequential growth, but they would have the opportunity to achieve an exponential quantum leap in performance if they used the *value-creating* approach that we describe in this book and introduce in this chapter.

This chapter describes how to determine whether or not your company is ready to acquire another company (or be acquired) and then shows how to get ready to acquire another company. It also reviews the two traditional approaches to M&As—one that focuses on cutting costs and one that focuses on growth—and then offers a third approach that fuses the two traditional approaches into one overall approach that focuses on creating value in the newly combined company. Finally, it describes what you need to do to acquire a company that will truly catapult you forward in your marketplace.

Why M&As Are More Important than Ever: The Increased Value of Knowledge and Intangible Assets

Merging with or acquiring another company is more important than ever because of several dramatic changes in the current business environment. First, the emergence of the knowledge era since the 1980s has brought significant change in both global and local markets. Second, the value of knowledge-based, intangible resources has grown geometrically in companies. These intangible assets include

- The experience and talents of your employees (human capital)
- Your relationships with your customers (customer capital)
- The specific structure of your company, including your processes, systems, and leadership approach, along with such intangible assets as patents, trademarks, brand value, business model, and business logic (structural capital)

These weightless assets now have a greater value in organizations than physical or financial assets have. This has been coupled with fundamental changes in legal, competitive, and global requirements.

For example, one such quantum shift is the advent of the European Union (EU), with its dismantling of boundaries and reduction of trade barriers. The emergence of the EU has also led to a shift in the regulatory environment in Europe, creating pressures to combine organizational strengths simply to be able to compete on a larger scale.

Another quantum shift in the importance of intangible assets is demonstrated by the rise of Chinese and Indian competitors in areas ranging from software outsourcing to manufacturing consumer and capital goods. Corporations now must have a "China strategy" and must also be ready to acquire emerging companies in India in order to maintain and grow their strategic position in world markets. Moreover, Indian and Chinese companies are not exempt from the effects of globalization. They are beginning to realize that they also need to consider actively acquiring companies in other parts of the world in order to have a more formidable competitive presence in the Americas, Europe, and the Middle East.

Knowledge, as a core organizational resource and the basis for the development of organizational capabilities, is playing a key role in driving these changes. Companies' knowledge-related capabilities are far more significant than they were even just a decade ago. Prior to the last several decades, leadership in organizations cared much more about tangible assets and attributed much less of the organization's value to intangible assets. There was substantially less concern about preserving knowledge or limiting knowledge leakage. The result was a marginal valuing of corporate knowledge and very limited efforts at building knowledge-based capabilities.

Case Example: The Acquisition Frenzy in India

Many large U.S.-based companies are acquiring many middle-level information technology (IT) outsourcing companies in India. For example, IBM moved into this market by acquiring several information technology companies to become a very significant player in outsourced technology in India—in fact, because of these acquisitions, IBM is now a dominant force in that market.

For defensive and offensive reasons, many other major Indian providers of information technology outsourcing services (such as Infosys, founded in 1981, based in Bangalore, India, with offices in 30 countries and $3 billion in annual revenue from IT services and consulting; and Wipro, also based in Bangalore, with offices in 40 countries and $500 million in annual revenue from R&D) have also become active in the acquisition arena, something that they would not have anticipated several years earlier. The market has now matured to the point where growth by acquisition has become a key factor in companies' ability to compete for clients, not only in India, but anywhere in the world. Therefore, a company's need to upgrade its ability to compete often makes the most compelling case for acquisitions.

Currently, however, organizations are beginning to give more attention to their intangible assets—i.e., as listed earlier, their employees' experience and talents; the quality of their company's relationships with its customers; and their internal processes, systems, and leadership context (which will be discussed in more detail in Chapter 2). Companies are finally viewing these intangible assets as the catalysts for creating value and building competitive advantage. Furthermore, many firms are bringing their intangible and tangible resources together to generate and renew their corporate capabilities, enabling higher levels of performance. These capabilities are the link between a company's strategies and its performance.

Organizations can be seen as an amalgam of capabilities that they harness to achieve their strategies. In that perspective, a key challenge for companies is to shape the capabilities they need to meet their growth goals. Your company has two basic choices to achieve this:

1. You can grow organically.
2. You can acquire other companies to obtain the capabilities you need to achieve your growth objectives.

Of course, many companies choose a mix of these two options. To build the configuration of capabilities that your company desires, it's crucial for you to understand the role that your company's intangible assets will play in planning and implementing effective acquisitions that will achieve the quantum leap gains you seek.

Are You Ready to Acquire Another Company?

At one time or another, all companies are either potential acquirers or potential acquisitions. A company could be an acquirer one year and be acquired the next. As a case in point, in 2007, just after Alcan, a Canadian-based aluminum producer, acquired the French state-owned aluminum manufacturer Picheney, it was itself acquired by the global mining firm Rio Tinto. The ink had not even dried on this transaction when BHP Billiton, the world's largest mining company, was making a hostile bid for Rio Tinto. Therefore, every company must consider possible acquisition activity as part of its strategic plan, and that perspective needs to cascade throughout all parts of the company. Exhibit 1-1 lists a few questions you should ask about your company.

Exhibit 1-1

Are You Ready to Acquire Another Company?

☐ What are the acquisition opportunities that we should pursue?

☐ Could we be acquired?

☐ What are the market dynamics that would lead to either of these scenarios actually taking place?

Although it is not possible for you to know exactly when your company is going to be in play, you need to be prepared for all eventualities related to either acquiring or being acquired.

Also, be aware that there are very few "mergers of equals." Even when these appear to happen, the new company eventually finds that shared ownership is unworkable, and sooner or later, one of the two original companies takes control of the newly combined company. The truth is that almost all of these transactions are "mergers" in name only; when the veneer is stripped away, one company has acquired another company—for example, the "merger" of Daimler and Chrysler, which wasn't a merger at all. Therefore, if one company is really *acquiring* another company, it's better to call that combination an acquisition rather than a merger so that you don't have to spend time and energy posturing and pretending that you're merging when you're really acquiring. Instead, you can concentrate on the real issues that you need to deal with, and you can position your newly combined company for the best competitive advantage.

Making a clear statement about an acquisition up front will help pave the way for an effective integration. Once you've made a clear statement on this matter, it becomes that much more important to put in place the principles that will guide the integration, in order to avoid negative power-based dynamics that could set in very early in the life of the new company. Although the transaction is an acquisition, to achieve quantum gains, partnering has to play a strong role in the process of integrating the new organization.

Preparing Your Company for Acquisitions

To ensure greater acquisition success, you need to prepare in two ways:

1. You need to build your company's "acquisition readiness."
2. You need to develop a *value-creating* approach to the acquisition, which is different from the two traditional approaches to acquisitions.

Let's look at each of these factors in more detail.

Building Your Company's "Readiness" for Acquisitions

Building acquisition readiness consists of continually developing a core set of capabilities that allows your company to respond successfully to acquisition opportunities whenever they may arise—and to integrate those acquisitions successfully. These capabilities are not applicable only to acquisitions; instead, they are generic to how excellent organizations need to operate. In other words, your company can develop these capabilities without necessarily using them specifically for integrating a company you may acquire. To ensure that you're ready to acquire another company, you need the six core capabilities listed in Exhibit 1-2.

A company can never dictate precisely when the opportunity for a smart acquisition will arise. Therefore, developing your company's acquisition readiness capabilities is the best way for you to be prepared to take advantage of acquisition opportunities that present themselves.

Exhibit 1-2

Six Core Capabilities That Every Company Needs to Be Ready to Acquire Another Company

1. *Strategic agility.* You need to be able to create strategies and shape action plans that take advantage of market opportunities and organizational strengths.

2. *Market agility.* You need to be able to respond to the changing dynamics of the marketplace and to uncover new possibilities to serve customers.

3. *Organization building.* You need to be able to build the right culture, implement the right leadership principles, build trust, forge robust processes, and incentivize the engagement of all of those involved in the company.

4. *People management.* You need to be able to recognize talent, build on strengths, select people quickly, and make sure that people are placed at the right level of challenge, neither underestimating nor overestimating their abilities.

5. *Project and process management.* You need to be able to put the right integration plan in place and to implement that plan effectively.

6. *Knowledge management, learning, and innovating.* You need to be able to share knowledge throughout your company to ensure that rapid learning and deep, experience-based knowledge continually sharpen your acquisition and integration practices.

Two Traditional Approaches to Acquisitions

Building acquisition readiness sets the stage for our approach to integration—i.e., one that *creates value*—which is the second pillar of acquisition success. Major acquisitions all seem to adopt one of two alternative approaches:

1. The *expense* synergy approach—i.e., cutting costs
2. The *growth* synergy approach—i.e., growing the business

The prevalent thinking is that these two approaches are mutually exclusive, so a company has to adopt only one of them. However, our research and experience show that this is a false dichotomy; let's look at each approach a bit more closely to show why.

Approach 1: The "Expense Synergy" Approach to M&As—i.e., Cutting Costs

Expense synergies are realized by streamlining the cost base of the company infrastructure. Sources of cost savings can range from cutting jobs to streamlining the IT infrastructure. Although pursuing such savings can be justified, an excessively limited focus on cost cutting can turn out to be shortsighted.

The expense savings approach strives to capture economies of scale by eliminating duplication. Unfortunately, in transactions where cost savings and expense synergies are the dominant concern, the M&A integration team tends to pay scant attention during the due diligence and integration phases to actual and potential capabilities of both the acquirer and the acquiree that could be uncovered and leveraged in the newly combined company. When this is combined with the typical time pressures associated with integrating a new company, many integration efforts become "clear-cutting" operations where only the *acquiring* company is left standing. A single-minded focus on targeted cost savings can easily destroy the value and the capabilities of the *acquired* company. The premise becomes simply to maximize efficiency without regard for what might be a different but effective way of running operations or approaching the market. There is no doubt that it is important to realize expense synergies in order to justify the cost of the acquisition, but a tight focus on savings can become counterproductive when managers either ignore or eliminate many opportunities for growth. Cutting costs is important, but no company achieves sustainable growth solely by paring its expenditures.

Case Example: Hewlett-Packard's Acquisition of Compaq Computer

When HP acquired Compaq in 2002, it did achieve huge cost savings, but it didn't achieve its long-term performance objectives. Shortly after the acquisition, the media reported that "executives with Hewlett-Packard Co. told securities analysts that savings generated by the acquisition of Compaq Computer Corp. could reach $3 billion by 2004, $500 million more than what the company had projected during the lengthy buyout process."[2] Even if these projected savings were realized, did this approach lead to greater success for Hewlett-Packard? The actual corporate results a year later were more than disappointing.[3] Only after several years, with new leadership and a refocusing of the company, is Hewlett-Packard back on track.

Approach 2: The "Growth Synergy" Approach to M&As

The alternative to a focus on financial or *expense* synergies is to concentrate on the growth option. The case for this approach stems from the point of view that the combination of two companies will produce compelling growth opportunities. Instead of just adding 1 + 1 to get 2, this approach seeks an exponentially higher outcome. For example, the product lines of two merging organizations will be able to use expanded distribution channels to reach more customers and achieve greater volume—in other words, 1 + 1 = 3.

Unfortunately, the track record of companies with a single focus on taking the growth synergy approach is poor. All too often, the combined operations and offerings remain much the same, and the promise of the growth option is only partially fulfilled.

Approach 3: The "Value-Creating" Approach

There is a third approach: the *value-creating* approach, which fuses the positive elements of both of the other approaches to allow for breakthrough performance as the outcome of acquisition activity. The goal of the value-creating approach is to use an acquisition as a springboard for a *quantum leap* in your company's performance. The time, effort, and financial investment required for a significant acquisition are both extensive and intensive, and the acquisition is associated with substantial risks, with executives often ending up "betting the farm." So why would you want to engage in such a major and high-risk investment unless you can achieve an outcome that is far above standard expectations, both financially and strategically?

There are many reasons that companies acquire other companies, but most of them reflect much narrower potential gains. For example:

- Some reasons reflect an *offensive* market posture—e.g., a company wants to become dominant in a market.
- Some are more *defensive* in nature—e.g., a company wants to acquire another company so that it won't be outflanked by its competitors.

Those are sensible reasons, but the question is, "Are they *optimal* reasons?" The implementation of a sound acquisition strategy can significantly enhance a company's position in the marketplace, while simultaneously providing some protection from the attacks of competitors. Carrying out a sound acquisition is an integral part of a company's strategy. In this view, the company's strategy becomes the beacon that points to acquisition opportunities that have a high potential to enhance the position of the company. An effective corporate strategy also includes criteria that

Quantum leaps result from applying capabilities to opportunities to achieve unprecedented gains. These gains are made by linking cost cutting and growth opportunities. The outcome is that these acquisitions will be the springboard that will allow a company to outdistance its competitors.

outline when it would make more sense to be acquired. The companies that are prepared for both alternatives will achieve the highest returns for all of their stakeholders.

Making the Breakthrough to Creating Value

The focus of this book is on how the value-creating approach is used to prepare for acquisitions and to carry out the integration process effectively in order to achieve breakthrough levels of performance and value. The integration stage is where most of the value of an acquisition is created or lost. Readiness prepares the company to act on acquisition opportunities.

The first step in the value-creating approach is to uncover potential capabilities during the strategic planning, targeting, due diligence, and negotiation stages. The merged company then concentrates on identifying how the capabilities in each company can be complementary to one another, unbundling those capabilities, and ultimately reintegrating them in the new company.

The value-creating approach sees the exchange of knowledge as the basis for developing the capabilities that will lead to high levels of performance. This exchange sets the stage for quantum leap improvements in how these capabilities are approached, integrated, and eventually transformed into the newly emerging company.

The value-creating approach brings the expense synergy and growth option approaches together into a wholly new perspective:

- It asks how we can integrate the complementary capabilities of the two combining organizations.
- It links the organizations' value creation and knowledge-based relationships to derive the greatest benefit from the capabilities of the new company.
- This brings each company's set of capabilities into play and also leverages both companies' value creation through new and greater interaction opportunities among the combined human capital, structural capital, and customer capital.

- The wealth generation arising from these relationships creates value by more effectively engaging existing customers and bringing in new ones.

Dominant Business Logic

The dominant logic of a company is embedded in the operating procedures and shapes not only how members of the organization act, but how they think as well. While useful for alignment purposes, the dominant business logic can over time limit the ability of people in the organization to drive innovation or see new opportunities and threats.[4]

—C. K. Prahalad

The value-creating approach employs expense reduction in areas where there is duplication. In this approach, cost reduction is pursued very carefully, while looking at the gains that can be achieved. The acquiring company is quite careful not to shut down something just because it is not in keeping with its own narrowly defined dominant logic. Instead, it is understood that the acquisition is an opportunity to *redesign* the dominant business logic of the whole company and join together the capabilities required to implement a reformulated business strategy with renewed growth objectives. In the value-creating approach, everyone has to change—both the acquirer and the acquiree. The reality is that not revising the dominant business logic is at the root of many acquisition failures.

Setting the Stage for Quantum Leaps

In the knowledge era, the intangible assets of your company are key to its survival. Yet these very assets are frequently the targets of the predominant expense savings model of acquisitions (i.e., Approach 1, described earlier in this chapter). If you acquire and then integrate another company using only the expense savings approach, you're not allowing any possibility that the intangible assets of both companies can be reframed for an optimal outcome. In contrast, our value-creating approach brings the expense and capabilities approaches together as one, to achieve significant breakthroughs.

In addition to changing the basic approach to the mechanics of the acquisition process, our approach includes affirming a set of values and leadership principles that are the basis and guide for taking action in all acquisition activities. In other words, the acquisition process needs to flow out of the processes, values, and strategies of your company.

Leadership has to be involved at all stages of the acquisition process:

- In planning—i.e., in determining how an acquisition would add resources and an edge that your company would not otherwise have
- In developing the strategy for the acquisition
- In communicating and monitoring the behavior of all involved during the negotiation of the acquisition
- In carrying out due diligence
- In planning and executing the integration of the acquired company

In short, the major benefit of using the value proposition of the value creation approach is that it can achieve the greatest gain for the company and result in the greatest possible financial performance. With the value-creating approach, your company can not only realize cost savings but also leverage the acquisition as an opportunity for transforming the newly combined companies. This approach allows you to develop a strategically driven integration plan that will result in breakthrough performance.

The Path to the Quantum Leap

Companies need to chart a pathway to achieve their quantum leap. The more prepared you are with your integration readiness capabilities and the greater your capacity to use the value-creating approach to integration, the more effectively and rapidly you will achieve a quantum leap breakthrough.

Exhibit 1-3 provides a model to show how your company can create its pathway. There are several stages to go through to achieve a breakthrough. Many companies have succeeded with different elements of what is necessary to move upward along this path, and there is a great deal that can be learned from them. Some companies have become outstanding in the way they approach and manage integrations. However, as good as some companies have become, we have not found any company that has successfully brought together all of the dimensions necessary to achieve a quantum leap breakthrough. In Exhibit 1-3, the vertical axis indicates the value-creating approach capacity and the horizontal axis denotes the level of readiness capabilities. Each quadrant represents a stage of acquisition capability.

Exhibit 1-3

The Four Stages of Acquisition Capability

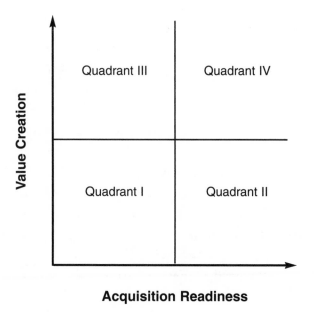

Acquisition Readiness

Quadrant I: Low Readiness

Companies with very limited readiness capabilities are in Quadrant I. Although a company could adopt a value-creating approach without having developed any readiness capabilities, it is not likely to do so. Many companies in Quadrant I have little preparation, in any sense, for an acquisition or for being acquired and therefore have the highest risk of failure or minimal gains if they become involved in an acquisition.

Quadrant II: Getting Started

The companies in this quadrant have significantly developed their readiness capabilities, but they have developed only a limited capacity to carry out a value-creating acquisition. Typically, these companies have a fair amount of experience in acquisitions. In many cases, they expect to be involved in an acquisition and have done some preparation for that eventuality. At the same time, they have only a limited amount of systematic capabilities, structure, and skill sets in place to take full advantage of acquisition opportunities.

Most of these companies tend to focus on expense synergies, given the capabilities at their disposal. However, it is possible for them to decide to put far more emphasis on potential capabilities synergies than on cost-saving synergies. Given their lack of ability to undertake a value-creating approach, this approach to the acquisition is likely to fail to bring any payback. Although organizations in this quadrant may choose to make substantial acquisitions, they are unlikely to be able to realize their business objectives. These companies run a significant risk of failure at the integration stage. For example, DaimlerChrysler, Sprint Nextel, and AOL Time Warner are all examples of companies that could not mobilize the capabilities required to successfully integrate the two merging company into one more effective company. All of these mergers were originally touted as mergers of equals, a description that was not borne out in the years following the transaction. Each has been negatively affected by strong clashes of culture that were not appreciated or provided for during the integration. This has led to an underlying current of distrust. Each has been characterized by destruction of market value, financial instability, impaired strategic position, organizational weakness, damaged reputation, and, in the case of DaimlerChrysler, alleged violations of ethical norms and laws.

Quadrant III: Advanced Organizations

The companies in Quadrant III have carefully codified the knowledge that they have acquired through their integration experience. They are likely to have established well-organized and thoughtful knowledge centers for acquisitions (as well as for other combinations and divestitures). These acquisition centers have created a network for companywide learning and best-practice knowledge sharing. Organizational capacity building for acquisitions is part of the way these companies do business.

The challenge often found in these organizations is the disconnect between the people who look for and validate acquisition opportunities and those who are responsible for leading the integration—i.e., between those who plan the acquisitions and those who carry them out. The planning part of the process is seen mostly as a financial function and is kept separate from the people with knowledge and experience of the integration process. As effective and efficient as these organizations are, either they have a pronounced focus on financial (cost-saving) synergies and view growth synergies as "icing on the cake," or they need to more fully develop and balance their expense synergies and growth synergies. These companies have built an excellent foundation for becoming quantum leap organizations, but they need to develop a mindset and cultivate the tools to more fully recognize and integrate all potential synergies.

For example, Dow Chemical, SAIC, and BP have all built an excellent foundation for becoming quantum leap organizations. Each has worked to draw on and codify the knowledge and experience from earlier acquisitions. Each has a process of working with business unit leaders and staff to explain to them how to carry out an acquisition that will link to both corporate and business unit goals. Each has amassed templates and tools to use during the implementation of integrations. These firms could move to the next stage of development by modifying their organizational mindset to adopt the value creation approach and to employ that frame-work to enable them to identify core capabilities, capture them, and then leverage them so that they are the basis for continuously creating high performance and value.

Quadrant IV: Quantum Leap

Companies that have built substantial capacities in both readiness and value creation are in Quadrant IV. They have the necessary capabilities in place to enable them to act on acquisition opportunities or, if need be, to make themselves a highly valued and collaborative target com-pany. These organizations see that acquisitions are a viable option for enabling them to achieve their organizational goals. They embed that option in their strategy making, and they proactively screen target can-didates by looking at companies that offer key capabilities that fill out or complement their own abilities. They collaborate closely with their due diligence teams to identify and validate opportunities. They know how to judiciously value all assets: tangible, intangible, and financial. Finally, they have solid skills in business planning and project manage-ment to plan and implement a speedy, comprehensive integration and postintegration transformation. They can manage the predictable and exploit the unpredictable elements of the acquisition process to a suc-cessful end. These companies have the choice to grow appreciably larger or not, but in any case, they will achieve their strategic goals, while at the same time transforming themselves through their acquisi-tion initiatives.

Moving from Quadrant I to Quadrant IV

Ideally, a company would move from a starting point in Quadrant I to Quadrant IV, having built its readiness capacities concurrently with having developed its understanding and implementation of value-creat-ing knowledge, framework, and actions. Because of the predominant

> ## Case Example: Boeing
>
> An indication of moving in the direction of becoming a quantum organiza-
> tion is Boeing's chartering two sets of synergy teams after its acquisition of
> North American Rockwell in 1996. Alan Mulally, then head of Boeing Space
> and Defense Group and now CEO of Ford, saw that there needed to be two
> major teams put in place to capture the synergies afforded by the North
> American Rockwell acquisition. The efficiency synergy teams addressed
> eliminating redundancies and integrating, while the growth synergy team
> looked for breakthrough opportunities.
>
> *The growth synergy teams were chartered to "analyze market segments,*
> *customers and competition, and to assess future trends relating to prod-*
> *ucts and programs" . . . these teams were co chaired by Boeing and*
> *Rockwell executives. To achieve growth, it was reasoned, the two sides*
> *would have to work together collaboratively, and co chairs were both a*
> *substantive and symbolic way of stressing the importance of mutuality.*
> *. . . Transition team findings were sifted and reviewed by 400 or so exec-*
> *utives from both sides.*[5]

thinking that financials are overwhelmingly what matters, however, the
most usual trajectory is to start from Quadrant I, with some companies
spending time in Quadrant II and others advancing over time into
Quadrant III. In other words, most companies become increasingly effective and efficient in the financial synergy approach. They are getting
more creative, comprehensive, systematic, speedy, and practiced, and
their success rate shows that.

However, it is only when a company integrates that financial perspective with a capabilities perspective that the company moves to
Quadrant IV to achieve quantum leap gains. This is where the company
takes advantage of *all* of the synergies as part of the whole acquisition initiative and has the skill base to carry that off. All the resources of both
organizations—i.e., the acquirer and the acquiree—are examined and
leveraged to the benefit of all customers and all external stakeholders as
the two companies transform themselves into a new company.

The next sections of this chapter describe some important considerations when looking at an acquisition to catapult your company forward.

> **Case Example: Siemens**
>
> Siemens has also taken an important step toward becoming a quantum organization by making it a priority to partner with organizations when it is acquiring their information technology units to turn them into outsourced elements for that organization. Siemens makes an extensive effort to learn what its new customer values and integrates that into the service plan it devises. It sees its new employees as its human capital, supporting them by bringing in highly qualified managers to work with them, and making all of Siemens technology and experience know-how available to them so that they can better serve their new customer. That is more in the spirit of what is necessary to move from an advanced organization to a breakthrough quantum leap organization.

Target an Acquisition That Fits Your Strategy

Well before you even formally consider doing due diligence, your company needs to determine whether it would be best to grow organically, through acquisition, or possibly through a combination of both. The answer to this question depends on how you can best obtain the capabilities you need to catapult your company forward. This has to be an ongoing conversation because a company must constantly reevaluate and reposition itself to take advantage of the market and (even more important) to shape the market. These conversations frame the choices a company needs to consider to achieve its goals.

Without a market-based strategy, a company cannot make the best choices, determine the appropriate targets, find the answers to its most important questions during due diligence, negotiate for the right assets at the best price, and then move effectively into the integration stage. Each stage is the basis for the success of the next. However, even the best strategy, targeting, due diligence, and negotiation will come to naught if the company doesn't do solid integration planning and implementation. Moreover, if the acquisition and integration process is done incorrectly or is handled poorly, the result not only will be financially costly, but will damage, perhaps irreparably, the company's ability to respond to its customers and its changing marketplace.

Once you have concluded that acquisition is the best route to take to provide the capabilities you need to meet your strategic growth goals, you need to put a set of principles into place before moving forward, as described in the next sections.

Clearly Define the Leadership Principles of the Newly Combined Company

When you're considering significant acquisitions that have the potential to reconfigure your company, you must clearly define the leadership and organizational principles that you will use to guide the process. These principles will serve to shape the way your company will interact with the acquired company during the due diligence process and the eventual integration of the two companies. Therefore, these principles take on a fundamental role because they set the tone and the climate for the "new" company that will emerge from the acquisition process.

Integration can be seen as a window of opportunity for changing every aspect of the companies being combined. All aspects and elements of the combining companies are open to review, realignment, and transformation as they are shaped into a new company. A key difference between most efforts at integration and the quantum leap approach is the overall context of engagement of all the employees of both companies. Their engagement forms the basis for developing a trust level that will be conducive to partnering and collaboration. This is the key to managing the integration so that it will have a vital, renewing, and potentially transformative effect on the newly combined company. Effective leadership ensures that the exchange of knowledge, insights, and experiences flows freely up, down, and across the combining companies.

Leadership plays a key role in modeling the collaboration, strategic orientation, and coherence that will provide a viable platform on which the integration will take place.

The integration of two companies following an acquisition is best accomplished by creating a strong partnership between the two organizations. Only in-depth conversations in a context of trust can make it possible to move through the extensive number of decisions necessary for the new company to be successful in the marketplace. These conversations can help in the following ways:

- Build effective partnerships at all levels.
- Develop high levels of trust across both companies.
- Ensure that people feel respected as the integration proceeds.
- Facilitate effective management of employee performance and accountability.

Even if everything (leadership, values, strategy, technological support, and a goal-driven process) is in place, there is still the sizable challenge of engendering trust in an environment in which a great deal of change is taking place at an accelerated pace. However, if you have developed effective leadership principles, this will prevent trust from deteriorating as you make the complex and difficult decisions required when integrating two companies. Communication and knowledge exchange are essential to successful integration. Effective leaders engage the people involved in an ongoing conversation. This provides the opportunity to voice issues and model how these issues are meant to be resolved. The conversations that relate to the resolution of real problems are where these leadership principles are affirmed within the company and in the minds of all those involved.

These conversations add to the clarity of the evolving strategy and support coherence as the emerging company takes shape during integration. As the new company emerges in the market, it is likely that its business strategies and its approach to customers will change substantially. Leadership has to be exercised with agility to ensure that strategies and performance reflect the integration plan, while keeping pace with changing conditions in the marketplace. In such an intense, high-pressure environment, effective conversations are the basis for people to renew their understandings and build the trust that is necessary to give shape to a high-performance company.

Elicit a Sense of Commitment and Ownership from Everyone

All parties must understand that, although there is respect for all those involved in the acquisition and integration process, this process is taking place in a highly purposeful, result-driven context. All the people involved have to assume their responsibilities and exercise their accountabilities in line with well-defined principles. It is important that leaders are clear about which principles are most important. Leaders must also communicate those areas in which people should feel free to exercise initiative. It is incumbent upon leaders to recognize and deal with differences in strategy and culture that need to be reconciled if the integration is to proceed with coherence and accomplish the commonly held goals.

Leaders must foster trust-based strategic conversations that target the critical elements of the acquisition process. The shared values of the two companies will provide the basis for the mutual understanding and trust that are required if these conversations are to take place. Such a climate cannot emerge if there is no respect for the differences that necessarily characterize companies that have evolved on separate paths for decades or more. Organizations need to celebrate the diversity in culture, leadership, and capabilities, rather than denying these differences. Then, leaders must quickly find the commonly held beliefs and values that will bind the two companies together. This process of amalgamating the values of the two companies forms the basis for an effective integration by weaving the newly emerging culture right from the start. The same allowance for the appreciation of differences in values between organizations applies equally to the processes and people of both organizations.

Effective conversations enable the companies to develop the strategy of the newly combined company based on customer needs. With an outside-in perspective (described in detail in Chapter 5), the company can focus on its customers and the needs it can meet in the marketplace. Then, with an inside-out perspective, the business leaders involved in the integration can map out how to bring together the right capabilities and eliminate the duplication of resources to reframe the company in a way that will lead to breakthrough levels of performance.

Recognize the Need for Speed When Integrating Companies

Acquisitions are pursued to achieve a competitive advantage that will position a company in the marketplace for accelerated growth, but that competitive advantage comes from being able to move quickly through all phases of the M&A process and to leverage current and emerging capabilities in the market rapidly. These transactions are complex and time-consuming undertakings that require considerable energy, time, and attention. Without building the capability for speed, the unexpected and frequent result is that a company often ends up becoming so involved in a draining integration process that the transaction can lead to significant drops in productivity, loss of key customers and staff people, and in some cases failure and divestiture of the acquisition.

Furthermore, while the two companies are consumed with their internal questions, your competitors will not be sitting still. In fact, the news of an acquisition often galvanizes competitors to make a concerted assault on the existing franchise of the companies involved in the acquisition. In addition, the strategic evolution of the two combining companies is brought to a standstill by the intensity of the effort required for the integration process.

Picture a python that has successfully captured and swallowed a goat: it takes a long time for the snake to digest its "acquisition." In the meantime, its competitors are running circles around it, with the python itself being exposed to the danger of becoming a meal for yet another predator. Typically, a company that is acquiring another company is just like that python: it is also open to being attacked and dissected by all predators. The time and energy involved in integrating an acquisition can arrest strategic development. Very often, acquisitions take two to three years to digest, with unresolved issues that can continue reverberating for more than a decade. During that time, people are hard pressed to have the time or the attention span to ensure that the integration serves to accelerate the strategic development of the company, instead of bringing it to a halt.

Too often, the business leaders involved in an acquisition become almost entirely consumed by tactical questions and issues. Understandably, they focus on the myriad of activities and decisions associated with the acquisition. In fact, they often become so overwhelmed by these activities and decisions that their focus on the strategic intent of the new company becomes impaired. As a result, the energy required to manage a major acquisition diverts attention from the company's overall strategic intent. This is an intangible cost related to acquisitions that is rarely taken into account by a prospective acquirer. The strategic inertia resulting from an important acquisition could very well cancel out the benefits of the acquisition, depending on how fast the market is moving and how well positioned the acquirer already is in its market.

To avoid falling into the trap of strategic inertia, you must regularly turn your mind to the strategic intent of your newly combined company. You must keep an eye on the dynamics of your markets and on fast-changing customer needs. Through it all, you have to maintain a high level of agility so as to not end up with a strategic deficit that leaves your company behind your competition when you're ready to get back into the game. You must stay in the game at a strategic level throughout the acquisition and integration processes. If you have an effective project management capability, a strong communication strategy, and the ability to delegate, you will be able to set aside the time you need to ensure strategic coherence with the dynamics of your marketplace. It is also imperative that you act with a sense of urgency. Speed remains one of the most important conditions for the success of an acquisition: the integration must take place quickly. It is only when the process is moving purposefully that the trust of the acquired company can be maintained.

This presents one of the key dilemmas associated with leading the integration process. There is a need for both swift decision making and the flexibility to shift gears as required. There is a need to move quickly, while respecting differences and making the distinction between the capabilities that must be preserved and those that should be discarded to avoid unnecessary expense. Once you've launched the integration phase, people in both organizations expect the process to unfold rapidly. They often feel that letting uncertainty reign for too long shows a lack of respect for them. Excessive lulls promote dysfunctionality. In contrast, rapid integration keeps people's attention focused. Keeping a rapid pace infuses a great deal of discipline and healthy tension.

While speed is of the essence, expending the necessary level of energy is also key so that you can achieve all of the following goals:

- To keep the company's overall strategic intent at the forefront
- To sharply define accountabilities

- To maintain clarity in the steps involved in integrating the two companies
- To ensure that your customers are served well
- To keep the day-to-day operations of your newly emerging company running smoothly

This is a tall order. Only experienced, skillful, and well-prepared business leaders can meet the tremendous challenges involved.

If you do not maintain the appropriate level of purposeful tension in your company, internal politics (instead of market realities) tend to take over, with an understandably negative impact on results. Managing the rhythm and cadence of the change is essential for making an integration successful. Even in the largest integration project, there is an 18-month window where the integration can be most effective. After that period, bad habits, ineffective practices, and duplication of resources become anchored and increasingly difficult to rectify. It is important to build positive momentum. You lose a great deal of opportunity for change when the sense of urgency and decisiveness falters. This causes delays, which suck in additional expenditures of energy, attention, time, and ultimately, financial resources. It is often not possible to ever recoup the resulting financial penalties. At the point when an acquisition is publicly announced, communicating a well-developed game plan and showing resolve to move with a sense of urgency are key. Speed enables your company to minimize the costs of financing the integration, lowers the investment in getting the new company into operation, and enables the newly combined company to reach optimal levels of performance faster.

Make Sure You Have the Right Mindset and Attitude

Mindset and attitude are important variables in charting and carrying out the acquisition. All too often, a "conquistador syndrome" prevails, with the acquirer declaring to the acquired company at every turn, "My stuff is better than yours"—often arbitrarily. Such a mindset prevents the acquiring company from recognizing the value of the capabilities and the resources that the acquired company brings—whether these be people, information technology systems, customer strategies, or supply chain practices. When an acquiring company has the conquistador syndrome, it ignores the capabilities that the acquired company offers, severely undermines morale, and can quickly destroy the value of the acquired company. It sets up a "win-lose" and eventually a "lose-lose" reality.

The issue is only compounded by the need for speed. People have an inherent bias toward their own ways of doing things and toward preserving the resources and procedures with which they are familiar. This is reinforced by the mindsets prevalent in the company and the resulting blind spots. Mindsets are forged through experience and become part of the tacit knowledge of a company and its people. Because different companies have different histories and experiences, it stands to reason that collectively held mindsets also differ from one company to another. These mindsets become the lens through which business leaders perceive value. If you are unable to recognize and transcend these mindsets, you will be ill equipped to make the right choices. In addition, the uncertainty surrounding integration projects often causes people to operate in "survival mode," with the resulting inflexibility and lack of trust, which locks existing mindsets in place.

Those who fall prey to the conquistador syndrome assume that they have the best way by definition. This blindness to their own mindsets leads them to reject anything that is different from their own experience. This, in turn, tends to trigger a similar reaction on the part of the people in the acquired company. The context is now set for win-lose interactions, in which there is little room for mutual influence. This only worsens when people lose all trust and start operating in survival mode. This has powerful implications for determining the appropriateness of decisions concerning which capabilities and resources are to be kept and enhanced and which are to be discarded. If the conquistador mindset prevails, then competition for limited space becomes the focus, and the partnering that could optimize gains and create a new company with a far more expanded range of possibilities falls into serious jeopardy.

Pay Attention to Both Success Factors and Derailing Factors

To achieve a quantum leap in performance, the acquiring company needs to pay careful attention to managing factors that can have either a positive or a negative impact on the performance of the new company. In many cases, the derailing factors are the mirror images of the success factors. For example, a constant inflow of freshly discovered knowledge may enable a company to recalibrate its method of negotiations. On the other hand, prematurely closing on a decision to acquire without subjecting that decision to ongoing validation based on the emergence of new knowledge may lead a company to discount the risks and overestimate the benefits. Very expensive mistakes have been made by companies of all sizes and types when these derailing factors are not taken into account.

To make sure that an acquiring company can achieve a quantum leap, each chapter of this book describes the success and derailing factors for that stage of the acquisition process.

Develop an Acquisitions Team or Manager to Oversee the Integration Process

Every company needs someone or some group, in one form or another, to take responsibility for the lessons learned from acquisitions and other external ventures of the company. Some companies develop a formal, budgeted, and staffed "acquisition team." Other companies assign this responsibility to a senior person or a group of senior leaders and key managers. For simplicity's sake, we'll refer to this function as "the acquisitions team."

The acquisitions team oversees, guides, and acts as a catalyst for all aspects of the acquisition process. It ensures that there is a repository of knowledge on all of the aspects of acquisitions. The acquisitions team also assumes the roles of educator and facilitator to help determine

- Whether an acquisition is the best choice for achieving strategic goals
- How to gauge readiness for an acquisition
- How to plan and organize for the acquisition

- What tools and techniques are appropriate for what type of effort, whom to involve, and in what ways (both internally and externally)
- How to develop an effective transitional structure and provide for tight accountabilities
- How to identify and mitigate the risks involved
- How to manage the intensive change surrounding the integration while making it into an organizationally transforming event

Based on experience and accumulated feedback, the acquisitions team develops a core set of practices. This is a body of knowledge that is made readily available to the company. One of the acquisitions team's core functions is to regularly engage people in the company to refine this knowledge as a standard part of its review and action planning, part of "how we live." The acquisitions team maintains an infrastructure of processes and knowledge that supports seizing opportunities when they present themselves for optimal results.

Case Example: Dow Chemical

Dow Chemical has a formal Mergers and Acquisitions Expertise Center, which has been instrumental in being exactly that kind of catalyst. The center was formed in 1999 to help manage Dow Chemical's $11.6 billion acquisition of Union Carbide. The leaders of the center realized that the company needed to develop a whole set of processes and templates to handle massive global acquisitions of this caliber comprehensively. The center is the lead internal entity for acquisitions, as well as joint ventures, partnering of all sorts, divestitures, and plant shutdowns. It has a team made up of a small group of experienced professionals who have both operational experience and a solid background in another area (e.g., finance or human resources).

Organizations may have a different or less formal structure, but ultimately someone or some group must make sure that all of the following are in place:

- The company is ready to make acquisitions.
- The company is making the best strategic choices.

- People are adequately equipped.
- Milestone measures that support a proven, reliable acquisition process are defined.

Each company has to find its own form of the acquisitions team to fulfill this important role to ensure that the company is ready to start acquiring other companies. The form given to this role has to fit with the company's structure, its strategy, and its specific way of doing business. The acquisitions team provides the navigational infrastructure that is essential for achieving breakthrough levels of performance through acquisitions.

Conclusion

Now that we've introduced the basics of our approach to effecting a successful acquisition, Chapter 2 goes into more depth on the intangible assets involved in combining companies.

Success Factors

- Building the capabilities for readiness
- Embracing an approach that creates value, bringing together both expense synergies *and* the growth option for breakthrough outcomes
- Understanding the value of intangible knowledge-based assets as well as the traditional physical, financial, and labor assets
- Developing a core set of capabilities that allows your company to take advantage of acquisition opportunities as well as being in the best position if it becomes a takeover target
- Understanding the requirements for a successful acquisition and integration
- Developing a custodial capability to capture and leverage the know-how and know-what of successful acquisitions so that this can be used across all business units of your organization

Derailing Factors

- Having a limited skill base to take on an acquisition and integration
- Being captive to a one-sided view that financial synergies are the primary driver for your acquisition's success

- Taking an attitude that the acquired company has no important capabilities to capture, combine, nurture, and leverage
- Not seeking to learn from your experience in acquisitions
- Discounting the need to partner with the leadership and staff of the acquired company to build the new company
- Being satisfied with cutting financial costs

Questions

- What do we think will be the key issues that we will face in an acquisition and integration?
- How open is our company to systematically looking into growth option opportunities as well as expense synergies?
- What unprecedented gains could our company achieve through a major acquisition as far as performance and value creation are concerned?
- What could block us from achieving those gains?
- What could enable us to achieve those gains?

Notes

1. Peter Beusch, "A Tentative Model for Management Accounting and Control in the Integration Processes of Mergers and Acquisitions," p. 2; http://www.handels.gu.se/epc/archive/00004170/01/Antwerp, Belgium (2005).pdf.
2. "HP: Merger Could Net $3B in Savings," PC MAG.com, June 4, 2002.
3. "HP's Compaq Acquisition (C) | Business Strategy Case Studies, ICMR; http://www.icmrindia.org/casestudies/catalogue/Business% 20Strategy3/BSTA022.htm. This business case study discusses the prospects for the success of HP's Compaq acquisition, as seen a year after the acquisition. It discloses that "HP shocked Wall Street by missing its earnings targets by a massive margin in the third quarter of 2003. Fiorina commented, 'I'm very disappointed that we missed our (earnings per share) growth target this quarter due to the confluence of a number of issues that we now understand and are urgently addressing. I accept full responsibility for the shortfall.' HP continued to lean heavily on its profitable printing business while its PC and server businesses struggled to generate profits. In personal computers, Dell was giving HP a run for its money while IBM outrivaled HP in the global markets for corporate computing. Though HP announced strong results in the fourth quarter, much of it stemmed from cuts in research and development, and from a lower tax rate and not from improved financial performance."
4. C. K. Prahalad, "The Blinders of Dominant Logic," *Long Range Planning* 37, no. 2 (April 2004).
5. Mitchell Lee Marks and Phillip H. Mirvis, *Joining Forces: Making One Plus One Equal Three in Mergers, Acquisitions and Alliances* (San Francisco: Jossey-Bass, 1998), pp. 128–129.

The additional material in this chapter comes from the authors' interviews and experiences.

2

Leveraging Intangibles:
A More Effective Business Model for
Mergers and Acquisitions

In the current business context, what creates value in a company has radically changed: *intangible assets* have become the most valuable resources your company (indeed, any company) can acquire. These intangible assets include your company's overall knowledge of your business, your relationships with your customers and suppliers, and all the other weightless wealth of your company. These assets have become the drivers for generating most of your company's value and future.

Although physical and financial assets are still essential ingredients in any company's recipe for realizing its goals, the driving force for success and competitive advantage is your company's ability to respond to your customers' needs rapidly and often globally, and that response is based on having the intangible assets you need available and being able to mobilize them well to address your issues. These include your understanding of market conditions, business philosophy, strategies, technology platform, relationships with customers and suppliers, vision, culture, values, quality of leadership, and level of engagement of people through-out your company, The fate of your company depends on the quality and vibrancy of your intangible resources.

This chapter describes these intangible assets and shows how you can use them to enable your company to hit your growth targets and remain competitive *after* your merger or acquisition has been completed. Intangible assets complement the much more universally acknowledged financial assets. Your intangible assets are where you can achieve synergy after a merger or acquisition; therefore, integrating and leveraging these intangible assets successfully is critical if you want to achieve quantum leaps in performance and increase the overall value of your newly com-bined company.

Three Types of Intangible Assets

Most managers in most companies believe that a successful acquisition is defined as one that yields certain types of results, including these:

- Enlarging the physical plant's capabilities
- Expanding product lines
- Increasing financial assets
- Cutting redundant costs substantially
- Increasing market share
- Increasing overall operational efficiencies

In other words, the perception is often that a company that is pur-suing a merger or an acquisition is buying "things." Although this is true, there is also a whole array of powerful intangible capabilities that under-lie the ways in which these physical and financial assets are used to create value. These intangible capabilities include the systems, practices, values, behaviors, and relationships of both the acquiring company and the company it acquires. To better understand what intangible assets are and the role they play in companies—especially in *your* company—let's look at intangible assets in terms of these three inputs (which interact dynamically with one another):

1. Human capital
2. Structural capital
3. Customer capital (also called relational capital)

These three intangible assets are the critical drivers for creating your company's wealth or value. For these three areas of capital to have true value, you must ensure that they ultimately come together to yield financial value for your company. So let's look at each type in more detail.

Intangible Asset 1: Human Capital

Human capital is the sum of all the capabilities of everyone who's currently working in your company—i.e., the cumulative knowledge, experience, attributes, competencies, and mindsets of all your employees, managers, and leaders. These individual capabilities of your employees create value for your customers. In any merger or acquisition, your most important challenge is to first *assess* the human capital of both companies and then identify how you can best *realign and reposition* the human capital from the new company with the human capital resources you already have.

In other words, you can't just bring people together; if you do, all you get is 1 + 1 = 2. But if you *realign and maximize* all the knowledge, talent, and experience of both groups of employees, that's when you can start to see that 1 + 1 = 3 or 4 or 5. The challenge is to engage *all* your employees—new and old, at all levels across the company—as you form and integrate your newly combined company. As Seamus Mulligan, executive vice president for corporate development of Elan Corporation, said, "If you access a company at a senior level, and get the chief executive officer to endorse your technology, you're still as good as dead in the water if you also don't get the endorsement at the lower level—the technicians. That goes for acquisitions as well."[1]

Intangible Asset 2: Structural Capital

Structural capital consists of the strategies, structures, processes, and leadership that translate into a company's specific core competencies. These *organizational* capabilities leverage your employees' *individual* capabilities to create value for customers. Structural capital also includes the organizational capacity and physical systems used to transmit and store intellectual material. Structural capital is composed in large part of your company's organization, innovation, and processes; again, let's look at each of these in more detail.

Organizational Dimension

This is your company's investment in your systems, your operational philosophy, and your supplier and distribution channels. It is made up of the systematized and codified competencies of your company, as well as the systems for leveraging these capabilities.

Innovation Dimension

This is the capability to renew your company along with the outcomes of innovation, which include

- The ability to anticipate market needs and lead the market in responding.
- The ability to bring new products to market rapidly.
- Intellectual assets and intellectual property (which include copyrights, patents, trademarks, and trade secrets).
- Your company's *brand* and your *theory of your business.* Although the best-known innovation capital is usually intellectual property, these are perhaps even more critical to your company's well-being.

Process Dimension

This comprises all the processes of your company that enable you to create and deliver goods and services to both internal and external customers. These can be your production, design, and product development processes;

your people development processes; your communication processes; your strategy-making processes, and your knowledge development, capture, and leveraging processes. Unfortunately, many companies never think to value many of these processes at all. However, when a process is effective, it produces wealth for a company. When it is ineffective, it produces that much less gain, and possibly even a negative outcome.

A look at customer service processes shows the differences in the value of processes quite clearly. Some companies, like Dow, are highly focused on customer satisfaction and have several alternative methods for gathering knowledge of customer experiences, needs, and expectations. Dow has an emphasis on providing its customers with a seamless experience during an acquisition and the follow-up integration period. It has developed extensive sets of indicators, profiles, and links to its product and service development teams, and it adjusts its practices in light of new information on potential disruptions of service or product availability to customers, including making sure that its customers are satisfied with their sales representatives.

Companies that have not developed a similar capacity, but concentrate instead on cutting production costs, emphasizing efficiency over providing the necessary attention and resources to meet customer service requirements, will be at a competitive disadvantage. For example, after America West acquired US Airways in 2005, it focused on cutting costs to achieve a certain level of profitability. A casualty in this effort was customer service; inadequate attention was paid to the deteriorating level of customer service, which included dismal rankings on on-time flights, baggage handling, and other critical customer service measures. Three years later, after customers' disaffection with and defection from the new US Airways, the company continues to have great difficulty framing and implementing the kinds of effective customer service practices and processes that would restore high levels of customer satisfaction.[2] Hoping to boost its chronically poor rankings in on-time flights, baggage handling, and other critical customer service measures, US Airways has added a chief operating officer to its executive ranks to be responsible for flight operations, in-flight services, maintenance and engineering, airport customer service, and reservations. One frequent flyer commented, however,

"They have already alienated such a big part of their frequent-customer base, I don't know if there's anything they can do to recoup that business."[3]

Carrying out mergers and acquisitions can be seen as a process; therefore, the better the process, the higher the level of performance and outcome. Many acquisitions fail, and much of the responsibility for that failure can often be traced back to how a company views and manages its M&A process. Many of the companies discussed in this book—including Dow, Siemens, BP, Elan, Symantec, and Clarica—have worked extensively to develop proprietary M&A processes and templates, and systematically use and enhance them through ever-growing experience and insights. These companies are continuously developing their acquisition capabilities, enabling them to minimize disruptions during integrations while leveraging for the greatest possible acquisition gains.

Intangible Asset 3: Customer Capital

Customer capital is the sum of all customer relationships, which can be defined by four parameters:

- *Depth*—your penetration or share of customers' wallets
- *Breadth*—your coverage or share of the market
- *Sustainability*—the durability of your relationship with your customers
- The *profitability* of your company's relationships with all your customers

Although customer capital includes all external relationships, we focus on customers and suppliers. Our goal is to focus on the people who are directly involved in creating value for your customers and for your company as a whole.

If you view a merger or acquisition from a customer capital perspective, you can reshape your company's emerging structure, strategies, processes, practices, and product and service lines to create even more powerful customer and supplier strategies. However, more often, acquiring companies overlook the way their newly combined companies will

Case Examples: Wells Fargo and Bank of America

When Wells Fargo acquired First Interstate Bancorp in 1996, rival California banks portrayed it as "huge and uncaring" as they attempted to capitalize on Wells Fargo practices that produced customer dissatisfaction stemming from the acquisition and the less-than-seamless integration of First Interstate.[4]

When Bank of America acquired MBNA, two consumer Web sites posted complaints about BofA's unfriendly tactics toward its customers. The Consumerist blog (consumerist.com) complained that BofA "greeted their new customers by charging them a new fee. Now if you don't pay off your entire balance in full every month, BofA will impose a $1.50 minimum finance charge."[5] That fee may be small potatoes to customers, but it still rankled many—which is obviously not a good way to start a relationship with a new customer base. In addition, consumeraffairs.com accused BofA of adopting "some of its some of its former prey's most prized tactics—spiking interest rates, charging late fees even when your balance is paid, and customer 'service' that leaves cardholders feeling worse than before they called."[6]

affect their customers and suppliers; they're left out of the M&A equation simply because they are *outside* the company! Yet, obviously, any interruption or decline in your customer service creates a space for your competitors to capture your disaffected customers and disrupt sensitive supply chain relationships.

A merger or acquisition can open up and recombine the resource sets of the two companies involved. Exhibit 2-1 shows that the intangible, financial, and tangible assets of Company A are joined with the clusters of those resources from Company B. In a merger or an acquisition, there are unprecedented opportunities to bring these resources from the acquiring and the acquired companies together in novel ways—and in ways that were not previously possible—to produce significant gains in your company's overall performance and wealth. This is the potential promise of a merger or acquisition. It is not merely *adding* the cumulative resources of one company to those of the other, but a *recombining* of all resources: financial, tangible, and all the dimensions of intangibles.

For example, this can be seen in Symantec's acquisition of Axent Technologies in 1999. That "acquisition was also the catalyst for changing

Exhibit 2-1

Joining the Different Assets of Two Companies

Company A	Company B
Intangible Assets	Intangible Assets
Human Capital	Human Capital
Customer Capital Structural Capital	Customer Capital Structural Capital
Financial Assets	Financial Assets
Tangible Assets	Tangible Assets

(The two company boxes are joined by a "+" symbol between them.)

Symantec processes to support an enterprise business. Axent had systems in place for serving major corporate customers, and just as important, its senior executives had an understanding of the service and support needs of that market. As the former Axent executives assumed leadership roles at Symantec, they helped guide the company's investment in and deployment of new systems to undergird the new enterprise thrust."[7]

One way to look at this is to think of all of the ingredients in a recipe. In the hands of a good cook, the right ingredients will yield an outstanding outcome. But in the hands of an inexperienced, inattentive, or poor cook, the results can yield a far lower-quality, less nutritious, and considerably less appealing outcome. This is the heart of the quantum leap approach to M&As.

Using a Knowledge Capital Model to Combine Intangible Assets Successfully

The knowledge capital model offers a perspective that can help you identify and manage the intangible assets of both your existing company and the company (or companies) you're acquiring, from the strategic planning phase through the postintegration phase of the acquisition. It enables you to systematically develop, recombine, manage, leverage, and renew your company's intangible assets and the new intangible assets you now have available because of the merger or acquisition.

You and your colleagues in the acquiring company need to be thoughtful, discriminating, and imaginative in how you nurture and manage your new bounty, because with each interaction among these knowledge capital elements, you will either create or deplete the value of your assets. As shown in Exhibit 2-2, human capital interfaces with customer capital and structural capital to create knowledge value capital.

For example, you will create value in the following ways:

- If there is a positive relationship between your sales force (human capital) and your customers (customer capital)—i.e., your sales force provides rapid, knowledgeable responses to customer questions or complaints—and if that relationship is reinforced by the new company's effective knowledge-retrieval system (structural capital), then your customers will have rapid responses that are tailored to their specific needs. This affirming

Exhibit 2-2

The Knowledge Capital Model

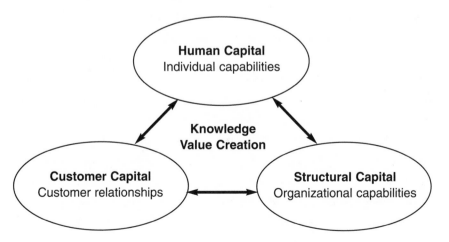

experience can stimulate strong interest in the newly available product lines and services that your company can now provide.

- As your company works to make sure that your core values (structural capital) are second nature to your employees (human capital) and your network, you ensure that your brand (structural capital) is embedded in the performance of your employees and is part of the customer experience (customer capital) on an ongoing basis. The implementation of your brand (structural capital) throughout all of your company's activities smooths the transition of customers and suppliers of the acquired company to having active, solid relationships with the new company.

- Customers give feedback (customer capital) to your company that is picked up by your employees (human capital), if they are sensitized to that, and communicated throughout the acquired and acquiring companies (structural capital). You can then use this fresh knowledge to realign the way your company operates and the way all your resources are used.

Exhibit 2-2 shows how customer capital creates value by its interaction with structural capital and human capital. If customer relationships are rich, customers will partner with the company to co-create new offerings. This linking of customer relationships with your company's organizational capabilities and individual capabilities creates an engine for constant organizational renewal and repositioning in the market. Your company's products and/or services will be targeted to your customers, with employees and the supplier network geared to be able to readjust to the pace of change in the market. When that capability is tied into your company's acquisition strategy and integration practices, you have a basis for continuous exponential growth.

On the other hand, if there are poor-quality links between the customer capital, structural capital, or human capital involved with your company, each interaction can be detrimental. If, during the integration phase, your customer service agents are not well engaged with the new company's vision and offerings, those agents will relate poorly to customers, who will then be dissatisfied and therefore will be open to the overtures of competitors. Key employees themselves may vote with their feet on how they feel about the new company: they may either move to your competitors or just leave. Often it is the best employees who feel that they can find other opportunities that are more satisfying and leave the firm. A lower quality of human capital inputs weakens your company's relationship with your customers and can result in inferior levels of performance and poor communication of key knowledge throughout your newly combined company.

The knowledge capital model has two assumptions:

1. *A company's intangible assets are made of capabilities and relationships that are built through the exchange of knowledge.* Value is created as knowledge flows among the three types of knowledge capital (human, customer, and structural). Knowledge exchange serves as the basis for accelerating learning and systematically developing individual and organizational capabilities.

It is essential that you promote and facilitate the free flow of knowledge across your company. Achieving high levels of performance and quantum leaps through acquisitions relies on a company's ability to establish trust through relationships. Trust determines the bandwidth of knowledge exchange and the extent of value-creation potential.

2. *A company's intangible assets form a system that you must manage through an integrated approach.* It is impossible to realize the potential of the capabilities of any one of the three areas of knowledge capital if they are isolated from one another. The greatest benefits happen only when your leadership team develops all three areas of knowledge capital effectively in tandem, integrates them, and ensures that they dynamically support one another.

Acquisition and integration can place extensive stress on all customers and employees, and on the ability of the structure to support carrying out critical functions. However, if you understand how the three types of intangible assets are interrelated and how to manage them, you can significantly minimize these stress levels. The choice here is between allowing entropy to take place by default and working unyieldingly for synergy. If you don't tend to these intangibles, your merger or acquisition can easily fail; on the other hand, if you actively incorporate them into your M&A strategy and integration implementation, you can achieve unprecedented gains for your new company.

Stocks of Knowledge and the Flow of Knowledge

There is a key difference between managing intangible assets and managing traditional tangible assets and financial assets. That difference is that intangible assets are renewable, whereas tangible and financial assets are expended when they are used. Because intangible assets have become the greatest share of the value of most firms, you need to actively manage these assets in order to optimize your company's performance in your marketplace.

There are two aspects of intangible assets:

- The *stock* of working knowledge, which can be inventoried
- The *flow* of working knowledge, which is a process

The Stock of Working Knowledge

Stocks of working knowledge represent the accumulation of the three types of intangible assets:

- *Human capital*, in the form of the accumulated individual capabilities of the members of your company—i.e., your employees
- *Structural capital*, in terms of your company's organizational capabilities
- *Customer capital*, found in your company's relationships with your customers

You can evaluate your company's stock of knowledge as the amount of capital that has been created by increasing your company's capabilities.

An important characteristic of the stock of knowledge is that it is (to a large degree) measurable. Knowledge stock includes all of the following:

- The specific skill sets of your employees
- Intellectual property
- Databases
- Company values
- Company processes
- Company strategies
- The length of the term or depth of your customer relationships

All three stocks—human, structural, and customer—are connected and grow based on the exchange of knowledge between individuals, your company, and your customers. These exchanges or flows allow you to use your knowledge stocks to create value.

The Flow of Working Knowledge

The flow of knowledge enriches the stock of working knowledge in companies where knowledge flows easily and reliably. Quantum leap companies use their existing capabilities to generate new capabilities that will enable unimpeded knowledge flow, which in turn creates new knowledge stocks, increasing the company's intangible assets.

In companies where the flow of knowledge is unnecessarily restricted, distorted, or simply blocked, that flow becomes degraded and corroded, with the result that knowledge-based capabilities and value wind up being destroyed instead of being created.

How stocks of knowledge flow depends on the type of knowledge involved:

- *Explicit knowledge* is knowledge that is articulated or codified in words or numbers, such as tools, procedures, and templates. It is formal, systemic, and easily shared and communicated. It is found in the words we speak, in any written commentary (such as product specifications, scientific formulas, or computer data), and in any recorded data. Knowledge sharing is enhanced by technology to make sure that knowledge is captured, made explicit where possible, and accessible throughout the company.

- *Tacit knowledge* is knowledge that resides in an individual. It is intuitions, perspectives, beliefs, values, skills, abilities, and know-how. Dorothy Leonard of the Harvard Business School and Walter Swap, formerly of Tufts University, who have done extensive research in this area, call tacit knowledge "Deep Smarts."[8] Tacit knowledge is what people "know" through experience that is not documented anywhere. It is their practical wisdom, their accumulated knowledge, know-how, and intuition gained through extensive experience. Tacit knowledge is shared personally among work teams or communities of practice, where people come together to exchange knowledge and create solutions.

Knowledge architecture is a blueprint that outlines the approaches for achieving a company's knowledge strategy goal of placing the collective knowledge of the company at the disposal of everyone. It supports the interchange of stocks of knowledge. Knowledge access and knowledge exchange are two components that support the flow of tacit and explicit knowledge.

Your *knowledge strategy* defines how your company encourages knowledge creation and exchange. The knowledge strategy guides how you will use new and existing knowledge to enhance your company's capabilities. It also provides the vision and direction for investing in knowledge capital.

If you're acquiring a large company, people involved in developing and managing both the knowledge architecture and the knowledge strategy must realize that their approaches are possibly going to be stretched beyond the original intentions. The knowledge strategy may no longer be suited to the new organizational configuration. You need to reshape the collaboration spaces to ensure that knowledge is being exchanged between relevant parts of the company. You must ensure that both your knowledge architecture and your knowledge strategy are viable enough to accommodate the needs of all the stages of the acquisition process and can recalibrate themselves to meet the requirements of the expanded range of stakeholders of the new and more complex company you are forming.

Conclusion: Looking Outward

In addition to requiring a good set of lenses to see the sources of creating value, if your company wants to make quantum leaps via M&As, you need to examine how your company currently operates, as well as how it relates to your customers and your suppliers, in view of changing business conditions.

To be a quantum leap company, you need to maintain a dynamic of looking both outward *and* inward to sense the changing requirements of your customers and the marketplace and your company's capacity to respond to those requirements. You need to look outward to continuously search out signals of changing needs and conditions. You can then bring that information inward and combine it with your company's experience and innovation perspectives to create a steady stream of new responses. You need to be a sense-and-respond company: you need to sense what's happening in the outside world and then rework your processes and practices to keep on target with your customers and your network. You must be able to transmit high-quality knowledge effectively throughout your company and also with and between your customers and your employees.

A truly quantum company not only looks outward to respond to current needs, but also looks to the future, anticipating customer desires and being just enough ahead of the customer to create a successful market. In this approach, a merger or an acquisition is not just an opportunity to capitalize on the resources of the acquired company for short-term goals, but also a chance to leverage those newly acquired resources to become the company of tomorrow.

A high level of flow and a good quality of knowledge stock will enable your company to stay closely linked to your customers and the marketplace so that you can develop products and service offerings based on a sense-and-respond mode of doing business.

As seen in Exhibit 2-3, the way to be a winner in our evolving marketplace is for your company to improve its organizational capability at a pace that stays just ahead of the market demand. That gives your company a chance to *create* the market, an enviable position to be in. Anything less sets up a situation in which, even though organizational capabilities are improving, they are not in keeping with market demand, and an expectation gap opens ever wider.

If you acquire another company using the quantum leap approach, this presents a major opportunity for you to boost your organizational capability significantly. By facing outward toward the world and your customers and by mobilizing that new knowledge internally for breakthrough responses, you can renew your operations and perspectives to become an ever more powerful, competitive, and strategic company. Chapter 3 describes in detail how you can develop your company's overall strategy to help you achieve a breakthrough acquisition.

Exhibit 2-3

Market Demands

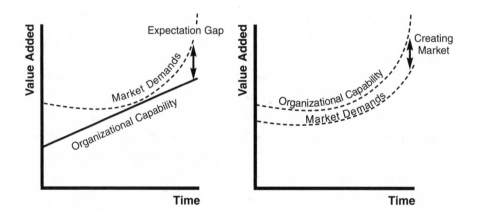

Key Learning Points

- A company's intangible assets are made up of capabilities and relationships that are built through the exchange of knowledge.
- Intangible assets now represent the most important source of value.
- A company's intangible assets form a system that must be managed through an integrated, values-based approach.
- You can increase the quality of knowledge flow in your company by understanding the strategic context of your business.
- Developing any capability begins with the customer, and strategy is no exception.
- Value is either created or depleted with every single interaction among the elements of knowledge capital.
- All other capabilities combined cannot fill the void left by a misguided strategy.
- A strategy is an objective that you arrive at, a conclusion. Strategy making is an action, a process that you follow, a capability.
- Predetermined strategies are excellent for dealing with recurrent acquisition issues. Having the capacity to handle emerging situations is equally necessary for dealing with novel issues that can stymie or derail an acquisition.

Questions

- Are there any stories from the merger (or mergers) we have been involved in that especially evoke the achievements and problems we encountered?
- What do we believe are the key issues experienced by our company during the acquisition and integration processes?
- What lessons did we learn from the M&A process?
- Have we incorporated those lessons into the way our company approaches mergers and acquisitions?
- Looking back, would we have done things any differently to make more of a quantum leap in performance enabled by the M&A?

Notes

1. Lawrence M. Fisher, "How Elan Grew by Staying Small: Growing a Business with Shrewd Acquisitions," *Strategy+Business*; http://www.strategy-business.com/press/16635507/19343.
2. Dawn Gilbertson, "US Airways Names Airline Veteran to Tackle Customer Service Woes," *Arizona Republic*; http://www.usatoday.com/travel/flights/2007-09-07-usairways-new-coo_N.htm.
3. Ibid.
4. Larry Kanter, "Wells Fargo Works to Reassure, Retain First Interstate Customers—Wells Fargo and Co.; First Interstate Bancorp—Special Report: Banking & Finance," *Los Angeles Business Journal*, May 27, 1996; http://findarticles.com/p/articles/mi_m5072/is_n22_v18/ai_18690455.
5. http://consumerist.com/consumer/complaints/boa-buys-mbna-starts-charging-customers-extra-for-not-paying-balances-off-in-full-251283.php.
6. http://www.consumeraffairs.com/news04/2005/mbnbofa.html.
7. Lawrence M. Fisher, "Symantec's Strategy-Based Transformation," *Strategy+Business*; http://www.strategy-business.com/press/16635507/8424.
8. Dorothy Leonard and Walter Swap, *Deep Smarts: How to Cultivate and Transfer Enduring Business Wisdom* (Boston: Harvard Business School Press, 2005).

The additional material in this chapter comes from the authors' interviews and experiences.

3

Framing Your Company's Strategy to Achieve a Breakthrough Acquisition

To achieve breakthrough performance following a merger or an acquisition, you first need to fully understand how your company operates currently, *before* you combine with another company. That may sound obvious, but many M&As fail because the acquiring company didn't have this basic understanding! Therefore, it's worth stating that you need to be fully aware of all of the following:

- Your company's strategic position
- Your company's business logic
- Your company's strengths and weak points

Full understanding of these three critical areas will enable you (the M&A decision makers) to anticipate shifts in customer preferences and the capabilities that you need to build to satisfy customers' expectations.

This chapter reviews why you should avoid the "quick-fix" approach to acquisitions and why you should be wary of letting people outside your company target possible acquisitions for your company. It also describes four scenarios for the types of customers and business solutions you're looking for in the companies you're considering acquiring and four ways in which you can integrate those companies into your own. Finally, this chapter offers detailed case examples of how many companies, including Symantec and Siemens, tackled these problems and acquired other companies successfully after honing their company strategy.

Developing Your Post-M&A Strategy

Strategy is a response to what is happening in the marketplace. It provides direction for the achievement of organizational goals. Strategy is a plan of action that encompasses the sum of a company's objectives, including the company's broader goals and the actions involved in accomplishing those goals. *Strategy making* is the organizational capability that underlies strategy, involving the capability to renew strategies constantly based on trends both inside and outside the company that affect its performance.

There is a need for a constant flow of new knowledge to keep strategies calibrated to the customer. It does not matter how effective the other organizational capabilities are; performance will falter if the company's strategy is not relevant to the customer.

Two Dimensions of Strategy

There are two dimensions of strategy: the strategy capability that deals with *predefined conditions* and the strategy capability that deals with *emerging conditions.* In a merger or acquisition, both dimensions must be involved. There will be a number of actions that are routine and can be planned for in every acquisition. However, the strategy capability must also allow for novel circumstances and conditions that are unique to each specific transaction. Working from the viewpoint of strategy making allows you to detect and respond to emerging conditions and opportunities.

A company can have predefined practices for dealing with routine acquisition issues. This allows it to carry out much of the acquisition process in an efficient and rapid manner. At the same time, it needs to continually search out and be able to respond to emerging problems and opportunities. The company needs to be able to shift gears as needed. It needs to have two different kinds of responses and to be able to handle these two different types of situations in the context of an acquisition. The chapter also explores three basic risk management issues.

In most companies where there is acquisition and integration planning, those efforts are primarily geared to tackling the predefined requirements of the acquisition. The challenge most often is to build the capacity to respond to emerging conditions. The acquisition can often be stymied and flounder unless this capacity is brought into play.

Four Strategic Elements

In the quantum leap model, four strategic elements define an effectively evolving company. These strategies are interlinked, flowing from one to the next and supporting one another to achieve the company's strategic goals:

1. The business strategy
2. The customer strategy
3. The organizational strategy
4. The knowledge strategy

1. *Business strategy.* Your company's overarching *business strategy* defines your broad strategic intent and strategic imperatives. You need to be constantly renewing your strategy to align it and keep pace with the evolution of customer and marketplace needs. It is the largest context for your company's strategies.

2. *Customer strategy.* Your *customer strategy* defines the way you take customers from transaction-based relationships to business-solutions relationships to partnering relationships. It should map out where your company wants to position itself with these various segments of its customer population and what steps you need to take to achieve the transition to increasingly value-rich connections. Your customer strategy should support the accomplishment of the goals of your business strategy

3. *Organizational strategy.* Your *organizational strategy* focuses on how to structure the value-creating processes and design the best way of organizing your company in order to build your customer strategy and pro-

vide the right solutions for those customers. Building the right organizational structure is about creating the right tension and giving the right degree of management attention to the various components of strategic intent.

4. *Knowledge strategy.* Knowledge is the tissue that holds this all together. Your *knowledge strategy* should put in place the mechanisms that provide for accessing and exchanging knowledge. It also enables the development of generative capabilities, such as learning, collaborating, and strategy making. By providing for greater connectivity across the company, a well-formulated and well-implemented knowledge strategy builds coherence and increases speed and agility in your company. To make this business model work, your knowledge strategy needs to support and enable all your other strategies.

The *knowledge strategy* encompasses understanding of the company's organizational strategies, the implications of those strategies, and making sure that these are well understood by everyone who is working on an acquisition project. An effective knowledge strategy surrounding acquisitions and their integration will serve to ensure the sustaining and further development of the core capabilities required for the realization of the acquiring organization's goals. Those capabilities are developed by putting in place effective tools and processes to exchange and access knowledge.

Intangible assets can be even more encompassing than knowledge, although they are the eventual outcome of creating, nurturing, and leveraging the knowledge capabilities of the company.

Having an appreciation of intangible assets allows you to complement the value of tangible, physical, and financial assets. In fact, not including intangibles severely distorts the worth of an acquisition and fails to recognize the capabilities that drive performance. Why would any company want to ignore the basis for performance in a company it is considering acquiring?

Value-added intangibles are created when there is an interaction between human capital, structural capital, and customer capital for knowledge-value creation. Every company has its own set of capital dimensions in play to produce value and yield financial gain. The opportunity in a merger or acquisition is to unbundle the capital dimensions of both the acquirer and the acquired company and then recombine and integrate them for a quantum leap in value creation, performance, and competitive advantage.

This interactive model provides a perspective for managing intangible assets and leads to recognizing, leveraging, and renewing them in the context of an acquisition. It makes explicit and transparent all assets of the target company: tangible, financial, and intangible. Not only that, but it also shows how these assets dynamically interact to produce outcomes. Grasping the real value of the full spectrum of assets is essential for thinking strategically about a significant acquisition. This type of strategic thinking then continues when selecting appropriate targets, raising the right range of questions during due diligence, making sure the company is negotiating on the real value of the target, and ultimately mobilizing the integration to optimize the full set of values possible from the acquisition.

This model for understanding value creation in companies offers a set of lenses for grasping and realizing the possible gains and potential drawbacks of any acquisition in the knowledge era.

Acquisitions Offer a Window of Opportunity for Growth

The goal of a merger or acquisition is to provide a company with high-growth opportunities where it can move quickly to be first to market and capture unprecedented gains before the window on these opportunities closes. An acquisition is a critical opportunity, because it provides a unique period of time when you can

- Carve out new areas of potential strength and expertise.
- Establish an enhanced presence in current market sectors.
- Develop a foundation for having significant impact in new market sectors.

To take advantage of the acquisition-related high-growth opportunities, your company needs to acquire companies that *complement* your strategic logic. That requires elasticity in your dominant business logic so that you can reconstitute your company as a newly emerging combined entity. You can then chart out your strategic issues and determine what will be the makeup of an acquisition or series of acquisitions that will enable you to achieve that quantum leap.

Don't Be Seduced by the Quick-Fix Approach to Acquisitions

As mentioned in Chapter 1, companies can grow organically, by acquisitions, or through some combination of both. Many companies avoid acquisitions because they believe that they have very good prospects already with organic growth. Also, they may not want to get caught up in the kinds of entanglements that can accompany an acquisition. Furthermore, many companies do not have any significant experience in attempting or carrying out acquisitions. Acquisitions can be daunting; they may appear to be an activity in which they have little competence or skills. Because they don't have that experience or practice, they are apprehensive, fearing acquisitions will be more difficult, complicated, and hazardous than their "tried-and-true" incremental organic growth.

In many companies that do seek to grow by acquisition, the leaders who decide on making acquisitions very often just stumble upon acquisition candidates, rather than targeting them specifically. These leaders frequently develop a very short list of companies they know, or apparent competitors, or people with whom they have worked; then they approach those people. There often is no thought about whether the target company is a good fit or about the strategic implications of acquiring that company. These leaders are simply acquiring a company similar to their own because *that is what they know.* They are not thinking (as they should), "If I did this instead of that, what would that do in terms of our strategy and our competitive position?"

> *That is the problem with the current merger-lust. There are few examples of companies entering into a merger with a conscious plan to redesign the rules of their industry. Buying "bulk" doesn't make you innovative.*
>
> *Ultimately, innovation requires a carefully conceived plan to do things differently: to listen to new voices within one's own company, to open up the strategy process, to devise new measurement tools for determining whether a company is innovating, rather than merely getting bulkier.*
>
> —Peter Skarzynski, CEO, Strategos[1]

These companies tend to have little or no strategic focus. Therefore, when they acquire companies that are the same as themselves, they are simply *adding bulk* and obtaining some cost synergies. However, these acquisitions may even arrest their strategic evolution because of the energy and attention required to integrate the new company.

Hone Your Company's Overall Strategy *before* You Acquire

In his book *Good to Great*, Jim Collins notes that companies that did not fare well in attempting to achieve breakthroughs via acquisitions never addressed the fundamental question, "What can we do better than any other company in the world, that fits our economic denominator and that we have passion for?"[2] He goes on to say that these companies "never learned that, while you can buy your way to growth, you absolutely cannot buy your way to greatness. Two big mediocrities joined together will never make one great company."

However, you can initiate and implement an acquisition in such a way that your company can continue to build your strategy and evolve as you carry out the acquisition. To achieve this level of successful acquiring, you need to be ready for the acquisition process, and you need to adopt the value-creating approach that we described in detail in Chapter 2. This means that your company needs to be building an effective acquisition capability.

> *Acquisitions need to be a by-product of your basic strategy. We would never want to do scattershot acquisitions and then have to think up strategies to justify them. We believe that the best way to build value is to focus on a few markets where we can achieve national leadership.*
>
> —Kerry Killinger, President, Chairman,
> and CEO, Washington Mutual[3]

Every company needs a strategic plan—i.e., a strategic set of aspirations over the short and the long term. Your leadership team must have a sense of what your company is about so that you can achieve your stretch goals. In the quantum leap context, your company should use acquisitions as a catalyst to facilitate your way to those goals.

Your company has to determine your strategic imperative, which is something that must happen in order to sustain your current market position, and your strategic aspirations, which is where you would like to be or what you would like to become. You need to know what is happening to the markets in each segment you're involved in. Your company's strategists have to identify success factors for penetrating those sectors so that you can determine what capabilities and products or services you can add through different acquisitions. You can then decide what acquisitions would add to your set of distribution capabilities, product capabilities, or customer relationship capabilities. This is a strategy that deals with the whole company and focuses on what will be required once you put an acquisition into play.[4]

Emerging and often unexpected opportunities are the great variable in acquisitions; however, the constant is *leadership* that is grounded in strategic focus and business logic so that you can use your strategic perspective to clarify the kinds of acquisitions that will add to the capability of your entire company. Your company's strategic framework, culture, and business logic are all intangible assets. Unfortunately, in the current financially dominated approach, these guiding factors are often marginalized. It takes a good deal of rethinking to give due weight to these nontraditional ingredients in the acquisition recipe for success.

Case Example: How Dow Chemical Develops Its Strategy

Randy Croyle of Dow Chemical's Mergers and Acquisitions Expertise Center describes how Dow approaches meeting its emerging organizational needs:

> *Dow has what we call an SDP, Strategic Decision Process, where the CEO and senior leadership take a look at our overall particular business statement and we identify gaps, i.e., where we are in relation to the competition, where we see there are areas for opportunities. Then we ask ourselves, "What is the best way to fill those gaps? Is it through internal resources, or does it go into the M&A space?" M&A is just one potential avenue once you have identified a particular gap when you have done a strategic assessment of a particular business line.*

Don't Let Outsiders Convince You to Acquire Companies That Don't Fit Your Strategy

Often, the first response by a company that has limited strategic capability is to hire a consulting firm or investment bank to map out its acquisition strategy. The investment bank or consulting firm gets its fee and goes hunting for opportunities as it sees fit. People from the firm go into the field and find out what might be available. After doing a financial analysis, they determine the rough size of the companies that their client company could afford to buy. At that point, they determine what it would take to buy this set of companies.

The next step for the investment bank or consulting firm is to find out which candidates can be pried away from their current owners. With that information in hand, they come back to their client and say, "You can buy this and you can buy that, or you could buy this other company." Unfortunately, the investment bankers or consultants may have only a superficial understanding of their client company's strategy. As more distant external advisors, they are often unaware of the capabilities equation involved.

Using the value-creating approach, though, a company must be more aware of its current strategic position in the market. You need to define what you want to do from a strategic point of view and then say, "These are the kinds of companies that we need to look at." You can then be in a position to take advantage of opportunities more effectively in terms of what companies to select within your strategic purview—in other words, you won't be merely opportunistic, which is a behavior that often leads to companies making significant and expensive mistakes by acquiring companies that don't really fit with their overall strategy and goals.

As your company learns to operate within your overall strategic intent, as you better understand your company's strategic logic, and as you establish replicable sets of practices, you will increase your knowledge of how best to use outside resources, particularly consulting firms.

Managing the Risks

The acquisition and integration of companies are all by definition high-risk ventures. To achieve great gains, business leaders must be rigorous in sifting through the downside risks as well as the upside benefits that are part of any major acquisition. The upside benefits of an acquisition are far more promoted and the downside risks rarely mentioned, but you must recognize both and put in place strategies to manage them.

Case Example: An Equipment Company Targets an Acquisition on Its Own

Instead of paying a substantial amount of money to an outside consulting firm to search for a fitting acquisition, one equipment company decided to determine on its own what its core business was and what type of company it should consider acquiring. This self-evaluation process took almost a full year.

Unexpectedly, the CEO decided to call one of the largest equipment makers in Europe. The CEO of the European company was very receptive to being purchased. He had led an acquisition that had gone wrong 18 months before, and now his company was going bankrupt. Because the North American equipment company's leaders had identified their company's strategic logic and had evaluated its current capabilities and the capabilities it was seeking, the equipment company was able to take advantage of this unanticipated opportunity. The acquisition took place shortly afterward.

Risks are inherent to all business decisions. There are a great many unknowns and numerous occasions during an acquisition and integration where conditions change unexpectedly. The better prepared you are for different types (some of which are described in the next sections) and degrees of risk, the greater the probability that your company will be successful in carrying out your integration and realizing breakthrough outcomes. As your integration team and your new management team gain practice at anticipating and managing risk, you will be better equipped to deal with a broad range of eventualities. As the ancient Chinese strategist Sun Tsu wrote: "If you know the enemy and know yourself, you need not fear the result of 100 battles. If you know yourself but not the enemy, for every victory gained you will also suffer a defeat. If you know neither the enemy nor yourself, you will succumb in every battle."[5]

Essentially, there are three different types of risk in an acquisition and integration. They involve mindset issues as well as market issues. They are:

1. Risk because of the inability to see how things can go amok in a volatile integration process.
2. Risk because company leaders have mindsets that are overly rigid.
3. Risk because the legacy companies fail to develop a partnership with each other. Skillful partnering builds trust. The lower the trust coefficient, the higher the risk of losing value in merging the two companies.

Let's take a closer look at each of these three types of risk.

Risk 1: Being Unable to Anticipate Problems during the Integration of Two Companies

If your company is expecting that everything will go according to expectations, you will be taken by surprise when your integration team and the new company overall come up against strategic risks that you did not envision. Strategic risks are the ones that can significantly impair essential elements of your new company's business. Some of the strategic risks that you may need to anticipate in the course of the acquisition are

- The emergence of a new technology or innovation that changes the way your market operates
- A shift in the way your market is organized or regulated
- A disruption in the availability or a change in market price of basic resources needed to produce your products (such as jet fuel if you are an airline)
- The arrival of a key competitor in your market space
- The departure of key leaders to competitive companies
- The failure of a critical R&D or market initiative that would have given your new company a unique competitive advantage

As the leadership of the new company goes through alternative risk scenarios, it can see critical issues in ways that it may not have been attuned to. It is not only senior leadership that needs to understand the variety of potential risks; leaders at all other levels of the company need to participate. One segment of the company may be aware of and affected by a different configuration of risk factors from another business unit. For example, a production function may be aware of potential technical breakthroughs that competitors are developing; a service department may have intimate knowledge of changing customer options; a safety group may know what kinds of environmental or regulatory changes are coming on line that will affect operations. Those perspectives need to be shared across the company to identify the most critical set of risk factors that the company will be facing. As the significance of these risks is defined and the probabilities for them are gauged, countermeasures can be developed to prevent or mitigate these risks, or perhaps innovative ways to turn these risks to advantage can be determined.

Exploring alternative case scenarios gives the leaders of the new company the opportunity to find out what the company can do to compensate for any advantages its competition has and any deficiencies it has. In good part, this involves reviewing the company's own capabilities and the capabilities of competitors to deepen its knowledge of what capabilities it needs to cultivate and how to shift its game plan to minimize any negative exposures.[6] Engaging in these reviews allows the new company to anticipate the type and extent of the risks that it could face, and use the lead time it has to generate responses to counter them.

For example, an energy company may determine that there is a substantial and growing risk of scarcity of oil and gas reserves. It may be facing diminishing outputs from its oil and gas fields, and/or promising new fields may be in areas where political turmoil makes it difficult to engage in new production. The company can see how the capabilities gained through an acquisition can assist it in pursuing alternative solutions to this dilemma. If its current capabilities fall short of what it sees as its requirements, it might seek to counter this risk by additional acquisitions or strategic alliances to obtain new technologies for gaining greater yields from existing or available fields or by investing in the development of nontraditional energy sources, such as shale, wind, or solar energy.

Being sensitive to strategic risks enables the new company to manage its risk exposure by adjusting its strategic plan and developing a specific set of countermeasures.

Risk 2: Having a Rigid Mindset and Failing to Be Flexible

Having a particular mindset helps leaders make sense of the complex world in which their company operates. Based on lessons learned through experience, leaders use a set of ground rules that worked in the past. The problem with mindsets, however, is that they can limit leaders' field of vision. Mindsets can prevent leaders from seeing the risks inherent in either business or organizational patterns. A company may be captive to the belief that only growth in absolute size will enable it to achieve its earnings goals, disregarding issues involving a changing market or internal issues of structural and cultural fit that may make proceeding with the acquisition or integration no longer economically sensible.

In the context of an integration, people from both companies are busy interpreting what they see through the lens of their respective mindsets. The leaders of the acquiring company tend to be more rigid in adhering to their own mindsets because they feel that the superiority of

---

Case Example: JC Penney's Failed Acquisition of Eckerd Drugs

When JC Penney acquired Eckerd Drugs in 1995, the company quickly and unfortunately discovered that it was a strategic mismatch. Penney did not have the capabilities to provide good management in the drug chain business. After nine years of not being able to resolve Eckerd's continuing poor performance, Penney sold off the drug chain in 2004.[7]

---

their approach has been validated by the fact that they are the acquirer. As we have often seen, however, just because your company is acquiring another does not guarantee that all of your senior leaders' mindsets will necessarily help your new company achieve breakthrough performance. Moreover, the pressure and haste involved in postdeal integration tend to bring more rigidity and impair the ability to see any approach but one's own as having any validity.

Only by being open to engaging in dialogue can a high level of trust come about. Trust is the necessary condition for participants to genuinely look for the best answer to the mindset challenges they are encountering, rather than seeking the familiarity of old approaches. In the pressure of a fast-moving integration, leaders often do not have adequate tolerance to grasp the true value of what has emerged from the other company, but tend to reject it out of hand. The inability to transcend one's own mind-

---

Case Example: What Happens When You Alienate Key Executives

One financial services company acquired another financial services firm, in good part based on the belief that the acquired firm had key marketing and technological capabilities that would enable the acquirer to resolve its sales and technology support issues. Within two years after the acquisition closed, however, it had so alienated the leading executives of the acquired company by continually disregarding their inputs that most of the these executives had voted with their feet and left, taking their capabilities to bring about the desired changes with them. The acquirer paid a premium to gain access to these resources, but because of behaviors stemming from its domineering mindset, those resources were driven from the company.

sets is a considerable handicap in dealing with and bridging what significant differences there are between an acquiring company and the company it is taking over.

Risk 3: Failing to Develop a Partnership between the Two Legacy Companies

A third risk factor that has to be managed during the transition is the inability to establish an authentic partnering relationship with the acquired company. If your company (i.e., the acquirer) makes an extensive effort to reach out to people in the company you're acquiring, you will build a basis for the trusting relationships necessary to meet the strenuous demands involved in moving your new company into a breakthrough mode. If your company is fair and open to the views of the acquired company, that will give the leadership and employees from the acquired company the opportunity to join the new company as peers and to invest themselves in creating a common future.

On the other hand, if your company sees itself as a conqueror that can be as ruthless as it wants solely through the right of ownership, you will undercut the very ground you need if you are to reach the high-performance and value creation goals that you profess to seek.

Case Example: A Conglomerate Alienated New Manufacturing Employees

A large conglomerate used its rapid-paced integration process to integrate and reorganize a sizable plastics manufacturing company that it had acquired. The management of the acquired company, which had a track record as a successful, profit-making enterprise, was disturbed by the abrupt change in management policies that ran counter to its effective production processes and disrupted its carefully developed customer relationships. The haste with which the acquiring company moved did not allow for acknowledging the value of the capabilities of the acquired firm or its employees. A significant portion of the value of the acquisition was impaired by not engaging the new employees in the transition process and allowing the option of taking the additional time needed to integrate such a nonstandard acquisition.

Knowing Your Customers Guides You to Acquire a Company with Complementary Capabilities

A company that is seeking significant and continuing growth has to make it a priority to understand how it is addressing its current and potential customers. Exhibit 3-1 lists some initial questions to consider when developing strategy.

Exhibit 3-1

Questions to Ask, before You Merge or Acquire, about Your Customer Relationships

- ☐ What are the customer relationships that we want as a company?

- ☐ Where do we want to be in the value chain that brings our products and services to customers?

- ☐ Do we want a close partnering relationship with our customers, or are we going to be more of a commodity player and relate to them through intermediaries?

Where your company wants to be in its relationship with your customers determines what you need to acquire, in terms of the value chain you will operate in and what particular place you will have in that chain. Thinking of your customers gives you a powerful perspective on the strategic role of the acquisition you're considering. At this strategic context stage, you can look at critical relationships. You can think of how things would be different from the following four vantage points:

- New customers
- Old customers
- New solutions
- Old solutions

Exhibit 3-2 shows different customer/solution possibilities.

Exhibit 3-2

Various Customer/Solutions Capabilities following a Merger or Acquisition

Old Customers/ New Solutions	New Customers/ New Solutions
Old Customers/ Old Solutions	New Customers/ Old Solutions

Scenario 1: Acquiring a Company Similar to Your Own

If you purchase a very similar company, you will expand your current customer base with *more* customers, but you will have much *the same type* of customers, and you will offer them much the same solutions. For example, Hewlett-Packard bought Compaq Computer, which operated in much the same customer space as HP, but with some complementary market segments as well. In this scenario, the question is whether the cost synergies you will achieve through acquisition will significantly improve your strategic position or simply make your company vulnerable because of the time, effort, and expense involved in integrating the other company. HP had to work very hard to differentiate its customer segments as well as its product and service lines. Unless your company's capabilities are markedly different from those of the company you're acquiring, this type of acquisition will primarily add bulk and will grow your customer base only marginally.

Scenario 2: Acquiring a Company with a Different Customer Base

If you purchase a company that has the same solutions as your company, but different customers, you will grow your customer base, but with much the same set of products and/or services. For example, if a cell phone company in North America with a regional customer base acquires a similar company in Asia, the products and services will be very similar, but the customers will be significantly different and will increase the customer base substantially. This is one form of a growth stretch through acquisition.

Scenario 3: Acquiring a Company with Similar Customers but a Different Way of Doing Business

If you acquire a company with new solutions but a customer base similar to your own, there is an opportunity to cross-market new products and services to a whole new population. For example, if you're a specialty manufacturing company and you acquire another company that makes a standard line of equipment, you will have an expanded line of products and/or services to make available to an expanded set of customer segments. This type of acquisition can present significant opportunities to bring together different technology or design capabilities and come up with product or service offering innovations that neither company would have been able to produce before. This is a growth stretch that presents challenges, but it's not completely alien because both companies are manufacturing companies.

Scenario 4: Acquiring a Company with New Customers and a Different Way of Doing Business

The greatest stretch comes when a company with one set of solutions and customers acquires another company with a significantly different set of both solutions and customers. The opportunities for new markets and customers are maximized here, but *so are the risks*. The danger is that you may underestimate the effort required to capture the anticipated capability synergies, and therefore, the result may be significant financial and strategic losses. For example, when AOL merged with Time Warner, the stretch was too great to allow the newly emerging company to carry out an effective and successful integration.

The implications of "what kind of solution?" and "who is the customer?" have strong consequences, as can be seen in the following case example.

Case Example: How One Company Decided *Not* to Acquire Another Company

A midsized pump company was considering making an acquisition. It was thinking through the "new customers/old customers, new solutions/old solutions" matrix. The leaders of the company were asked whether they wanted to continue selling only water pumps for buildings or to expand their product line to include selling water pumps for golf courses. Initially, they did not know how to sort out this issue.

Then they were asked, "Are you dealing with the same customer group?" They said, "No!"

"Is it the same technology?" They replied, "It is related, but it is not the same technology."

"Do you have any knowledge of the products that would be required for a golf course pumping system?"

"No; it is really quite a different technology."

"Are you interested in starting a different company?"

"No."

By considering these questions, the leaders of this company realized that this acquisition would not provide their company with a rightful claim to ownership for two reasons:

They could not make the new offering work from a financial point of view.

They did not have an idea about how to run the newly acquired company.

The principle of rightful ownership is that you can realize the most value by acquiring that company. In this situation, the value gained would have been marginal. The exploration revealed that the acquiring company would end up running two organizations, which it did not want to do.

If a company goes into a new customers/new solutions acquisition, is it, in fact, starting a different company instead of bolting something onto the current company? This is a judgment that has to be grounded in the company's individual circumstances. Some companies decide that when they make an acquisition, they are going to become an entirely different business. They may become more of a holding unit, as opposed to actually running the new company. In other cases, they want to change their business. In any event, they need an adequate set of capabilities both to carry through the acquisition and to integrate the acquired company effectively so that they can achieve both their short- and their long-range goals.

The question is whether the acquiring company wants to add a capability to serve its existing customer populations or to bring in a different group of customers that it can now reach with this particular acquisition. The challenge to the acquirer is how much of a stretch it wants to make. Therefore, before you merge with or acquire another company, ask yourself the questions in Exhibit 3-3.

Exhibit 3-3

Questions to Ask, before You Merge or Acquire, about How Much You Want Your Company to Stretch

☐ What is too short a stretch?

☐ What is an overstretch?

☐ Where do we begin to optimize both expense and capability synergies?

Positioning Your Acquisition for Maximum Strategic Advantage

A company can do everything else right, but if it has the wrong strategy, the acquisition will turn out to be a mistake. Conversely, if your strategy reflects your company's actual strategic intent and business logic, there is a great opportunity for you to fashion an imaginative strategy that can strengthen your company's future and powerfully realize your vision.

In some cases, this may mean creating a schema of what your company believes it needs to become over time and the key acquisitions that will bring in capacities that allow that to happen. In other cases, it may mean that your company understands that it needs to basically transform itself into a fundamentally different kind of company, with different customer sets, income streams, and markets.

An acquisition is an important option to consider when a company is deliberating on how it will achieve stretch strategic goals. The question that is always in the background of an acquisition is whether it will be worth the effort and expense, or whether the company will be better off if it develops its own capacities organically over time to achieve those same ends. Having an effective strategy-making capability and making the best decisions is the first step in that process. How well a company proceeds with its acquisition and integration process will then create the basis for the company to know if its choice of acquisition was the best way to go.

Four Ways to Integrate an Acquired Company

There are four types of integration that a company can consider. Any of these types may be appropriate for a company at different points in time. Choosing one type versus the others has to do with the gains you're seeking from the acquisition and the expenditures of time and other resources that each type will entail.

1. The "Add-On"

In this case, the acquisition is an addition to an existing business umbrella portfolio. Pragmatically, the acquirer is a holding company that is seeking to keep the new acquisition relatively untouched and unchanged, except for, perhaps, holding it to standard of performance measures. Examples include conglomerates like Loews Corporation and Fortune Brands:

- Loews is a holding company that is one of the largest diversified financial corporations in the United States, with holdings in the areas of insurance, hotels, movie theaters, watches, cigarettes, and oil and gas pipelines. Loews's principal subsidiaries are CNA Financial Corporation; Lorillard, Inc.; Diamond Offshore Drilling, Inc.; Texas Gas Transmission, LLC; Loews Hotels; Bulova Corporation; and Gulf South Pipeline, LP.
- Fortune Brands is a conglomerate with a continuing acquisition program for a wide range of consumer brands in the areas of spirits and wines, household items, and golf and recreation products.

Add-on acquisitions can be appropriate for such highly diversified conglomerates.

2. Dominant Absorption

In this type of integration, one company acquires the other and absorbs it completely, with the acquired company taking on the prevailing owner's business management philosophy, management systems, goals, and practices. This approach focuses on cost-cutting synergies and rapid absorption of the acquired company. It often takes place when a company acquires other companies from the same industry.

The advantages of absorption are that you can achieve considerable cost savings (by eliminating duplicated functions) and you can integrate the new company into your own company rapidly. The disadvantages are not only that you may lose valuable people during the integration process, but that you also are unable to take into account the differentiated capabilities of the acquired organization. See the case study at the top of page 75 for two examples of dominant absorption integration.

3. "Best of Both"

This approach involves engaging in a systematic reevaluation of both companies' management structure and practices, followed by an objective selection of the best approaches to governance, values, structure, modalities of operating, and culture, which then become the basis for the newly combined company's approach. In a sense, this could be considered seeking to become the "best of breed." This approach takes a great investment of leadership and commitment to working through difficult issues if it is to succeed. In some instances, this approach works, as in case of the acquisition of Wells Fargo by Norwest Corporation in 1998 (see the case study at the bottom of page 75), but in many others, it gets very politically entangled in battles over whose practices are best.

4. Breakthrough

The goal of a breakthrough integration is to go beyond the "best of both" approach by incorporating not only the breakthrough aspects of both com-

Case Examples: America West and Bank of America

Two examples of the dominant absorption type of integration are the America West acquisition of US Airways in 2005 and the Bank of America acquisition of LaSalle Bank in 2007:

- America West acquired the debt-ridden US Airways at a bargain price and took on the better-recognized brand name of its much larger acquisition target. By doing so, it gained an instant presence in every major market along the east coast of the United States.
- With the $21 billion LaSalle acquisition, Bank of America became the second-largest U.S. bank after Citigroup and gained a significant foothold in Chicago and Michigan.

panies, but also selected aspects of other outstanding business models. This may include incorporating cutting-edge technologies, marketing capabilities, or approaches to innovation. The outcome of this approach is achieving new levels of performance and significant increases in the value of the combined companies. Breakthrough is an attitude—a way of perceiving and operating during the acquisition, during the integration, and afterwards. The breakthrough approach embodies innovation and continuous renewal; these are at the core of how the newly combining organization approaches the company, its relationship to all of its stakeholders, and the changing market environment.

Case Example: Norwest's Acquisition of Wells Fargo Bank

Norwest adopted the Wells Fargo brand name after the acquisition, which doubled the newly combined bank's assets to $198 billion. Considerable care was taken to determine the best way to govern the combined bank in terms of

- How it navigated its legal and regulatory environment
- How it selected its technology
- Its emphasis on speed to market
- Establishing a mutual understanding of risk
- Making customer service a priority
- Doing whatever was necessary to build a strong brand based on its vision and values

These efforts brought the new bank to a higher level of performance and profitability.

> ## Case Example: Symantec
>
> Symantec chose the path of becoming a transformational acquirer. It made several serial acquisitions, and then acquired Axent Technologies for $990 million in stock at the end of 2000. With the Axent acquisition, Symantec augmented not only its technical capabilities but also its sales and marketing capabilities, and it became a global player.
>
> When it acquires companies now, it has learned to move those new products and services onto a common architecture. The ability to use acquisitions as a springboard for transformation is in good part rooted in attitude. Symantec CEO and chairman John Thompson brought that kind of attitude into the foreground of how Symantec does its business when he said:
>
> > *Companies that win in this industry are willing to make big bets, and they're able to get their team rallied behind what they're trying to do. The fact that somebody bigger than you has an idea doesn't mean you should run away from it. I can outrun. I can outthink. I can outexecute. If you can do these things, size doesn't matter.*[8]

The emphasis in this book is on major acquisitions, where there is the opportunity to use an acquisition as a catalyst to achieve breakthrough (i.e., extraordinary) performance and substantially enhance the value of the combined companies. In a globally competitive environment, adopting the breakthrough acquisition approach may be the only schema for achieving a sustainable competitive advantage that meets a company's short-range and long-range strategic objectives.

Developing a Growth Strategy Based on Acquisitions

Acquisitions can either be strategic or tactical. The difference is how well the acquisition aligns with achieving the strategic goals of the company. In many companies, acquisitions are tactical. These acquisitions satisfy the goals of a business unit or perhaps the company's CEO or CFO, and that may be satisfactory when there are limited goals for the company. However, if the company has quantum leap goals, operating on the tactical level is not adequate. Considering the level of energy, expense, and time required for a major acquisition, creating an ongoing *strategic* acquisition orientation and capability is the key to making acquisition investments become higher-yielding, transformational initiatives.

Case Example: How Symantec Completely Reshaped Itself

Symantec is an example of a company that used acquisitions as part of a strategy to recast itself and transform its business base. Over a five-year period starting in 1999, it transformed itself from a consumer software publisher with a disparate product focus and little brand identity into a provider of enterprise security systems used by large corporations to protect their computer networks against spyware, cyber attacks, misuse and abuse, viruses, spam, and other unauthorized network access. As technology analyst Lawrence Fisher put it, "Symantec's transformation involved acquiring technology and management capabilities, learning new sales and marketing approaches, and skillfully positioning business leaders to drive change and execute strategy."[9]

Symantec's strategy has been working. The company moved to the number one position in the worldwide security market, with a 12 percent share, leading the list of the world's top 21 security software vendors.[10]

As with other companies that have embarked upon a major transformation strategy, the realities of carrying off such a large-scale initiative are uneven, especially when the company is faced with conditions that border on being highly volatile.

An organization needs to be resilient as much as it is flexible to recover from stumbles along the way. And recover Symantec did, taking its market capitalization from about $600 million to more than $6 billion within three years, even as the stock values of most software companies were plummeting.[11]

Did Symantec have a choice? According to a Symantec board member, "It was either fix the company or continue to unravel and go into a death spiral."[12]

It was at this time that John Thompson, an IBM veteran, became the CEO. He gathered senior managers to map out a new direction for the company. In addition to concentrating on security, which was an existing strength of Symantec's, the company decided to restructure itself by customer sets, instead of by products or geographic factors.

The company recruited a core leadership team to oversee its consumer business, new company initiatives, finances, communications, and brand management. The next step was to get key middle management support, because such a broad transformation needed a sizable cadre of collaborative, experienced, and respected people who were committed to the change initiative and could lead and influence the change at their levels of responsibility.

After that, Symantec dealt with was building up its capabilities so that it could become a serious player in the enterprise security market. It needed new product development processes and capacities for performance testing to enable it to serve multiple thousands of users. In conjunction with that, it had to establish close relationships with its customers.

Symantec realized that because it did not have time to *create* a technological base, it had to *buy* that base. Therefore, the company made a series of acquisitions that both broadened its security base and added to its pool of human capital. At the time, during the dot-com boom, Symantec was not seen as being a dynamic, competitive opportunity employer. The acquisition strategy had the advantage of adding key talent to the company immediately.

Symantec's 1999 acquisition of Axent Technologies gave it key products and technology capabilities, but also a substantial sales and marketing capability with a global reach. As Symantec's CFO, Greg Myers, said, "Early on, we bought technical talent, not sales talent. In the second phase, we've started to bring into the company people with strong direct-relationship sales capabilities."[13]

The Axent acquisition was the catalyst for changing Symantec's processes to support an enterprise-based business (instead of individual consumers, which had previously been Symantec's customer base).

> Axent had systems in place for serving major corporate customers, and just as important, its senior executives understood the service and support needs of that market. As the former Axent executives assumed leadership roles at Symantec, they helped guide the company's investment in and deployment of new systems to under gird the new enterprise thrust.[14]

This section provides case studies of various companies that used a strategic perspective when they developed and implemented mergers and acquisitions. These case studies illustrate key principles involved in how companies can create an M&A strategy that is a good fit for their company and enables them to achieve significant performance and revenue leaps. No company stays the same for long, nor do the conditions that it operates in stay the same. The lesson to be learned is that when a company operates from a strategic perspective and aligns all its operations, including mergers and acquisitions, it can make great leaps. This strategic perspective must be recalibrated on an ongoing basis to match both the internal and the external changes in the company's circumstances.

Finding Your Own Path

Every company needs to find its own path. The key differential is that a company can operate on either a tactical or a strategic basis. When it operates on a strategic basis, there is a strategic vision that uses acquisitions to fill and bolster strategic capabilities, which are instrumental in enhancing

Case Example: How a Large Technology Consulting Company Intentionally Built Its Acquisition Capability

SAIC is a large technology consulting company that had traditionally been a highly decentralized, employee-owned company. When a new CEO came in, he saw the need to double the company's revenue in a three-year period. That stretch goal required the company's mostly autonomous business units to reconsider the approach to growth that they had used for decades.

Although these separate business units had engaged in acquisitions, and in many cases were skilled and knowledgeable in their acquisition efforts, their acquisition initiatives had been more opportunistic and tactical than intentional and strategic. The new revenue requirement, however, demanded acquisitions that would take on a much more significant role in growth plans and that would be aligned with the growth of the entire company, in addition to the growth of individual business units. This shift demanded a basic rethinking of how these business units went about creating their futures and how they managed their operations. Acquisition quickly became a key element in intentionally making the revenue and strategic leap envisioned by the CEO.

SAIC's central organization developed a strategy for this transition. It used the leaders of its knowledge management component to bring together the most experienced SAIC M&A practitioners, not only to develop a database of the company's best practices, but also to initiate and weave together a network of colleagues across the company with the skills (human resources, accounting, legal, technical, and so on) required for successful acquisitions and integrations. The goal was to take the company's *tactical* acquisition capabilities to a *strategic* level. Communities of practice, knowledge repositories, expert yellow pages, and other vehicles are being used collaboratively by knowledge management staff and business unit staff to build on existing strengths to form that strategic, companywide capability. For SAIC, stretch goals and the means to achieve them are not an option; instead, they're a requirement and a core part of its new way of doing business.

both market presence and positioning. Companies as varied as Siemens AG (one of the world's largest electrical engineering and electronics companies) and the much smaller Elan Corporation (a pharmaceutical company) have developed a sense of where they needed to be in the future and targeted the companies they needed to acquire to achieve the configuration that would give them the capabilities they needed. In both cases, the company had the set of capabilities to make it ready to formulate its strategy and to integrate the acquired company effectively.

> ### Case Example: Siemens's Acquisition Strategy
>
> Siemens Business Services Division wanted to establish itself as a cutting-edge company in a newly opening media market, so Siemens targeted acquiring the BBC's Technology Information Group. This was a break-through strategy that showcased Siemens's IT outsourcing capabilities to a vast and previously untapped media sector. Siemens's readiness capabilities included a strong customer partnering capacity, which allowed the BBC to feel that Siemens would carry out its IT requirements of global support 24 hours a day, 7 days a week, more effectively than the BBC could do itself. The BBC also had the opportunity to draw on Siemens's companywide innovation program to manage its resources more effectively, increase the levels of its performance, and support it in moving in new directions as far as its technology and how it ran its organization were concerned.
>
> The leverage point for the acquisition was that Siemens marketed itself as a good acquirer; it was not just providing services less expensively but also providing services differently and at a higher level than the target company was able to produce itself or purchase from others. That is the focus of the Siemens client-centered component approach.
>
> Siemens has also developed a set of templates and processes for carrying out acquisitions and integrating acquired companies successfully. The company has a game plan that kicks in at the beginning of the whole acquisition process. Sellers know that when Siemens comes in, it is ready to make the acquisition process work. Siemens does not just offer a platform. It has a whole set of templates for how to go through the process, from strategy to integration.

Business Strategy and Knowledge Strategy

A sense of what knowledge is needed for a successful acquisition under-pins the full extent of the value-creating approach to the M&A process mapped out in this book. In the strategy stage, a company needs to ask itself a key question:

> "What are the knowledge implications that flow from the understanding that we need to grow by acquiring other companies as well as growing organically?" That is, what kind of knowledge structure, learning capabilities, communication skills, and so on do we need to have to support our growth model, and who needs to be involved in developing and maintaining our knowledge capability and in what ways?

Case Example: Elan Corporation

Elan Corporation is a global pharmaceutical company based in Ireland that has grown by a mixture of acquisitions, licensing of products, and strategic alliances. It began as a contract provider of drug delivery technology in the 1970s and the 1980s, a role that required little capital because its development costs were covered by its client companies. However, by the late 1980s and into the 1990s, Elan became aware that it was reaching the limits of its contract-provider business model. In that model, clients brought the already developed and approved drugs to Elan, which added a time-release capability and other formulations that increased the efficiency of or added life to the already existing drugs.

Elan rethought its position and determined that it needed to become a fully integrated pharmaceutical company, with the capability to develop its own drugs and take them to market. The first major step on that path was taken in 1996, when Elan acquired Athena Neurosciences for $638 million in stock. This acquisition gave Elan a niche set of licensed neurological drug therapies, as well as a sales force and products that generated revenues. Elan had a practice of retaining key managers, one of whom became Elan's president and COO.

When Elan was frustrated by finding that there were few viable drugs available to bolster its market niche, it made another major acquisition in 1997, buying the Neurex Corporation, which concentrated on treatment of intractable pain. Elan subsequently acquired Carnick Laboratories, another company involved in pain treatment. These acquisitions also expanded Elan's new advanced medications and provided sales forces that knew the specialist customers intimately.

Elan used a strategic planning team to keep track of more than 100 companies that were potential acquisition targets and to keep a closer watch on 20 of these. This team continually screened these companies, first for their science capabilities, and then to see if they were growing as fast as Elan needed.

In short, Elan changed its strategy as it saw markets emerge and change, and shifted its acquisitions accordingly. Elan's shifting fortunes demonstrate that even with several advantages—i.e., an experienced and resourceful strategic acquisition capability, an orientation toward entrepreneurialism, the ability to retain talented people, and a track record of significant success—no company is immune to market shifts or reversals based on unanticipated problems with products, service, or its own leadership. Elan's stock went from $60 a share in 2002 to $6.80 in 2005, but it has since rebounded from that low point. Questions of safety of one of the company's products were resolved, and Elan continued to develop a pipeline of upcoming drugs that show significant promise.

Elan's case demonstrates how important it is for a company to retain its integrity, rethink market conditions and strategy, and utilize its capabilities to respond; these qualities are what enable a company to reposition itself for viability and success. When that integrity is compromised and those capabilities are not sufficiently renewed, the company will find that its ability to maintain its past successes is seriously jeopardized.

Generally, you first need to ensure that your business strategy is in place; then you can develop your knowledge strategies to support your business strategy. At this stage, company leaders and strategic planners should ask these further questions:

- "Where does our company need to have structural growth?"
- "Would bringing in an external element—i.e., acquiring another company—provide what we require?"

The knowledge implications of these questions may be that you need to be searching for the right acquisition opportunities. Your search team must be able to tap into the strategies of companies that would fit *your* company's strategic requirements. It is not as much a question of knowledge strategy here as it is a question of what the knowledge implications of this are, what the knowledge requirements of such an exercise are, and how the company goes about getting those needs met.

If a company has a knowledge strategy in place and if that knowledge strategy is supported by a well-designed knowledge technology platform, people in the company will be familiar with the ways in which they can access and exchange necessary knowledge throughout the company and how they can use this knowledge every day in their own work. A natural extension of this is that when an opportunity for an acquisition arises, everything is in place to connect to that knowledge resource, and everyone will be ready to take on the roles they need to play in an acquisition and the follow-up integration processes.

Every company has a way of *handling* the knowledge that is required to carry out each of its activities successfully. Underneath every company's activity, there is some method of *transferring* knowledge. The question is whether this method is as systematic as it needs to be—which is where a knowledge strategy can make a key contribution. A knowledge strategy makes the transfer of knowledge more effective, more systematic, less segmented, and more complete. It also involves learning how to use technology more systematically and in ways that are compatible with and attractive to people, because over the years, people typically develop ways of working that ignore the capability of their company's technology platform. A goal of the knowledge strategy is to deal with the strategy/execution split. People in the company have to learn how to use the technology to access, use, and share essential knowledge effectively. To accomplish this, the company needs to develop a knowledge strategy that enables it to be ready to acquire other companies. Doing so makes it possible for a company to have the capacities it needs to ensure that an acquisition fits strategically and that the acquired company can be integrated effectively.

Case Example: An Embedded Knowledge Strategy at Clarica

Clarica, a Canadian insurer, made several acquisitions to build its market share between 1998 and 2002. Clarica was itself acquired in 2002 by Sun Life Financial Services of Canada. One capability of Clarica's that Sun Life sought to build upon was its ability to design and carry out mergers and acquisitions.

Clarica's knowledge strategy provided a framework for its new initiatives, which were aimed at leveraging Clarica's intangible assets. This strategy provided a context for growing those assets through the exchange of knowledge inside the company, as well as externally in its partnerships and with customers. The strategy outlined the processes, tools, and infrastructure that enabled knowledge to flow effectively to accelerate the development of a capability. The knowledge strategy also delineated a phased approach that took into account Clarica's absorption capacity.

Everyone at Clarica was a participant in the knowledge strategy in one form or another, but the core developers were members of the Knowledge Team of the Strategic Capabilities unit. This Knowledge Team was responsible for

- Shaping the company's intranet
- Facilitating communities of practice
- Supporting different business groups to implement knowledge initiatives

A virtual team of IT professionals became part of the Knowledge Team to ensure that the necessary "sociotechnical" dimensions were reconciled for maximum impact.

From Strategy to Acquisition

Strategy maps out the goals and how they will be accomplished throughout a company. Without strategy, there is no direction, coherence, or basis for measuring degrees of success. Action without strategy is meaningless and a costly, wasteful expenditure of resources. The business strategy names the key reference points and establishes the necessary threads that have to be established and woven together by a company over time to become the whole cloth of the newly emerging company. Growth by M&As is often a core element of that business strategy.

Strategy sets the stage and charts the path, but it isn't everything. M&A strategy is derived from company strategy. Once you've set your strategy and defined and stated what you need to do to implement that strategy, your company will be positioned (and will have a firm basis) to select M&A targets that will complement your existing capabilities and meet your strategic goals. The targeting process, along with due diligence and negotiations, begins Stage 2 in the M&A process, which we'll describe in Chapter 4.

Success Factors

- Have a clear view of your market and the evolution of your market, and have a proactive view of where your company needs to be.
- Questions the assumptions and the mindsets the team holds with regards to its evolution as a firm. There has to be debunking of any dominant mindset, regardless of how well established it is, in order to understand what course of action and what candidate target companies would provide sufficient efficiency *and* growth synergies for your company.
- Deal with the risks of volatility, mindsets, and establishing partnering.
- Work through both downside and upside scenarios.

Derailing Factors

- Your company has no strategy to start with.
- You don't have a clear view of the dynamics of your market or you don't understand market trends. This can lead to your acquiring a business unit or another company that adds a burden to your company rather than enhancing it, thereby drawing your company into a dangerously disadvantageous competitive position.

- You let the pet peeves of certain people take over, or your management team doesn't truly thrash out the pros and cons of a possible acquisition. Decision makers can get enamored of one idea or fall in love with a target and then ignore the strategic dimension. A fascination with the target can overshadow strategic logic, and decision makers may think that this might be the "big" one, either because of an ego-based need for growth at any cost or simply because of a desire to put a competitor out of business. In each of these cases, you risk losing the thread of your company's strategic logic.
- You minimize the risks of the acquisition and integration.
- You misunderstand your company's own capabilities and what you're lacking. Many companies tend to be not very clear on what the holes in their capabilities are; they often think that they are a lot more capable than they truly are. They need to face the harsh reality and accept the idea that another company might be better than they are at some function or in some market or with some type of customer. This is something that very few companies are able to do because they typically believe that their competitors are not as competent as they are. This leads to a "conquistador" mentality, in which the acquiring company either ignores or eliminates the people, processes, and practices of the acquired company in favor of its own people, processes, and practices (i.e., those of the acquiring company). Differences are considered impediments, and employees don't value those differences as learning opportunities and dimensions that could add value to the newly emerging company.

Questions

- How does our approach to M&As relate to the way our company is carrying out our strategic intent and enhancing our company's strategic position?
- To what extent have the M&As our company has previously undertaken been driven by our company's business strategy—i.e., pertaining to our customers, the products or solutions our company offers, and the organization required to deliver on these dimensions?
- What key motivations, strategic factors, or circumstances have prompted our M&A initiatives over the past 5 to 10 years?
- To what extent have our company's acquisition(s) realized the strategic intent that drove those acquisitions in the first place?
  - To what extent has each acquisition enhanced our company's strategic positioning in the marketplace?
  - Do we believe that each acquisition has accelerated or retarded the evolution of our company toward the realization of our strategic goals?

- How do we deal with risks involved in:
  - Failing to be able to anticipate problems emerging during the integration?
  - Having a rigid mindset and failing to be flexible?
  - Failing to establish effective partnering between legacy companies?
- What were the goals of our M&As?
  - To what extent were those goals met?
  - How did we measure success?
  - What financial synergies did our company achieve?
  - What capability synergies did our company achieve?
- Were our company's acquisitions driven by the need to create greater value for our customers? Or were other concerns more of a factor?
  - What roles did the different drivers play when our company decided to initiate an acquisition and when our company planned and implemented the M&A process?
- How does our company approach mergers and acquisitions?
  - Why does our company choose to pursue M&As, rather than strategic alliances, licensing, or other relationships?
  - How do we select potential target companies?
  - How did our leadership guide these decisions?
- When acquiring another company, what emphasis does our company place on intangible assets?
  - How have we taken into account the value of a target company's intangible assets (i.e., its structural capital, human capital, and customer capital)?
- Does our company have a knowledge strategy? If so, how does it relate to how we carry out our M&As?

Notes

1. Peter Skarzynski, "When Mega-Mergers Don't Make Sense," *Chief Executive*, June 1, 2000.
2. Jim Collins, *Good to Great* (New York: HarperCollins, 2001), p. 180.
3. George Anders, "7 Lessons from WaMu's Playbook," *Fast Company*, issue 54, January 2002, p. 102.
4. Ibid.
5. Lionel Giles, trans., "Attack by Stratagem," Chap. 3 in *Sun Tsu on the Art of War*, 1910; Project Gutenberg, http://www.kimsoft.com/polwar.htm.
6. Adrian J. Slywotsky, *The Upside: The 7 Strategies for Turning Big Threats into Growth Breakthroughs* (New York: Crown Business, 2007), pp. 9–10.
7. Constance L. Hays, "J.C. Penney Sells Drugstore Chain for $4.5 Billion," *New York Times*, April 6, 2004; http://query.nytimes.com/gst/fullpage.html?res=9B0DE6D81F39F935A35757C0A9629C8B63.
8. Lawrence M. Fisher, "Symantec's Strategy-Based Transformation," *Strategy+Business*; http://www.strategy-business.com/press/16635507/8424.
9. Ibid.
10. Ibid.
11. Ibid.
12. Ibid.
13. Ibid.
14. Ibid.

The additional material in this chapter comes from the authors' interviews and experiences.

4

Targeting, Due Diligence, Negotiation, and Deal Approval: Four Steps to Creating Value in M&As

---

When you're working through your company's strategic issues (as described in Chapter 3), you need to identify what capabilities you currently have, what capabilities you need, and how you will grow or obtain those needed capabilities. Once everyone has agreed that the way to acquire those capabilities is by acquiring another company, you can move on to the targeting, due diligence, negotiation, and approval processes—all of which are covered in this chapter. The aim of these acquisition processes is to bring substantial expense and growth synergies to your company.

In an acquisition, every stage of the journey adds to the basis and carries over to the next stages. Strategy development (covered in Chapter 3) forms the background for targeting possible companies to acquire, which in turn frames what is required in doing due diligence on the target company, negotiating the deal, getting approval for the deal, and integrating the acquired company into your existing company. A common error is to see these stages as completely separate efforts, often with distinctly different sets of participants. Although specific expertise and experience are necessary at each stage, so are inclusiveness, feedback learning loops, and continuity.

Case Example: How Dow Chemical Prepares for Acquisitions

Preparing for the acquisition is critical. Here's the way Randy Croyle, director of Dow Chemical's Mergers and Aquisitions Expertise Center, describes how he helps everyone involved prepare:

I personally spend a lot of time with that business leader, making sure they understand what it is going to take, what the time commitment is, and what the issues are. I spend a lot of time setting up their organizational structure to be able to handle that M&A, via putting together due diligence teams, or putting together the integration teams. We share with them the failures or the successes of Dow's M&As, where are the lessons learned. After they come into my office, they end up spending about two hours with me. By the time they leave their eyes are glazed over regarding all of the things they have to consider. Then we say, by the way, we are going to be right with you, mentoring you and your teams as we move forward. That is how we prepare these individual lines of businesses for their acquisition.

As they move from stage to stage, the better and more successful M&A efforts have intentional overlap of participants to support knowledge gathering, sharing, and learning during the entire process. Less successful M&A efforts do not have an adequate degree of preparation for the things that are necessary if the acquisition is to take place on the best terms, or even to happen at all, as seen in the next case.

The business planning process is not a form or procedure where one merely checks the boxes, nor is it something that can be done on the fly; rather, it is a cumulative, in-depth process that needs to begin immediately after you've identified your acquisition target. The business plan is a sketch outline at that point, but the knowledge gained at each stage shapes and continuously fills out the plan so that when you've completed your negotiations and obtained all necessary deal approvals, you will have a fully formed business plan, ready for implementation.

The stages of the acquisition process are multilevel and multidimensional. As the participants move from stage to stage, they move forward on several levels of the process, not just on that particular phase. This iterative approach requires a high level of readiness and integration capability but is central to capturing value throughout the acquisition process.

Case Example: The Failed GE-Honeywell International Merger

The $2 billion attempt by General Electric and Honeywell International to merge in 2001 unraveled when the merger proposal, which had met U.S. Department of Justice antitrust requirements, did not receive approval from the European Commission (EC) antitrust regulators. The EC claimed that the merger "would have severely reduced competition in the aerospace industry and resulted ultimately in higher prices for customers, particularly airlines."[1]

Would the outcome of this attempted merger have been different if GE had successfully prepared for the necessary regulatory approval by the European Commission? Would the result have been positive if there had been adequate readiness, preparation, and learning feedback at all stages of the preacquisition process that would have better positioned the companies for their regulatory review? There is no way to know definitely whether the gulf between the reality of the situation and what was needed for approval was too wide to be bridged regardless of anything GE and Honeywell could have done. However, we do know that this was a case in which there was a marked deficiency on GE's part of preparation for gaining regulatory approval in the hotly contentious European venue.

GE CEO Jack Welch himself got to the nub of the why the merger did not pass muster. On the day he announced the merger, he said, "We haven't touched every base," when he was asked whether GE and Honeywell had contacted regulators in the United States and Europe, as is often done when big transactions are proposed. Welch's decisiveness, which served him so well in his 20 years running GE, led him to put the deal together in just a few days without sounding out regulators. And when they balked, he refused to make enough concessions to satisfy them.[2]

"Honeywell made an eleventh-hour attempt to save the deal . . . , as it offered to accept a lower price if GE would make the further divestitures required by the EU [European Union]. But GE rejected the offer, saying it did not make sense for shareholders."[3]

Edward T. Swaine, professor of legal studies at the Wharton School of Business, agreed with Welch's assessment: "My sense is one of the reasons why this has gone so badly wrong is that the parties didn't do their homework—I think it's odd if GE and Honeywell were surprised by the road the EC took. I don't agree with the EC on the substance of its decision, but I can't say I was terribly surprised." Swaine concluded that the proposed GE-Honeywell case is "a cautionary tale (for all multinationals) about the need to seek specialized [legal] advice as early in the process as possible."[4]

Step 1: Engaging the Target

Targeting is the outcome of an ongoing search process. An acquiring company needs to design and implement a targeting process that carries out the strategy that it has defined for itself. It needs to determine which companies the acquiring company can be "rightfully the acquirer of" because of the expense synergies and capability synergies that can be harnessed.

Your targeting process should start with a wider picture of your company's strategy, and you should ask the questions listed in Exhibit 4-1.

Exhibit 4-1

Questions to Ask before You Merge or Acquire to Clarify What You're Targeting

☐ "Where do we need to add to our products and/or services, our customer relationships, our channels, and the various capabilities that we currently have?"

☐ "Where is it and what is it that would give most value to the whole?"

Once you have decided on those factors, then you can ask, "According to the concept of rightful owner, what are the types of companies that we can go to where our own business logic and our own integration will give us an ability to provide value to stakeholders that is superior to what the current ownership configuration can yield?" By using this kind of question set, the acquiring company can build a framework for determining the types of companies that are worth the effort of pursuing.

You can now start the process of tracking opportunities. A well-articulated targeting process allows your targeting team to systematically uncover opportunities within these well-defined targeted areas.

After you've determined your target, the next step is engaging the target, and Exhibit 4-2 lists a series of questions that you should consider next.

Exhibit 4-2

Questions to Ask before You Merge or Acquire about How You Want to Approach the Company You're Targeting

- ☐ "Who are we going to go after, and how are we going to go after them?"

- ☐ "How do we approach them?"

- ☐ "Is this a friendly takeover?"

- ☐ "Is this a hostile takeover?"

- ☐ "How are we going to go about it?"

Every company has its own version of how it carries out its targeting process. In too many instances, selection is based on mere casual familiarity, sometimes called the "marrying the girl next door" phenomenon. As noted in Chapter 2, the prospects that you are immediately aware of and feel comfortable with may not be the ones that are the best choices for the future of your company. In contrast, when acquisitions are seen as an essential part of a company's growth strategy and its way of doing business, there tends to be a more articulated, explicit, and tightly structured process for targeting and engagement. Having the ability to carry out an acquisition becomes a key capability of a company. Such companies develop a clear acquisitions structure, a clear decision-making process, and strong relationships among all parts of the company so that learning how to participate in acquisitions and integrations is, over time, built into all of the company's business units.

Developing this capability is a discovery process that happens when a specific acquisition demands a defined set of practices to make sure that the transaction will be a success. As a company confirms the validity and value of these new practices, the practices and the learning associated with them should be incorporated into an integration playbook that brings together the processes and templates that can be put to use in future acquisitions.

Each structure and process used in targeting acquisitions has to match the needs of your specific company and should be tied to the frequency and size of the acquisitions that might be involved. Although every company creates its own unique structure in response to the conditions it faces, all have a common set of principles:

- A clearly defined strategic intent
- A defined set of criteria that link to how that strategic intent will be accomplished by an acquisition
- A screening mechanism for targeting
- A set of measurable goals
- A learning process to bring other key participants in the company into the acquisition and integration process
- An appreciation of the needs of the acquiree and an effort to reach its goals as well[5]

Developing and Implementing Targeting Criteria

Every company needs to develop its own targeting criteria and targeting framework. Because your company's targeting activity is an extension of the company's strategy and intent, it will have to embody and incorporate those values and perspectives. The most successful targeting efforts are ongoing and are often operated by an element of the corporate strategic planning group. The advantage of having a continuous evaluation of opportunities is that it keeps information fresh so that when the right combination of factors converges, your company is primed to make its move.

Constant communication with the senior leadership and with the business units is equally important. Special knowledge may come through the business units earlier or more quickly than through conventional channels. Equally, senior leadership may be able to broach conversations with peers that may reveal emerging opportunities well before that information percolates to become more easily available knowledge.

The larger the acquisition, the greater the likelihood that it has been initiated by the company's board or at the senior leadership level. For example, when Dow acquired Union Carbide and when BP acquired Amoco,

Case Example: Washington Mutual's Targeting Process

Craig Tall was Washington Mutual's vice chair of corporate development and specialty finance until 2005, and according to him, "A week doesn't go by where we don't talk to someone about a possible deal. In a typical year, we may complete two or three transactions." Washington Mutual has clear criteria for its acquisitions.[6] Deals make the cut if they

- *Improve per-share earnings.* Any deal that your company proposes to do needs a clear statement of how that particular deal would create value for your company and improve earnings. Each deal needs to spell out an *investment thesis*, which is a defining statement, based on a clear understanding of how money is made in your business, that outlines how adding this particular business to your portfolio will make your company more valuable.

   Although this may seem simple and fundamental, a "survey of 250 senior executives across all industries revealed that only 29 percent of acquiring executives started out with an investment thesis (defined in that survey as a 'sound reason for buying a company') that stood the test of time. More than 40 percent had no investment thesis whatsoever(!). Of those who did, fully half discovered within three years of closing the deal that their thesis was wrong."[7] This is the first screening test for a possible acquisition target.

- *Fit into growth strategies.* As WaMu's president, chairman, and CEO, Kerry Killinger, put it, "Acquisitions need to be a by-product of your basic strategy. We would never want to do scattershot acquisitions and then have to think up strategies to justify them. We believe that the best way to build value is to focus on a few markets where we can achieve national leadership."

- *Bring minimal risks.* When Washington Mutual seriously pursues an acquisition, its formal deal team consists of three people: Tall and two assistants. They're also joined by as many as 100 regular bankers who have day jobs, but who clear out their evening and weekend schedules to help. That help from the front lines is invaluable in making sure that Washington Mutual buys the right targets for the right reasons—and pays an intelligent price.

   "Take something like risk assessments," Tall explains. "One of the bank's senior risk managers, Norm Swick, is fantastically quick and good. We use him every time we can." What's more, frontline managers who get involved in acquisition screening become much more committed to making the deal work. In other corporate cultures, where a big-deal team does all of the work, there's a much greater risk that the eventual handoff of the acquired business to an operating team will go badly.

As Tall and his team gauge risks, they pay attention to sellers' priorities: "Most sellers want this transaction to be a way to extend their business further than they can take it on their own," Tall says.[8]

It is important to note that while the framework for pursuing M&As is driven by achieving WaMu's strategic goals, a key part of WaMu's approach to making acquisitions successful is the effort that the company makes to actively extend itself as an attractive and desirable partner to work with. After a takeover, when a WaMu representative finishes a briefing on its approach to senior staff of an acquired bank, "The tension is gone. Managers at acquired banks suddenly see a brighter future. As one of them told a WaMu executive, 'This sounds like the company that I've always wanted to work for, but never knew existed.'"[9]

In short, the WaMu acquisition process starts with targeting, but it also incorporates everything that is necessary to make the acquisition work.

the targeting took place at the executive level. With larger acquisitions, targeted companies are analyzed for soundness by strategic planning groups, by M&A teams, and often by outside consultants. A difficult targeting situation arises when a senior leader proposes an acquisition that the acquisition staff views as not being strategically aligned or not a good candidate. The acquisition team may need good diplomacy skills to forestall acquisition initiatives that are not well grounded.

For example, a CFO who is focused on growing revenues and reducing costs may see a certain company as a good buying opportunity because it is financially vulnerable, and may push strongly for its acquisition. Yet that target may not be a good overall fit, or it may have a radically different culture that could cause serious integration problems down the road and eventually lead to divesting the acquisition. Therefore, it's important for all companies to be wary of senior managers who recommend companies for acquisition simply because they meet that manager's agenda rather than the goals of the company as a whole; making such acquisitions can have costly ramifications for the company.

The best methodology for targeting is to use a strong set of multidimensional criteria to evaluate any potential target against. With this procedure, no single dimension of the potential acquisition can dominate in the decision-making process. That set of evaluation criteria can also form the basis for the next stage in the preacquisition process: due diligence.

Case Example: Cisco's Targeting Criteria

Cisco has made acquisition a core business practice and has a core set of criteria that it must meet when selecting acquisition candidates. It first decides that it needs to be in a certain market. It then determines whether it can grow the capabilities needed to be a dominant player in that market organically. If it cannot, it will go outside of its structure to acquire a company that already has those capabilities.

Cisco intentionally developed and systematized its acquisition process so that it would become part of the company's regular set of practices. As a result of embedding this process in how it does its business, Cisco educated a significant number of its personnel to have expertise in its acquisition methodology. From 1993 to 2001, Cisco acquired 71 companies. These were mostly smaller acquisitions, but five were major, multi-billion-dollar transactions that challenged the company to revise how it carried out its acquisition and integration process. Cisco was strongly affected by the technology downturn in 2001, and there are significant questions as to how effectively it has repositioned itself after the dot-com meltdown. Nonetheless, there are many lessons to be considered in how Cisco pursued its acquisition program.

One of these lessons is that Cisco understands that "acquiring a company's technology without acquiring the future efforts of its people is a formula for an unsuccessful purchase. As a result Cisco, spends a lot of time evaluating a company before any purchase agreement is reached," according to Silicon Valley high-technology management veteran Ed Paulson.[10] To that end, Cisco has five basic criteria that must be satisfied to qualify a target candidate:

1. The target and Cisco must share a compatible vision of the future from both an industry and a product perspective.
2. The acquisition must produce a quick win for Cisco shareholders, preferably within 12 months of the purchase.
3. The companies must share a complementary culture, or what John Chambers, [Cisco's] chairman and CEO, calls the "right chemistry."
4. There have to be long-term wins for the company's four major constituencies: shareholders, employees, customers, and business partners.
5. For large acquisitions, the target must be geographically located close to a Cisco office.[11]

A target must meet at least three of Cisco's criteria to be looked at more closely. If it meets four out of five, a team determines if the areas of incompatibility will compromise the chances of success. When a target meets all five criteria, it will be actively pursued, but even then, Cisco may, at any time, choose not to acquire the company.

Case Example: Dow Chemical's Criteria for Targeting Acquisitions

Dow Chemical has its criteria for targeting potential companies, which Randy Croyle sums up here:

> We look to understand what their product lines are, look at what their financials are, try to get an understanding of what are the risks of that target company, be it their product lines, what is their litigation history. Typically, we will have that type of analysis done by individual businesses, or if it is a corporate play, where it is an acquisition that would cross over multiple business lines, we would be understanding exactly how each of those business lines would fit into the overall corporate business strategy. We look at potential acquisitions both from a corporate standpoint and from a local, individual business unit point of view.

Step 2: Doing Due Diligence on the Targeted Acquisition

Due diligence identifies and explores any risks or liabilities so that you can deal with those risks during the negotiation process. Due diligence helps you—the acquiring company—determine the price range you're willing to pay and guides you through the negotiations. If that price range heads into an area that makes the acquisition prohibitive and not appropriate, it becomes clear that it is time to terminate the acquisition initiative.

Although the greatest emphasis in due diligence is on finances, you need to examine all of the target company's relevant capabilities and key areas related to the success of the acquisition. Together, these provide a full picture of the potential acquisition.

For example, an information technology or pharmaceutical company that is targeting a company that is developing a unique application will want to see whether that firm has the staff to complete the development of the application; the legal capabilities to have the application protected by patent, trademark, or some other mechanism; and the marketing capabilities to bring the application to its potential customers. A construction company may want to know if an engineering firm it is seeking to acquire has the design and engineering capacity to develop

Case Example: SAIC's Criteria for Targeting Acquisitions

SAIC has had a more decentralized structure, and therefore most initiatives for acquisitions have originated in specific business units. An effort is currently underway to have those initiatives align with the new CEO's requirement to double the revenue of the overall company. Even so, that effort is leveraging the extensive capabilities that already exist within the business units to bring them up to the level where they meet the requirements to realize the corporate goals.

Concerning the selection of targets for acquisition, Kevin "Ed" Murphy, senior vice president and director of mergers and acquisitions of SAIC, states:

> The business units "know a dog when they see it" and feel less inclined to fall in love with the deal because they have their own strong base to fall back on. We have had folks who pass on several deals, although it looks like a decent deal, because it is not good enough for them. We look for the business folks, who are the sponsors, to apply their good business practices and judgment. If they are walking away from an acquisition that we think is a good deal, generally my approach is let them walk away from it, because you can't force them into an area of noncomfort.
>
> One area that has been a lesson learned is that the better-performing and better-talented business units do the better deals. This is not a coincidence. Also, if the target company's management is well skilled, and the day after the deal closes, from their point of view, all they have to do is figure out where the SAIC rulebook is. . . . In the past, our business leaders did not know how to do the integration. Their approach has been, "Here is how we do things." They are getting more sensitized now.

innovative and efficient buildings that will enable the newly combined firm to forge or penetrate new markets.

Some generic capabilities that can be highly relevant to whether the proposed merger or acquisition will succeed are whether the targeted company has the capabilities for

- Developing and retaining its people
- Generating innovation of market-defining goods and services
- Cultivating customers
- Supporting high-performance technological outcomes

> ### Case Example: How Cisco Handles Due Diligence
>
> Cisco has been so successful at acquiring other companies that an entire book has been written about its process: *Inside Cisco: The Real Story of Sustained M&A Growth*. Here's a brief excerpt about how Cisco conducts more than just financial due diligence:
>
>> *Due diligence at Cisco is more than just verifying the financial, legal and asset value status of a target company. It is a test—a test of ethics, honesty, team spirit, professionalism, and customer commitment. Notice that these items don't appear on a balance sheet, an income statement, or a statement of cash flows. . . . Underlying the due diligence process is the search for the answer to an overriding question: "Will these people, their products, and their culture merge well with Cisco's so that they will be seamless with Cisco within a few months?"*[12]

Structuring Due Diligence

Due diligence for different acquisitions will have the same basic elements but will also be shaped by the specific nature of each transaction and the needs of the acquiring company—and, to some extent, the needs of the acquired company. Each due diligence is an extension of your company's strategy and, at the same time, is a basis for the follow-up negotiation and implementation stages. If M&As are considered a major part of your company's overall corporate strategy, you may have be a formal center for managing M&As, as Dow Chemical has.

Every acquisition has elements in common with other acquisitions, but each, for any company, also has its own character and specific complexities. One acquisition may be made primarily for technology capabilities, another for sales and marketing capabilities, a third for product and service lines, a fourth for customer sets, and a fifth for physical resource reserves. In addition, there may be different degrees of integration for different acquisitions. Generally, the more fully the acquired company is to be integrated into the acquiring company, the greater the need to understand how the two companies can create value in as many ways as possible through capability synergies, while at the same time finding opportunities to capture expense savings. In some cases, integration will be limited and the acquisition will operate fairly autonomously. Even so,

Case Example: Dow Chemical's Mergers and Acquisitions Expertise Center

At Dow Chemical, all acquisition initiatives must go through the head of its Mergers and Acquisitions Expertise Center. That leader is in charge of a team with an array of skill sets in finance, negotiations, due diligence, operations, and processes.

After the center's leader accepts going forward with an acquisition, he and his staff decide how they will handle due diligence, negotiations, and, where possible, implementation as well. They map out the strategy and process for the preacquisition phases with the head of the business unit involved. As Dow's Croyle says:

> *I have a list of what I call functional focal points. I've got a very senior person in each one of our functions, and I routinely interface with them. So, if a deal is coming down, if we feel we need somebody out of HR, or we need somebody out of our environmental health and safety organization, I work through these functional focal points. Either they themselves will be the person or they will then delegate that to somebody within their organization. It is a big chunk of time that is involved. It is something that is over and beyond their normal day job. They have to make the adjustment if they are going to keep all of these balls in the air.*
>
> *We have a kick-off meeting with the due diligence team. That meeting gives them the scope of the due diligence—what is the strategic intent, what are we looking for, identifies what the boundaries are, gives them an idea of the time line. Then we go with them to the data room or to the site visits. At the end of that period of time, we will have a number of debriefing sessions. Before they are excused, they have to put everything in writing. We use those documents to help with the valuation, but those documents are also the start of our implementation plan.*
>
> *Every one of our functions has a checklist and a template that they use. That is something that we put together when we developed our "corporate M&A" process. Part of that was to get standardized checklists, protocols, templates, and other materials for all of our functions as they went forward on due diligence.*
>
> *Whoever is on due diligence, we try to get them involved during the implementation phase. Likewise, we try to put the folks who are on due diligence close to the negotiating team and, if possible, on the negotiating team. If the acquisition has a lot of manufacturing assets, we will try to put the manufacturing persons who were on due diligence on the negotiation team. Or, if we anticipate that there are a lot of HR issues, the HR person who is on the due diligence team will also be part of the negotiating team. Continuity of personnel across these different phases is very important.*

good leadership in holding companies and conglomerates can enable a flow of the best managerial methodologies and capabilities across all of these companies' autonomous business units.

For example, when Hajoca, a large construction supplies company, acquired Emco, one of Canada's leading integrated distributors of plumbing supplies, Emco continued to operate as an autonomous business unit, but it adopted a number of managerial processes that were developed in Hajoca's cluster of companies, including a new compensation approach for profit sharing.

Each due diligence emphasizes a different configuration of readiness and capabilities. The due diligence teams that your company assembles should reflect your company and its acquisition strategy. The team should gather and review different functional focal points with the view that the information it discovers will guide managers in making the following decisions:

- Whether to pursue the acquisition
- What pricing range is workable and acceptable
- What areas and issues to negotiate
- What inputs are needed for developing a business plan that will shape and guide the integration

Also, keep in mind that you need to balance the time spent on due diligence in order to achieve all of the following (and often conflicting!) goals:

- To optimize the limited time available for due diligence
- To take into account the degree of confidentiality or nondisclosure requirements involved
- To consider the need to gather adequate and relevant information for decision makers

This requires the acquisition team to define its due diligence objectives rigorously and communicate them clearly and fully to everyone involved.

Generally, the people on due diligence teams are drawn from across the company, and they participate in due diligence in addition to their regular responsibilities. They usually become members of due diligence teams on an as-needed basis, with some serving part time and some serving in a full-time capacity. By keeping them aware of what makes for effective due diligence, the M&A team can readily involve the members of the due diligence team as needed. In a sense, this is like having firefighters trained in a fire company drill so that they are ready when the call comes. Continuously building a network of qualified participants is another illustration of how organizational readiness creates the basis for the specific capacities to carry out the acquisition process.

Although the traditional emphasis of due diligence has been placed heavily on financial and accounting reviews, the due diligence team needs to consider a full range of issues, including

- Cultural factors
- Technology
- Leadership and human capital resources
- Communication
- Customer relationships
- Legal and regulatory requirements

The particular configuration of factors that is important to a company will determine any special emphasis on the team. For example, the due diligence team of a major chemical company for which R&D is a major driver includes participation by R&D staff, an intellectual property lawyer, and people from manufacturing technology. Other companies will have more of an emphasis on environmental safety, the ability to perform in financial markets, or other factors.

The Importance of Trust

The importance of trust in acquisition relationships is extremely critical. Making every participant take on the role of an ambassador changes the relationship from an impersonal (if not hostile) takeover to a

Case Example: How SAIC Handles Due Diligence

SAIC is a technology service firm that puts a strategic emphasis on serving its key customers. The loss of one of those customers would have a serious impact on the company's well-being; therefore, customer service is part of its due diligence process when targeting possible companies for acquisition. Here's how SAIC's Ed Murphy describes the process: "A critical piece of due diligence is talking to customers face-to-face. We are always thinking of the customer and making sure that they are comfortable with the company that we are buying as well as with us. We are very customer-centric in that approach.[13]

> SAIC is also careful to tell its due diligence and integration teams that they are not simply doing financial or technical due diligence. Beyond that, they are ambassadors to the company. Someone from a due diligence team has one chance to make an impression on the company. If team members go in and set the target company on edge, you can be nice the next five times and the target is still waiting for you to treat them poorly, because that is the impression you have left. We encourage people to be ambassadors, to do the job, but to have a balance.[14]

respectful, collegial knowledge sharing. If people at the target company come to believe that they are potential partners in a new company, they will be more collaborative and perhaps even indicate issues and opportunities that might not otherwise be noticed. Trust in a partnering orientation sets the tone for how negotiations and later integration will be carried out.

At the same time, due diligence is a process of refining what is known and what needs to be known. It starts out at a high level, and as information comes to light and is reviewed, more and more critical questions are asked until the knowledge obtained allows the acquiring company to determine whether to proceed (and how) or whether to terminate the acquisition initiative. Therefore, it is understandable for the target company to be prudent and reveal only what it needs to; after all, the deal may not go through, and even if it does, the target company still needs to be in the best possible position to negotiate the best outcome for *its* stakeholders.

Case Example: Clarica Life Insurance Company

Clarica demonstrated that having knowledge capture and transfer capabilities enabled it to move quickly when an unexpected acquisition opportunity arose. That capability made the difference in its bid for the Canadian operations of Metropolitan Life Insurance. At that time, Clarica was embarking on a highly resource-intensive shift from being a mutual life insurance company to being a stock company (demutualizing).

Just as Clarica was focusing significant resources on demutualizing, an extraordinary opportunity to make a major acquisition arose when the Canadian operations of MetLife became available. Clarica recognized that several other bidders would also be very interested. It knew that it would be successful only if it was able to move quickly, because the first bidder to complete the due diligence process and indicate a possible price range would probably get to the negotiation stage. It also needed to use the least amount of resources possible because it had committed substantial resources to its demutualization.

Within three weeks, Clarica organized 150 people into 16 teams, each targeting a component of the deal. From the beginning, the teams were linked by a common knowledge database, where they filed findings, raised questions, identified issues, and found creative ways to resolve those issues. This allowed every individual on any team to know what was happening with everyone else who was part of the process. Because there was very little time for managerial intervention, team members were the ones who identified issues, found solutions by building on each other's ideas, and then moved on to the next concern. Through the teams' efforts, the due diligence and business planning processes for the "integration" were completed in record time.

The quality of the preparation work was so good that the negotiations were carried out in a fraction of the expected time. Clarica negotiators found that they often knew more about the business being acquired than their counterparts in the target company who were sitting across the table from them. The knowledge acquired through the due diligence process put Clarica in an advantageous negotiating position because it could make and justify its offer much more quickly and better than any of the other suitors. The result was that Clarica was able to acquire a company that was 50 percent of its size at an advantageous price. Focus and teamwork, enabled by the knowledge strategy, provided a decisive advantage in speed and agility. Clarica replicated this same approach for other acquisitions and found that it could readily reuse the processes and templates from the earlier acquisitions with equal success.

Knowledge Capture and Transfer Capabilities

The strength of the business plan is in large part determined by the quality of the due diligence effort. Good due diligence information allows the company to identify possible expense savings and complementary capabilities. The knowledge derived from due diligence is used to build the foundation for the integration plan.

Due diligence is not just a requirement for determining value. It is also a way of thoroughly and tangibly operating. Although there is a due diligence stage in a merger or acquisition, the principles of due diligence need to be present and practiced *from the very beginning* and throughout the transaction process.

In the value-creating approach, due diligence applies the principles of strategy making, which means that the acquirer is constantly renewing its acquisition strategy to take into account new knowledge that emerges from the due diligence process. This dynamic strategy approach leverages the new understandings flowing in from the due diligence team, shedding light on how both expense saving and capability synergies can best be captured and leveraged at all stages of the M&A process.

The due diligence process needs to encompass the following practices:

- Using a "bifocal" approach that takes into account not only expense synergies (i.e., duplication of expenses) but also growth synergies. The result is that your company will get a longer and broader view of potential combinations, what value could be created through the acquisition, and what savings could be

Case Example: Dow Chemical

Dow Chemical makes a practice of knowledge capture and transfer, along with continuity of personnel from due diligence, as a critical input for its implementation plan. According to Randy Croyle: "We have continuity because when the due diligence team is visiting a data room or a site, knowledge that is picked up during that visit is extremely important and is transferred to the people putting together the implementation plan. The best way to transfer that knowledge is to have continuity of personnel. That is another key learning for us."

accrued. This sets the stage for determining what price you should be willing to pay for the target company.

- Using an "accretive" approach that enables your company to add to earnings per share as soon as possible. This approach looks for acquisition synergies that are expected to increase earnings per share. This may mean looking for opportunities for such things as cross-selling of the acquired company's services to the acquiring company's client list or turning the acquired company's research into salable goods and services, all of which will have a significant impact on your bottom line. The value-creating approach emphasizes pursuing both short-term and long-term opportunities for gains, but in a more holistic framework.

- Recognizing the relationship between the due diligence process and the shaping of your business plan. Doing due diligence provides information that leads your company to be more exacting when negotiating the deal and when integrating the company following the purchase. This knowledge helps frame your business plan; it enables you to look at a range of options to see what is possible and what is not possible; and it helps you determine what to give up on (and what not to) in the upcoming negotiation and integration phases. If you follow this process, at the end of the due diligence period, your business plan will be well into its development.

- Setting the ground rules for establishing an atmosphere of trust and a partnering context.

- Checking whether the assumptions of your business plan are holding during the due diligence process and beyond, and determining what modifications you need to make.

Step 3: Negotiating the Deal: Who Is the Rightful Owner?

Negotiations determine the cost and terms of the acquisition. To begin negotiations, and to get your price accepted, you have to be able to say,

"This is the best price we can pay, and because we are the rightful owner, it is probably the best price that anybody can pay." In short, you need to demonstrate to your target company that you can offer the best value.

The concept of the rightful owner is that the acquiring company finds target companies where its own business logic and its own integration capabilities enable it to provide greater value to stakeholders than the current ownership configuration can currently provide.

Your goal during negotiations is to achieve a value proposition where your company will gain a desired return on your investment in the target company. You need a payback at a certain rate and over a specific period of time to satisfy your company's threshold and hurdle-rate requirements and to ensure that you will realize a return on equity. If those results can be obtained in the first six months, then you can pay a higher premium for the target company. However, if you have to wait for, say, two years to get those results, then the integration process will incur more costs, which means that the amount you are is willing to pay up front will be less.

Negotiations are the venue to ensure that the elements for both potential expense synergies and potential capability synergies are incorporated into the final agreement. Negotiations also cover caveats, representations and warranties, and related risk areas in the agreement. If everything works out, your company will make payments to the target company, but if things fail to work out as agreed, the selling company is liable to compensate you, the buyer.

And this can involve a substantial sum; for example, one acquirer claimed back $180 million from the selling company out of a $1 billion purchase price; the claim went to court, and there was a settlement in favor of the acquiring company. In negotiations, the acquirer protects itself against eventualities in ways that will help it manage the risk. Good due diligence will indicate risk areas and enable the negotiation team to incorporate adequate recourse for areas with a significant but uncertain outcome.

Although the negotiations phase is primarily handled by the senior leadership of the acquiring and acquired companies, it cannot be detached from the things that have gone before or will follow in the acquisition process. In fact, it can be supported by a range of people from

Case Example: How Dow Chemical Handles Negotiations

Here's how Randy Croyle of Dow Chemical describes his company's negotiations process:

> There are always challenges. I would rather use [the word] "challenges" than "mistakes." Folks who are in negotiating sometimes do not understand a lot of the IT implications. Dow has an ERP system. We use SAP R2. We are so linked together by systems, so integrated between our customers, our supply chain, our manufacturing organization, our finance, etc., that we cannot make a decision in one area that won't have an impact someplace else. The problem is that when you are negotiating a deal, you may think, "Fine, we'll agree to this or that," but not understand that there are implications on the systems that can create significant heartburn and costs. That is the challenge.
>
> More times than not, trying to get folks with operational experience on the negotiation team is a big help. People just do not recognize how complicated it is to run a business in a fully integrated company.

across the company who know what special requirements and issues need to be addressed during the negotiation phase so that significant challenges are addressed.

Negotiations are also an opportunity to get close-up experience of the negotiating skills of the senior managers from the target company. If your acquisition is consummated, these managers may take on significant roles in the newly combined company. Negotiations can provide a good view of how these leaders determine value as well as how they think and act in important and intense circumstances. Good negotiation skills are a very valuable capability in any number of settings in the new company.

The goals of the negotiations process include the following:

- Put forward the case for why you want to acquire the target company.
- Present potential growth synergies to the target company.
- Map out the advantages created by these synergies (both expense and growth synergies) and how the added value generated by these synergies will be distributed to your company and to the acquired company.

- Protect your company against eventualities to help manage risk.
- Determine what is included in and what is excluded from the deal.
- Prevent your company from "falling in love" with your target and losing track of what your boundaries are in terms of hurdle rates. Your company should always be prepared to let the targeted acquisition go.

Step 4: Approving the Deal

Up to this point, the acquisition process has been between your company and your target company. Once you've completed your negotiations, however, the deal may have to pass muster with various different stakeholders. In some cases, the deal may require approval by your company's shareholders; this typically depends on the size of the transaction and other factors. In all cases, there is legal scrutiny, which can involve the following areas:

- Antitrust laws (which can be national and/or international in scope)
- Environmental concerns
- Industry regulations
- Other regulatory approvals of various kinds

The need for approvals may mean carving out a different deal. Your company might say, "We will buy your company, but we will agree that we are going to sell this part and this part and that part." These are the parts where there could be an antitrust issue if the newly emerging company is seen as too dominant and has a monopoly in the market.

During this approval phase, if the antitrust review says that your company needs to rid itself of parts of either your company or the target company, you may have to review your strategic assumptions and determine whether the deal is still worthwhile or whether you should terminate it. You have to determine whether the need to divest elements of the target company makes the acquisition a much less favorable deal.

When these approvals are critical, they can be deal breakers. Therefore, you need to understand the requirements of the deal approval phase at the early stages of the acquisition process so that you can minimize disruptions and reworkings of the deal—or at least better appreciate the implications of gaining the necessary approvals.

The proposed General Electric and Honeywell International merger (described earlier in this chapter) demonstrates that approval by antitrust governing bodies is complex, may involve very different views of what dominance of the market means to different antitrust bodies, and

Case Example: Sirius and XM Satellite Radio

Achieving regulatory approval within a country can be daunting and can have a serious impact on the success of a proposed merger. Approval of the merger between Sirius and XM satellite radio companies by the U.S. Department of Justice took more than a year. Sirius and XM still need to obtain another major regulatory approval from the Federal Communications Commission, which may impose an additional set of conditions on the merging companies.

Regulatory approaches developed during the industrial era are difficult to mesh with the way emerging technology companies work. In an increasingly technological and intangible resource era, regulatory agencies have to work through often complicated technology issues as well as a thicket of business issues, ranging from service contracts for providing satellite radio connections to competing automobile companies, to determine whether allowing companies to merge will be harmful or beneficial to consumers.

The length and possible stringent conditions of these approval processes lead to unending frustration for subscribing customers and uncertainty for investors, and they curtail the ability of both companies to invest or go forward with significant aspects of their strategic plans. Therefore, a clear and thorough analysis and strategy for gaining the required regulatory approvals needs to begin as soon as possible, preferably from the first day the merger is being considered. In major acquisitions, there are bound to be a range of complex and sometimes unprecedented regulatory issues that have to be dealt with.

Developing alternative scenarios is one way for those involved in the acquisition to prepare for the range of eventualities that may arise. This is a way to allow the merging companies to sort through, prepare, and ultimately be in the best position to deal with the requirements and possible collateral effects that occur in and as a result of a regulatory approval process.

can be strongly affected by regional and global politics. These complexities of the approval process must be fully appreciated, or the merger may be hobbled, stalled, or even aborted. The failure by GE and Honeywell International to gain the European Commission's approval made the proposed merged company unworkable as a global company, and the merger was terminated.

Only when your company has taken care of all of these approvals at various levels can you sign on the dotted line and take possession of the target company, which completes the preacquisition stage. The next stage of the process is to integrate your newly acquired company, which we'll cover in Part II of this book, in Chapters 5 through 10.

Success Factors

- Have a framework and dedicated resources to continuously scan for acquisition opportunities.
- Establish a mentoring function to educate lead people in the how-tos of an acquisition.
- Initiate the business planning process as soon as you select a target company.
- Be able to move rapidly through the due diligence process, with excellent communication between due diligence teams and senior leaders.
- Develop the basis for being the "rightful owner."
- Recognize the need for benefits for all stakeholders from both companies, and also for external stakeholders.
- Know when to walk away from a deal.
- Have a continuity enabler. The knowledge role becomes very important, tying together Stage 1 and Stage 2 of the M&A process. Everyone involved in integrating the acquired company, during Stage 2, needs to understand the work that was done during Stage 1, and that knowledge must be communicated and translated appropriately in Stage 2. You can't just say, "OK, we're done with Stage 1, it's closed; now we'll move on to Stage 2." Instead, key knowledge needs to be carried forward and made available, when appropriate, during all subsequent stages of the integration. The continuity enabler should oversee all of these communication functions.

Derailing Factors

- You target acquisitions primarily on familiarity—i.e., the "girl next door" phenomenon.
- The people in your company who will play key roles in leading the acquisition don't have the knowledge and experience needed.
- You have weak links (or no links!) between stages and teams in the sequential acquisition process—in other words, you simply "throw the deal over the wall to the next team."
- You fail to include enough representatives from operational staff in your due diligence and negotiation teams.
- You don't have a good grasp of all value elements so that you can make the best offer.
- You underestimate the requirements for necessary regulatory approvals.
- You "fall in love" with the company you're considering acquiring, to the point where you develop blind spots or ignore potential problems.

Questions

- How did we prepare our company for the M&A?
- How did we initiate the M&A?
  - How did we approach our target company?
  - Who was involved, and in what ways?
  - What was the response from the target company?
- Were we able to balance our due diligence investigations holistically between financial assets, fixed tangible assets, and intangible assets?
  - How did this work, and what was the outcome?
- How did we organize our due diligence process?
  - Who was involved?
  - What did our teams focus on?
  - What areas did they cover?
  - How did they communicate what they learned?
  - How was that new knowledge communicated to the leadership of the due diligence effort?
- Did we engage in any knowledge, culture, or human capital audits during the due diligence phase?
- How did we incorporate what we learned during due diligence into the negotiation phase?
  - Who was involved in the negotiations?
  - How well did the negotiations go?
  - Were there any surprises?
- Were any mistakes made in the context of the negotiations that had an impact on the performance of the integration?
- How could we have avoided these problems or issues?

Notes

1. CNNMoney.com, July 3, 2001; http://money.cnn.com/2001/07/03/europe/ge_eu/.
2. Andrew Ross Sorkin, "A Rare Miscalculation for Jack Welch," *New York Times*, July 3, 2001; http://www.nytimes.com/2001/07/03/business/03WELC.html?ex=1207108800&en=fdf4dc5bf54d9024&ei=5070#top.
3. CNNMoney.com, July 3, 2001; http://money.cnn.com/2001/07/03/europe/ge_eu/.
4. Knowledge@Emory, "Lessons from the GE-Honeywell Non-Merger," July 4, 2001; http://knowledge.emory.edu/article.cfm?articleid=366#.
5. George Anders, "7 Lessons From WaMu's Playbook," *Fast Company*, no. 54 (January 2002), p. 102; http://www.fastcompany.com/magazine/54/chalktalk.html?page=0%2C0.
6. Ibid.
7. David Harding and Sam Rovit, "Writing a Credible Investment Thesis," *Harvard Business School Working Knowledge for Business Leaders*, November 15, 2004; http://hbswk.hbs.edu/archive/4485.html.
8. Anders.
9. Ibid.
10. Ed Paulson, *Inside Cisco: The Real Story of Sustained M&A Growth* (New York: John Wiley & Sons, 2001), pp. 30–31.
11. Ibid.
12. Ibid., p. 165.
13. Ed Murphy, SAIC interview.
14. Ibid.

The additional material in this chapter comes from the authors' interviews and experiences.

PART II

POSTDEAL
INTEGRATION PHASE

5

Integration Planning:
Positioning the Acquisition to Succeed

The value and effectiveness of an acquisition depend on how well you carry out the integration—and that depends on how carefully, thoughtfully, and thoroughly you do your up-front planning. Unfortunately, too often, integration planning starts only at the closing of the acquisition agreement. This late start in planning the integration could be a key factor in reducing the success of your acquisition. The acquisition may be a financial coup, but a successful ultimate outcome will take place only if you follow up the deal effectively by ensuring that your integration team has clearly laid out how the integration will actually take place.

This chapter examines the elements involved in planning for the integration, along with who is involved, in what ways, and at what points in the preintegration and integration processes. A successful approach to integration planning incorporates the capability to carry out the following activities:

- Developing an *integration playbook*, which is a guide that your company can draw on to create specific integration plans

- Exploring your newly combined company's *new markets* and *new customer requirements*
- Auditing all the *capabilities* of your newly combined company
- Determining the *governance* of your new company in terms of leadership, values, behaviors, and overall identity
- Identifying and developing ways to respond to *risk management* issues
- Deciding how you will handle all the *people issues* involved in an acquisition—first to make sure that everyone is engaged in, committed to, and invested in combining the two companies, then to assign new or changed responsibilities to some employees, and to announce and manage any necessary termination of other employees or groups

The Integration Playbook

A playbook is designed to be a guidebook for incorporating the essentials of an integration. Playbooks are the comprehensive templates that are to be used in integration planning to leverage the cumulative knowledge and experience gained from previous integrations to inform upcoming integration plans and allow them to be produced with greater speed and with appropriate breadth, depth, and precision. Playbooks help create a continuity and a learning model from one acquisition to those that follow, providing a common approach, a shared set of guiding principles, and an ever-expanding toolkit of effective practices.

Integration teams have increasingly been adopting integration playbooks as a way to bring strategy making and project management together in a comprehensive and coherent way. Playbooks started out as a collection of templates and tools that were taken from different acquisitions, but they have gone significantly beyond that to become vehicles for governing the integration implementation itself. A playbook differs from an integration plan in that it is a repository of the cumulative learnings of how a company carries out a merger or acquisition, whereas the integration plan is the plan for the specific integration. The ability to put together a good playbook has become an important part of building a company's integration implementation capability. You can incorporate learning from past acquisition initiatives and from other companies into your playbook development process to renew it as a cutting-edge manual for current and future acquisitions.

A playbook provides an overall framework and template to support the formulation of an integration plan. In addition to providing definitions of key terms, the playbook gives a model for shaping all of the following:

- Guiding principles
- Roles and responsibilities
- Accountability structures
- A road map and timeline for the integration implementation

A playbook provides a framework that allows integration planners to go through all of the steps and stages of the integration process systematically, synthesizing all of the strands that need to come together during the integration implementation process. It presents you with an effective way to plan an integration process, countering the tendency for an integration plan to fragment into a collection of unaligned parts. It is a readily understandable operating manual for integration planning.

Because there is no such thing as a standardized integration, you use your playbook to provide an outline into which you can incorporate unique integration planning requirements. Playbooks are geared to address the approach and process for any upcoming M&A with a well-defined, step-by-step methodology.

Developing and Implementing a Set of Guiding Principles

Developing guiding principles is a core component of a playbook. Guiding principles flow from the mission and underlying values of the organization. They serve as the basis for all the decisions your company makes and all the actions your company takes during your integration implementation process, ensuring that everyone can act in an aligned, appropriate manner. Examples of such guiding principles include

- Giving the top priority to your customers' needs and running your core business
- Developing long-lasting relationships built on trust, collaboration, and mutual understanding
- Communicating with your stakeholders clearly and directly on a continuous and timely basis
- Staying in accord with the time frame for implementation and selecting a course of action that may not be perfect, but that you can achieve within specified timelines

The business leaders involved in the integration know that if they operate in accordance with the guiding principles, they can feel free to use their judgment to take initiatives that will open up important areas for examination and action.

Road Map: Key Stages

You begin developing your integration implementation road map once your company has negotiated the terms of the deal. At that point, you've identified the scope and objectives of your new company, and you've determined the extent of the integration. As with any integration planning document, the road map is reviewed and validated at the onset of the integration and throughout the integration.

In an integration implementation of significant size, there are several stages and substages. The integration road map is a visual guide to the multitiered, interrelated activities defined through the integration process. It gives everyone involved a ready reference as to how the integration will proceed. It includes the stages that the integration implementation will go through and what happens in each stage, along with the integration timeline. This road map helps team members to focus on the right issues at the right time.

The road map recognizes that the work of the integration starts in the predeal phase.

Case Example: How Alcatel and Newbridge Developed Their Integration Road Map

The road map for the Alcatel/Newbridge Network $7.1 billion acquisition outlines the companies' integration planning and implementation stages as a three-stage integration implementation process:

- Stage 1 involved integration planning, which took place prior to the closing.
- Stage 2 took place during the initial months of restructuring; it focused on quick wins with a substantial payback, planning for the changes that would take place in the next phase of the integration, the start of the long-term transformation of targeted elements of the new company (e.g., sales), and initiating and closing out of certain start-up action initiatives, all with the effect that customers experienced the new company in a "business as usual" fashion.
- Stage 3 emphasized the execution of significant planned changes, consolidating departments where possible and starting core initiatives, including product rebranding.

How to Use the Road Map

Your company needs to determine the specific range of activities that are required if you are to accomplish the strategic goals of your integration implementation; you should then incorporate those specific activities into your road map. Delineating phases maps when the different tracks begin and end, some sequentially and others in parallel. The road map imparts a sense of urgency and timeliness to your integration implementation. Regardless of how well the integration team develops the integration road map, there is always some degree of uncertainty involved in going down the novel path of every integration. To avoid slippage from the integration road map and timeline, everyone involved with the integration implementation needs to learn to operate in conditions of both uncertainty and urgency. To facilitate this, some companies invoke the 80/100 rule: you'll move forward 100 percent of the time even if a decision is only 80 percent right.[1] This is a process approach that is based on the point of view that you may make mistakes, but you can always revisit your decisions later. It is a way to stay in healthy control of the pace of the integration. It's more important that you keep your integration implementation keyed to the road map apace with your goals and in accord with your principles.

The Day Zero Approach to Integration Planning

Integration planning should occur simultaneously and iteratively as your company proceeds from the targeting phase through the due diligence, negotiation, and approvals stages (described in Chapter 4). The importance of a successful integration should shape the questions you ask during due diligence and should affect the pricing model and other requirements that your company brings into negotiations. In addition, you need to ensure that any modifications and adjustments that are necessary to obtain regulatory approvals will allow for a viable integration (see Exhibit 5-1).

There has to be continuity between integration planning and implementation. All too often, an acquiring company creates a new team to implement the integration that does not understand the background of the issues that were uncovered during the acquisition process. In contrast, a sound integration planning process prevents the deal from being "thrown over the fence" for the integration team to salvage. You need to complete your integration plan *before* the acquisition is approved, which allows you to create, organize, and staff your integration team on Day One. This is the "Day Zero" approach to integration planning.

Although you should start your integration plan when you identify your targeted acquisition, the plan should be based on everything that you've learned at every stage in the M&A process and should be shaped by your company's playbook. This begins with identifying your company's strategic intent (covered in Chapter 3) and continues as you develop your acquisition business plan. A robust, more explicit business plan will enable your company to move quickly, resolve issues faster, and streamline decision making. At the same time, a good integration plan cannot be based on a rigid set of procedures designed for efficiency only;

Exhibit 5-1

Integration Planning: A Developing and Interactive Process across All Preacquisition Phases and Core Capabilities

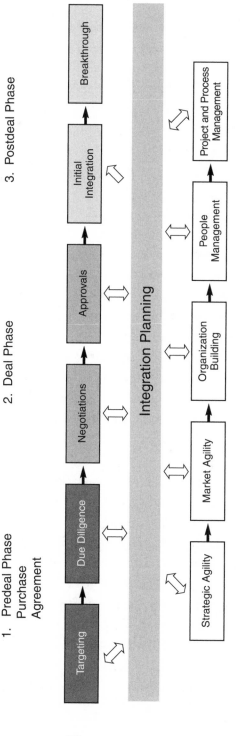

1. Predeal Phase
   Purchase
   Agreement

2. Deal Phase

3. Postdeal Phase

instead, it needs to be a flexible plan that can accommodate whatever new understandings and conditions may surface during the integration. A strong business plan with enough flexibility is the vehicle for carrying out an integration that will meet its strategic goals.

The main task of integration planning is to define the possible shape of the newly emerging company. The key question it aims to answer is, "What will this company look like once we are done?" When developing your integration plan, your integration team should do all of the following:

- Define the characteristics of the structure—that is, how the new company will be structured to carry out all of its functions.
- Identify the horizontal coordination mechanisms that will provide effective knowledge flow (e.g., the steering committee and other teams that coordinate across the integration).
- Project all ongoing costs and revenues.
- Note what different customer segments will be targeted.

The result should establish a new company that realizes synergy in both reducing costs and increasing capabilities. Exhibit 5-2 offers a list of questions that can help your acquisition team start thinking about the integration process.

Once you've answered the questions listed in Exhibit 5-2, the task of those involved in due diligence is to verify the set of hypotheses formulated in the course of the initial integration planning. The acquisition team can determine from the resulting data profile whether the key assumptions that the company made concerning the positioning and synergy configuration are true and support the business case that justifies the purchase.

When your company takes the approach of formulating your overall acquisition strategy at the start of your acquisition initiative, you will be shaping your integration plan to do more than the "standard" due diligence. Typically, due diligence focuses on much narrower questions pertaining to a target company's financial soundness, the scope of its liabilities,

Exhibit 5-2

Questions to Ask before You Merge or Acquire about How the Two Companies Will Be Integrated

☐ What will be the extent of the integration between our company and the acquired company?

☐ How should our new company be configured?

☐ What are potential obstacles to integration in the core areas of

- Leadership?
- Strategy?
- Systems?
- Structure?
- Culture?

☐ What will our new company's positioning in the marketplace be?

☐ What customer segments can our new company serve? And what capabilities will we need to be successful at that?

☐ What are the core capabilities of each company? And how can we capture and fuse them to create the next level of performance and value in our new company?

☐ What new sets of offerings would be made possible by combining the capabilities of our two companies?

☐ What would be the possible balance between expense and growth synergies? Where would potential expense synergies run the risk of *negating* growth synergies?

☐ How would our new company share knowledge and information?

and the range of its assets. However, when you include questions concerning integration requirements in your due diligence process, the answers can help you negotiate key issues and prepare your company to meet approval requirements; in addition, those answers also bring issues to the surface much earlier in integration planning.

Based on this information, you can start to formulate your integration plan. You will sketch it out in greater detail until it takes full operational shape and is ready when integration formally begins. Questions concerning what is required for successful integration planning are built into each preacquisition activity. This planning has to be designed so that it can benefit from learning through iterative feedback loops to define probing questions and refine the strategies for approaching, managing, and optimizing the integration plan.

As a result of unexpectedly lengthy regulatory approval periods, companies have, on occasion, been forced to wait for long periods of time before they could begin integrating their new acquisitions. In some cases, what at first seemed to be a highly negative *imposition* has turned out to be an unanticipated *opportunity* to deal with a sizable docket of questions and issues required to formulate a successful integration plan. In other words, for these companies, the cloud of delay turned out to become a valuable integration planning silver lining.

When approval for the transfer of ownership finally came through, these companies were ready to move forward and integrate their new company far more successfully than they would have been able to do otherwise. As a result, their well-thought-out integration planning allowed them to generate expense synergies beyond what had been anticipated, and to capture and enable fundamental capability development, all in much less time.

How to Develop Your Integration Plan: From the Outside In

The "outside-in" approach starts with the demands of the market, with market signals coming from the outside environment and stimulating responses from the operations and management inside your company.

Your company should begin with the new market conditions and center on your customers' needs; when you choose to go down that path, you are making the decision to become a more customer-centric company. You are moving from simply *determining customer needs* to actively exploring *how you could reshape your company* to meet those requirements by rethinking and redesigning the mix of customers that you're targeting, the solutions your company offers, and the distribution channels you use. Sorting this out first helps you map out what you need to do to ensure that your company has the internal capabilities to deliver superior value to your existing or potential customers.

Starting with the targeting phase and continuing through all phases of preacquisition, you can use business intelligence and market research to analyze current and new markets and to evaluate the impacts of anticipated innovations (both yours and your competitors). This creates a basis for fashioning increasingly detailed scenarios of how you can shape your newly emerging company. From this viewpoint, the acquisition period is a unique opportunity to reposition and reframe your company. The integration planning team can start saying, "We could do this with this, or we could put that there; we could have this kind of structure, or we could reach our current and many new customers with this array of products."

An Outside-In Approach Is Critical to the Strategy-Making of a Customer-Centric Company

When your company makes the fundamental decision to become a customer-centric company, you need to organize your structure and core processes to become responsive to the new information and requirements you're learning from customer interactions. Because market trends and customer needs are constantly evolving, your company must strive to focus your strategy on those trends and needs, in line with what customers see as exceptional value.

This is one of the key issues with acquisitions: most companies become internally focused, and the market passes by them—at a time when the process of combining two entities makes the need to engage in ongoing strategy making even *more* compelling. Markets move too fast to suspend renewal while your company is focused on integrating its newly acquired business.

Therefore, you must use the acquisition and the subsequent integration as an opportune time for renewing your fundamental strategy. This imposes more stringent demands on all business leaders involved, because you are already taxed to the limit with integration issues. The acquisition and integration processes are not for the faint of heart; leadership strength and bandwidth make the difference between a mediocre integration and one that truly generates value.

Your newly combined company is in a unique position to make exactly that sort of choice. You can take your assets, both hard and soft, and your capabilities and redesign your company as one that is capable of high performance and extraordinary value creation. However, you can make that choice work only by having all the elements of your company aligned with the goal of striving to provide an extraordinary value proposition to your customers. Your company has to gear your new offerings not to what customers have wanted in the past, but rather to how they see you responding to their emerging needs and providing superior value.

Commitment to becoming a customer-centric company requires a different way of designing the company. Instead of just operating several business units geared to produce specific products selected on the basis of your own internally driven perspective, your company needs to look outward to determine how you can best meet the evolving needs of the customers you seek to serve. Decisions about the design of your company's organizational structure and processes have to flow from a shared understanding of how best to reach these customers.

The shift to becoming a customer-centric company is fundamental. It does not happen overnight, and there is not a final "there" there; it is evolutionary, and it is never complete—first, because you will continue to uncover new layers of connectedness with your customers, and second, because your customers and their needs will change over time. For example, company leadership tends to learn from front-line sales and service representatives what customer opportunities exist and where those opportunities can be leveraged. This information can then be used as a guide to deepen the shift from a product-centered company to a solutions-oriented, customer-centered company. As most leaders are placed under stress during an integration, the temptation is to simplify and turn to a more familiar product focus, which is counterproductive to achieving quantum gains.

Over time, your company determines the degree and extent to which you need to form new structural elements, such as customer-specific teams, to establish the right balance of investment between what it would take to produce customer solutions and the type of structure and processes you need to support that focus. What is most critical is that all elements of your new company need to be invested in the common vision of building a customer-centric, high-performance, value-creating company. Then when opportunities arise, all parts of your company will, in the process of forging initiatives that shape customer solutions, knit together the evolving framework of the new company and simultaneously form its emerging culture and the way you conduct your business.

Leadership needs to guide this transition by putting in place a clear customer-centric vision for the new company. Such a vision will focus the collective resolve of the company and serve to refocus internally oriented energies on the market and your customers. This will reduce the internal tensions that come with integration and work to provide a unifying context for both managers and employees. The vision operates as a guide to everyone's day-to-day actions. It is incumbent on business leaders to support this new context by clearing obstacles that present themselves. This context also serves to guide strategic decisions, such as determining what new "solutions" can best leverage the combined capabilities of the new company.

Capabilities

Most executives believe that it is key for their company to acquire specific core capabilities if it is to achieve its strategic goals.[2] That understanding is an essential part of the early considerations that guide a company's decision as to whether it wants to achieve its goals by acquisition, organic growth, or some combination of both. You have to start exploring these capabilities during the targeting stage, and your exploration needs to become more specific during the due diligence stage. You can then use the knowledge you gain from these explorations in your integration planning to form a framework for accessing the essential capabilities that you need as quickly and effectively as possible.

Each company has its own key clusters of capabilities and needs to seek out the ones that are complementary or catalytic in an acquisition. Your company needs to determine which of its core capabilities are of primary value and which are of secondary value in this setting. This is a skill and capability all by itself. To do this, you need to structure and carry out a capabilities audit. (See Appendix C, "Auditing Strategic Capabilities in the Context of the Deal Exercise.")

The first step in this process is to develop a framework for categorizing capabilities and their value to your company. The framework can be as simple as asking companywide leadership and business unit managers to name the top three capabilities that enable the success of your company or of their specific operation. You can use that information to take you to the next level of analysis by asking the questions listed in Exhibit 5-3.

Exhibit 5-3

Questions to Ask When Auditing Your Company's Capabilities

☐ What types of capabilities does our company have, and what do those capabilities enable us to do?

☐ What core capabilities drive through our supply chain?

☐ How does our company compare to our competitors from a capabilities perspective?

☐ How would we rank our company's capabilities when considering our company's overall critical success factors?

The different types of capabilities that a company has and the ability to access those capabilities can make a distinct difference in making the decision to acquire. Capabilities are, by their nature, unique to a company. They are not just materials or procedures; they also include ideas and how those ideas can be acted on, and what people, skills, equipment, and conditions are necessary to generate significant outcomes involving those capabilities. You need to identify your own company's capabilities. It is equally essential that you have a process for tapping into and leveraging the capabilities of both your own company and the acquired company.

To carry out an effective audit of capabilities, the integration planning team needs to take the knowledge obtained from due diligence and other sources and develop a comprehensive profile of the capabilities of both companies. Moreover, you need to carry out and test your capabilities audit before integrating the company you've acquired so that you have a good grasp of your own capabilities profile and how it can be enhanced by the capabilities of the acquired company. In addition, your integration planning team has to educate those who will be involved in integration implementation in this capabilities auditing approach so that they can put it into practice as soon as the transaction is completed.

Where it is legally permissible, it is to your advantage to include conversations with your counterparts in the acquired company, prior to the closing of the deal, about the range of capabilities. These conversations may be acceptable if they are exploratory discussions and not action related. Being ready to conduct a capabilities audit will have sizable payoffs in terms of facilitating speed and gaining value from integration in the short and the long term. It is an investment that is worth all the time and effort that your integration team can devote to it, because your company will benefit by being better able to reach new potentials that were not possible before the acquisition.

Finally, you need to develop a methodology that your new company will use to transform the capabilities that are identified into your expanding operating capabilities. This will include a knowledge repository, provision for development and application teams, and a structure of accountability so that the work of developing the capabilities and making them available for companywide use is led and supported effectively.

Governance: Moving from Two Companies to One

Governance by the leadership of both companies (and over time, at all levels of the emerging company) maps out and operates the new organizational design and how it can yield optimal high performance and a quantum leap outcome. Governance comes directly into play in M&As because it is "the set of rules and procedures governing corporate decision-making, control, and monitoring processes."[3]

But governance goes beyond rules and procedures "to spread a corporate culture among staff and ensure both risk prevention and advisability of business decisions, using documents such as a code of ethics, governance manuals and organizational, management and control models to guide and orient corporate life."[4]

What Difference Does Good Governance Make?

Effective governance has to be part of a well-structured approach to the acquisition and integration process. Having effective governance will ensure that the values and principles guiding the integration are applied

> **Case Example: Pfizer's Acquisition of the Warner-Lambert Company**
>
> Pfizer executive vice president and CFO David L. Shedlarz shared his experience of how Pfizer benefited from its cultivation of its vital governance model in its $100 billion acquisition of the Warner-Lambert Company in 2001:
>
> *Pfizer has a long and strong history of being very sensitive to corporate governance issues and we tend to be at the cutting edge in this arena. As a result, I'm certain our access to the institutions was enhanced. I also believe our reputation in the areas of transparency, financial reporting, and accounting helped. Given the nature of the transaction, this went through extensive review by regulatory authorities. Without that past investment, this would have been a lot more difficult to accomplish [especially given the time limitations].[5]*

consistently. It will create an advantage by ensuring consistency between the company's actions and its principles.

Exhibit 5-4 provides another checklist of questions that you should consider when you are evaluating the business risks and the adherence to governance that your company requires in order to plan and implement an acquisition successfully.

Although defining governance and making it operational are challenges, we cannot overemphasize the importance of creating a viable governance capability. It is a requirement, not an option, for carrying out significant acquisitions of any scale, but especially for large-scale acquisitions that redefine a company. (In Chapter 6, we examine governance structures that were put into place to provide effective oversight of integration activities.)

Exhibit 5-4

Questions to Ask before You Merge or Acquire to Evaluate Your Potential Business Risk and Ensure that You're Meeting Corporate Governance Standards

☐ Have we evaluated all business risks and their potential impact?

☐ Have we assigned responsibility throughout the company?

☐ Are we encouraging responsible behavior among employees?

☐ Are we rewarding employees for achieving corporate governance goals?

☐ Are we looking after our shareholders?

☐ Are we aware of activities that could impair our company's image?

Everyone Needs to Be Engaged, Committed, and Invested

In the knowledge-capital era, a company's management, workforce, suppliers, and customers have to collaborate on what they know as well as how they operate in an extended supplier/producer/customer network; if you don't collaborate, you won't survive. This is important in any company, but if you're seeking to grow by acquisition, it is even more challenging. An acquisition requires combining companies that may have different backgrounds, operating structures, practices, values, and relationships. In addition, there is the uncertainty and stress of potential layoffs, possible movement to new positions and locations, the need to choose operating platforms, and many other factors that need to be addressed in order to achieve effective integration.

Traditional command-and-control practices and traditional contracts fall short of being able to rapidly define, reframe, and realign the crucial capabilities in these complex settings. In the newly turned soil of the acquisition and integration, all participants—both internal and external—need to be engaged, committed, and invested in grasping and reworking their roles, practices, and organizations to carry out these complex sets of changes.

For the company workforce to fully invest itself in the work of building the new company, its members must see a good, clear return on their investment for themselves, too. Just as financial investors bring their financial capital to the table and work out the best deal for themselves, individuals in the workforce are investors of their own human capital and seek their own best return on investment.[6] Each individual involved in this change is negotiating his or her own "deal" while participating in the integration. Even when operations are growing organically, this is not an easy process. Not just senior leadership but also each individual involved needs to have a set of negotiating skills to articulate his or her new roles, responsibilities, rights, and rewards in the new company. Members of the workforce must negotiate with company managers to forge these new social contracts in which individuals invest their capabilities so that the company's strategic goals can be reached.

The leadership of your company shapes the context for these deals so that people will invest their human capital resources (that is, their capabilities) to achieve strategic targets. Front-line employees, supervisors, and senior leadership all have to seek the best outcome for both the company and the workforce. The same holds true in the relationship between the company and the customers for its outcomes, with products and services being cogenerated with inputs from users. Although there was a time when these relationships could have been imposed by the acquiring company, the networked world in which your new company currently operates requires that all elements be collaboratively synchronized as you reshape your company and take on new markets. How a company can intentionally design the conditions for employee engagement and commitment is seen in the way Cisco structured its relationships with employees from companies it acquired.

The people planning element of integration planning is an extension of the core capability of people management. This is the capability to recognize talent, build on strength, select people quickly, and make

---

Case Example: Cisco

Cisco had a multiyear acquisition program that was well thought out and orchestrated. Cisco developed and used a clear format that rapidly integrated the companies it acquired. Often, the goal of the acquisition was to acquire core ideas, patents, and emerging markets; in addition, however, Cisco was keenly interested in having the developers of those ideas join Cisco, as these were the people who could make new product lines grow within the larger Cisco context.

The incentives for joining Cisco were not just financial reward, but also the availability of resources, access to markets that the larger Cisco could provide, and the opportunity for autonomy. This had enormous appeal, to the extent that in at least one case, the leadership of a targeted company accepted Cisco's offer over a larger financial package tendered by a competitor.

The leaders of Cisco's newly integrated units became quite wealthy as they were acquired. But Cisco's emphasis on quality and value went far beyond traditional incentives. Cisco knew that it was acquiring intellectual capital and capabilities more than products, however great the potential of those specific products might be. The combination of the right people with the right processes and the right context could leverage those talents and capabilities to a substantially greater degree than Cisco's competitors could provide. Cisco invested in developing the capability of knowing how to integrate while maintaining respect for people's talents and values, and that approach paid off handsomely.

sure that people are given the right level of challenge, neither underestimating nor overestimating their abilities.

A human resources plan is as critical a component of integration planning as any other element. An acquisition is a traumatic time for people. They want to know what their future will be. They want to be treated openly and fairly and not be unwarrantedly surprised. They want an environment in which they can trust the messages coming to them and expect to be informed about any changes affecting them. Building integrity into a rigorous communication plan allows much more management of people throughout the integration.

Planning for people involves three areas:

1. Planning for continuity across the acquisition and integration phases
2. People and the transition to the new structure
3. A people management plan for integrating the two companies

Planning for Continuity across the Acquisition and Integration Phases

People who are involved in due diligence need to be close to the negotiating team (if possible, on the negotiating team); where appropriate, they should be on the integration planning team as well. For example, if the acquisition has substantial amounts of manufacturing assets, the people who were on the due diligence team need to be a factor on the negotiating team. If it is anticipated that there are especially strategic or significantly impacting human resources issues, the HR person who is on the due diligence team should also be part of the negotiating team. Ensuring the continuity of personnel across these different phases provides the knowledge required to deal with the challenges encountered. This is an important condition for setting the stage for a successful integration.

People Planning for the Transition

In dealing with people management, it is important that the right knowledge is preserved for the new entity. Integration planning needs to take into account the substantial knowledge and know-how that is at risk when one company is integrated with another. If your company knows the role

Case Example: How Bristol-Myers Squibb Dealt with People Acquired from a Unit of DuPont

The Bristol-Myers Squibb company (BMS) acquired DuPont's major pharmaceutical business unit for almost $8 billion. A good part of the value of this acquisition was the pipeline research that DuPont Pharmaceuticals was in the process of developing, which could be useful in work that was already underway at BMS. This knowledge and experience was considered to have enormous value, in some ways a higher value than the physical plant and equipment that came with the acquisition.

However, access to the critical personal knowledge of DuPont's research scientists was questionable. Because those research scientists might have only a limited and short-term future with the newly integrated company, they would have little incentive to share their knowledge. At the same time, BMS had a very time-constrained window of opportunity to capture this critical knowledge before many of the DuPont research scientists found out whether or not they were being offered a position in the new company. Even if they were to be offered a new job, the DuPont scientists might choose to accept recruitment offers from other pharmaceutical companies, or they might simply decide to leave for any number of other reasons. The company needed to answer this question:

> How could BMS devise an approach that would encourage people who had such an uncertain future to collaborate on sharing their knowledge, which would be key to the strategic future drug pipeline of the newly integrated company?

To make this knowledge sharing and capture even more of a challenge, the DuPont research scientists were highly educated, well known in their respective fields, and quite well paid. Therefore, the next question facing BMS was this:

> What incentives would encourage the DuPont scientists to share important knowledge of projects that they had spent a good deal of their professional life developing?

The job of meeting this challenge was taken on by Melinda J. Bickerstaff, BMS's chief knowledge officer (CKO), and her knowledge management (KM) team. They looked at the situation and thought about what might be most valued by the research scientists from both companies, BMS and DuPont. After reviewing several alternative approaches, including traditional surveys and financial incentives, they came to the conclusion that the research scientists would share their knowledge only when a strong basis of trust and shared values existed. The most appealing way to stimulate this values-based knowledge sharing was to re-create the scientific review process that each company used to review their work. This format would be familiar to the scientists from both companies, but it would now be implemented in the context of an integration effort. This process would involve peer-to-peer conversations between scientists. Not only was this a format with which the scientists were already comfortable, but it also tapped into each professional's (i.e., each scientist's) desire to "tell the story of my work" to someone, regardless of what their future might bring.

The KM team recruited and briefed the BMS scientists to organize and to be participants in these strategic conversations. The BMS scientists mapped out a two-week schedule of briefings or scientific reviews, to be initiated immediately upon the closing of the deal. The DuPont scientists were given the schedule of reviews, and for a period of about two months, while the deal was being reviewed by regulatory agencies, they were hard at work preparing the "stories of their work." In the meantime, the KM team worked with the BMS scientists to help them be very specific about what information or knowledge they needed to make both the "asset" and the "people" decisions. They asked questions like these:

- What knowledge do you need?
- Where would you find it here (at BMS)?
- Where do you think it is in DuPont?
- What format is it in? A document? A database? Or does it reside in a person?

The work of the KM integration planning team paid off. When the deal closed, the two-week scientific review process commenced. The DuPont scientists were actively engaged in telling "their stories." Each evening, the BMS scientists would meet to determine what knowledge they had and what they needed to get the next day through the review process. This process worked remarkably well. Eight days into these reviews, BMS made all the "asset" decisions; and fifteen days into them, it made all the "people" decisions. Two and one-half months later, the integration was complete—in record time for this industry—and BMS achieved the financial synergies it had targeted as well. These were very significant indicators of the success of the acquisition venture.[7]

of knowledge assets and how to preserve them or bring them into the company, it can make a substantial difference in whether your company will generate value or lose value from the acquisition.

In most cases, this opportunity to generate and capture crucial knowledge is not actively sought out during the different stages of an acquisition. Certain knowledge may be available at one stage and no longer available after that point. It is more than rewarding for those on the acquisition, transition, and integration teams to make it a priority to bring to the surface and capture intangible assets at all possible opportunity points. The capability to cultivate and leverage this knowledge creates substantial value for the acquiring company (in the previous case, BMS). This initiative cost very little to carry out, and the key knowledge that emerged became inputs that were used by the acquiring company for building a significant part of its future.

Planning the "People" Integration

The goal of planning the people component of the integration is twofold: to keep two existing companies in operation to satisfy customer needs and organizational goals, while simultaneously leading the rapid transition of these two entities into one newly emerging company. That being the case, it is critical that you accomplish all of the following:

- You must retain key employees.
- You must build trust across the board, with all employees.
- You must ensure that employees take on new responsibilities in such a way that the outside world experiences the transition as seamless.

To achieve all those goals, the human-capital component of the integration has to be well planned, carefully orchestrated, thoughtful, and resilient.

Case Example: How Clarica Integrated People Acquired from Another Company

The approach that Clarica developed for its acquisitions provides a good example of the thinking and planning needed for a sound human capital integration plan. Clarica saw that it needed to determine in its business plan what employees and employee skill sets would be needed in the new company. From previous acquisitions, Clarica had developed a set of resources and support templates (which had become components of its reusable integration playbook) for employees affected by the acquisition.

Directly after the announcement of an acquisition, Clarica would hold an initial discussion with the senior management team from the acquired company that was working on the transition. Clarica then sent a memo to employees describing its commitment to timely communication, including a statement that it would confirm the status of employees by a specific date. This was the beginning of outlining Clarica's employment and severance terms to all the employees of the acquired company.

The next step was a series of face-to-face meetings in different work units to hear concerns and outline the process for moving forward. As promised, Clarica sent confirmation of the employment status of all employees who were affected be the acquisition. To continue to cultivate an atmosphere of trust, Clarica set up communication channels and available resources for support during what could be a very trying period for the employees who were affected by the acquisition.

A major ingredient of the success of the human capital component is that employees of the acquired company were treated with respect and appropriate dignity. Even if employees were to be terminated (either immediately or at some point after the closing date), Clarica found that the employees truly appreciated the company's direct, honest communication.

In one sense, the Clarica approach established a new social and employment contract with these employees, even if a temporary one. Part of Clarica's effort was to support its reputation as an employer of choice and to nurture a positive organizational climate that it could carry forward into the integrated company. If the employees felt that Clarica was treating them equitably, they would be much more likely to accept termination or a limited-term transition employment without that affecting overall employee productivity. To support that stance, Clarica committed itself to a series of meetings with open communication to ensure that it communicated as soon and as much as it could, as clearly as it could, and as often as it could.

After the announcement of the deal, but before the closing, Clarica established a transition council to set policy and make decisions on transition issues. Part of its role was to recognize cultural differences and to ensure that the company managed those differences and the ways they affected employees and other stakeholders (including customers, independent contractors, and suppliers). The transition council monitored the integration process with regard to people and business issues and oversaw the change management plan and communications.

As part of its human capital plan, Clarica also established what it called "due process." The due process ground rules included several principles and provisions that outlined how Clarica would go about human capital-related actions in the period leading up to and during the integration. These principles were posted on the Clarica intranet and communicated to employees of the acquired company, so that every person affected by the acquisition could be aware of the major points that were guiding the human capital plan. Provisions included the following:

- Decisions pertaining to the employment status of individuals are communicated one-on-one by the appropriate manager.
- All individuals will receive written confirmation of their status by a specific date, including timing and amounts if severed.
- Clarica will give as much advance notification as possible, with each unit speaking to its people when it is ready to do so.
- Positions will be identified first, with individuals to fill them chosen second.
- Individual consideration is given to all acquired company employees.
- Selection decisions for management positions are made first, and those selected assist in the selection of those who report to them.
- After a specific date, all staff members will have equal opportunity to apply for new roles as the new company evolves.
- Aside from performance issues, no one will be terminated prior to the closing date of the deal.
- Clarica commits to provide transition support to all employees continuing within the new company and those making the transition to other opportunities.
- A career center is established for all individuals looking for alternative career opportunities.

Bringing all of these elements together set up positive expectations for the employees of both Clarica and the acquired company. In an era in which people's skills and innovation may be a company's most highly sought-after resource, this counts for a lot. In Clarica's case, this stance enabled it to retain more than 90 percent of the technical staff of the company it acquired. Even when a company finds that acquisitions bring redundant staffing, it is considerably more effective for both the employees who are retained and those who are not to view the acquiring company as a fair, equitable employer of choice.

What to Do If the Conditions or Timing Aren't Right for Integration

Often, you may find that there are components of an acquisition that you simply cannot integrate readily without significantly destroying value. For example, any (or all) of the following elements of the target company might not be a good fit:

- Customer sets
- Marketing channels
- Suppliers
- Regulatory requirements
- Corporate culture

Or the timing might not be just right for the quickly moving processes of your integration implementation phase. At the same time, your company may have a strong desire to integrate that component later, when both you and the target company have created a better process or structure for such a migration. In this type of situation, your company should develop a process for evaluating how ready your company is to integrate and the readiness of the business unit you want to acquire.

If the conditions for immediate integration are not good, you can place your target business unit in an "acquisitions parking lot" until a more appropriate time to either integrate that unit or divest it arrives. While it is in the "parking lot," the acquired company can carry on business as usual, but it also has the option to either fully link into your company's key support services or have those services operate in an oversight role. These include such support areas as

- IT services
- Human resources management services
- Legal resources
- Marketing capabilities
- Any other departments where there is a complementary fit

Exhibit 5-5 shows how this migration approach could be structured. The business groups and their lines of business are "parked" in a defined market operating group for a period of time that you and the leaders of your acquired business unit have agreed is appropriate, until you can build more satisfactory bridges to your company and integrate your acquisition more effectively. These business lines are part of your company,

Exhibit 5-5

A Business Operating Model Allowing for the Gradual Introduction of Newly Acquired Business Units

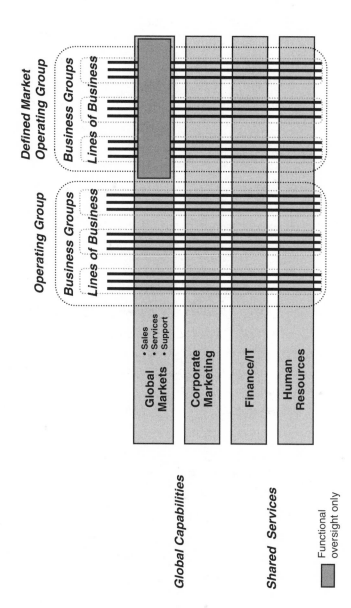

but they are at different stages of integration. You should review this arrangement regularly, and modify it as needed. It is important to make it clear that this "parking lot" arrangement is a temporary one until the right conditions have been found for effective integration without assuming excessive costs such as the departure of key staff. Criteria have to be spelled out to determine the readiness for a greater level of integration. Setting up such a unit in your organization allows you to acquire a new business and integrate it gradually without having to undergo extensive structural change in the acquiring company.

Conclusion

Once you have developed your integration plan and oriented employees on both sides of the acquisition to implement that plan, you can move rapidly, yet sure-footedly, from the day your transaction closes. Using this Day Zero approach, the integrity of your company's strategic intent will be a central thread running through all elements of your integration plan. The plan makes a great effort to ensure alignment in two ways:

1. Vertically, from senior leadership to the front line and back again
2. Horizontally, across all components that will be touched by the new emerging company

The implementation plan positions the company to succeed in its integration efforts by providing it with the framework it needs to reorganize the two legacy companies into one high-performance, value creation-focused company.

Success Factors

- Implement an integration playbook that is coherent and transparent to all employees.
- Set out a clearly defined road map and timeline for all major stages of the integration.
- Avoid the trap of developing the integration plan in isolation from the rest of the acquisition process.
- Validate your business plan with representatives of the new company you're acquiring. This is especially important because your business plan embodies your integration plan—including the milestones and outcomes you're seeking.
- Make sure your integration plan informs the acquiring company what its financial drivers are going to be and how it can leverage those financial drivers through the integration process. This is an especially important ingredient during the negotiations phase.
- Develop a capabilities audit framework.
- Identify what complementary intangible capabilities are central to the success of your newly emerging company and what synergies you expect to realize during the integration process.
- Make sure your integration teams establish a cascading conversation for carrying out your business plan throughout all levels of both companies.

Derailing Factors

- Beginning integration planning *after* the closing of the deal transaction
- Seeing the transaction as an add-on rather than an opportunity for organizational transformation
- Not providing adequate leadership or the structural, staffing, or material resources to support the development and implementation of the integration plan
- Preparing only a narrow communication and change management plan—or none at all

Questions

- Can we use our past experience and templates to build an integration playbook?
- What was the importance given to speed in the context of our most recent integration?
  - If it was seen as important, what steps did we take to accelerate the pace of the integration?
  - How did we work to have the change take place rapidly and expeditiously?

- Who was involved in the development and implementation of the business plan and the integration plan:
  - During the preselection phase?
  - During the due diligence phase?
  - During the integration phase?
- What areas did our business plan cover?
  - How did our business plan change over the course of the M&A process?
- How did we obtain critical information relating to the proposed acquisition from managers and others from the M&A target company during the due diligence and integration planning phases ?
  - How much importance did we place on building trust and partnering with the acquired company prior to the actual acquisition?
  - How successful were those efforts?
  - What could we have done better in this regard?

Notes

1. Mary Cianni in *Making Mergers Work: The Strategic Importance of People*, Jeffry A. Schmidt, ed. (Alexandria, VA: Towers Perrin/ SHRM, 2002), p. 131.

2. Chris Zook, *Unstoppable* (Boston: Harvard Business School Press, 2007), p. 119.

3. Brembo Web site, April 4, 2006; http://www.brembo.com/ENG/ AboutBrembo/CompanyOverview/CorporateGovernance/Corporate +Governance2Eng.htm.

4. Ibid.

5. Ellen M. Heffes and Phil Livingston, "Reflecting on a Mega Merger," *Financial Executives International*, 2002; http://www.thefreelibrary.com/ REFLECTING+On+a+MEGA-MERGER.-a075835706.

6. Thomas O. Davenport, *Human Capital: What It Is and Why People Invest It* (San Francisco: Jossey-Bass, 1999).

7. John Girard, "Words of Wisdom, An Interview with Melinda Bickerstaff." *KMPro Journal*, www.kmpro.org/journal/KMPro_Vol_ 3_No_1.pdf., p. 18.

The additional material in this chapter comes from the authors' interviews and experiences.

6

Getting Your Integration Structure Right

Chapter 5 examined how to set the basis for developing an integration plan that positions the new company for success. This chapter examines the framework that needs to be developed for the implementation plan and indicates how an accountability structure, linked to that framework, can ensure that the integration will be implemented in ways that meet your company's goals. Extending from that accountability structure is a set of measures that allows the steering committee and the integration team to evaluate how well the integration is being implemented. Having these elements in place builds into the integration plan the actions to be taken and the lines of responsibility necessary to maintain a continuity of the core businesses of the company, while at the same time carrying out the fundamental changes required to set the stage for the new, quantum leap company to emerge.

Integration Framework, Accountability, Metrics, and Continuity Structure

Every company needs to develop a framework through which it can support its acquisition and integration processes. The framework is the structure in relation to which the leadership and staff from both companies define their roles and institute the accompanying accountability and responsibility linkages. This allows for the continuity that the two companies need if they are to continue their operations and gradually emerge as one new and transformed company.

In a large-scale acquisition, the acquiring company needs to design its integration framework to accommodate the reality that both it and the acquired company have to change themselves in "midflight" as it continues to carry out business during the integration. In an acquisition of this scale, the acquired company cannot be merely bolted onto the acquiring company. Rather, the acquiring company has to assimilate what is positive about the acquired company. The acquiring company's framework needs to have the capacity to work through the major issues involved in fusing organizations that have business logic, structure, customer relationships, distribution channels, technology platforms, and other such elements. At the same time, the framework must support maintaining core business operations and flawless customer service. It has to achieve both continuity and change without stumbling or giving its competition the least opportunity to take market share away from the two companies as they are integrating. Planning the development of a robust framework that has the capacity to manage these demands is a must to avert the downsides and realize the upsides of the acquisition.

The framework has to be malleable because the challenges facing the acquisition and integration teams will change from phase to phase during the acquisition. It also must adjust to the changing tasks and responsibilities at each stage of the acquisition. If the framework's structure is too cumbersome or top-heavy, it could overburden the company, making the integration sluggish and disconnected. If the structure is too meager, it will provide inadequate support for the tasks that need to be accomplished. If the acquiring company has developed an integration playbook, it can draw on the background knowledge in that playbook to design its integration structure to be a good fit for the challenges it will meet in its implementation. The acquiring company can also look at major reorganizations it has gone through to see how well the framework it used enabled it to succeed, as well as where the framework fell short during those initiatives. In all of these cases, there are significant learnings that can be incorporated to guide the development of the framework structure so that it will facilitate the new company's reaching its integration goals.

Accountability

The definition of accountability is to be answerable for one's delegated authority and have the obligation to demonstrate and take responsibility for performance in light of agreed-upon expectations. Governance sets up an accountability structure that ensures that the people who are carrying out the transition to the new company implement the integration effectively and efficiently. Managers use the integration framework to guide how accountability is assigned and managed.

Just as each company has to design its own version of an overall structure for carrying out the acquisition, each has to design an accountability structure for roles that will achieve its particular goals. Implementing an accountability structure ensures that a company has integrity and cohesiveness, with integration goals that are able to be accomplished across the company at all levels and in all of its parts.

Metrics

Integration planning includes developing a framework of metrics. Metrics are company-specific; however, in general, there are two types of metrics: strategic metrics and integration metrics.

Metrics are an explicit reference that indicates whether the processes of integration are efficient and effective and how well the acquisition is going from a strategic perspective. Metrics provide a strong link to accountability, because they give clear reference points to gauge the immediate and long-term success of the venture. To ensure that you're considering all your key strategic metrics, ask yourself the questions listed in Exhibit 6-1.

Integration metrics are the way the company knows how effective it is as it goes through its integration process. However, a good integration process is not the only driver for success. The acquisition must also meet your company's strategic requirements, to determine if it is creating value for your company.

Exhibit 6-1

Questions to Ask before You Merge or Acquire to Ensure that You're Meeting Your Company's Key Metrics

Financial Metrics

☐ Have we exceeded the internal rate of return (IRR)?

☐ What is the net present value (NPV) of this acquisition?

☐ Does the stock price reflect a positive view of this particular acquisition by the market?

Integration Metrics

☐ Were we able to retain our customers?

☐ How do the new employees feel about the new company?

☐ How quickly were the new employees able to be integrated culturally into the new company?

☐ Are we retaining the key employees that will be required to carry the business through the transition and integration phases?

☐ What is the value of the synergies captured, both cost and growth synergies?

Continuity

The accountability structure must provide for the continuity of both businesses during the acquisition and integration stages. During the transition stage, both companies must continue to carry out their business as separate entities. After closing, integration formally begins so that the two companies can become one. Continuity is one of the major challenges during these transitions. People, processes, and business units are being unbundled and recombined into new configurations, with both old responsibilities being redefined and carried out and new responsibilities being taken on.

This transformation does not happen immediately on Day One, but rather takes place over the entire time period of the integration, and also in the postintegration period. During integration, you need to ensure that the integrity and relationships of each transitioning company are supported, and ensure that your customers and suppliers are continuously informed of the changes that are taking place. At the same time, you need to ensure that your customers (and the outside world in general) experience the change as seamless, with no loss in the quality of your service or disruptions in transactions.

Case Example: How Sun Life Financial Planned Its Integration of Clarica

The Sun Life/Clarica approach to integration planning is particularly interesting in terms of the unusually strong partnering that took place before the two companies were actually combined. The two companies engaged in active discussion and planning, but this was only *preparatory work* for the posttransaction integration. An acquirer can work to create a substantial level of partnering prior to the actual integration. This is part of the Day Zero approach (described at the beginning of Chapter 5). The higher the level of partnering, the greater the amount of effective preparation that can take place for a successful transition to the new company and the takeoff of the integration implementation phase.

Clarica had developed a template for its acquisition and accountability structure over the course of several acquisitions over a number of years. This capability to carry out acquisitions effectively and efficiently was one of the capabilities that Sun Life Financial (SLF) valued when it acquired Clarica in 2002. Based on that capability, Clarica staff members were given the responsibility of playing a leading role in developing and executing the integration plan after Clarica accepted Sun Life's offer.

Clarica designed and implemented a plan for transition and integration, using an architecture in which staff from both the acquirer and the acquired company could partner in carrying out the transition and acquisition process. The framework that was developed incorporated an accountability structure, a continuity strategy, and a communication plan, as shown in Exhibit 6-2.

For Clarica, the development of the accountability structure began with the acceptance of the letter of intent. A senior leadership team took responsibility for managing the acquisition process through closing. During this period, the business plan and integration planning were developed. At each stage, the responsibilities varied, with different people playing different roles at different times. As a result, the accountability structure underwent continuous redefinition. At the time of the transition to integration, much of the accountability structure for the integration was already designed. There was some change in the composition of teams and lines of accountability, but the basic structure that threaded through the company remained.

Clarica included in its framework the key imperatives of speed, clarity, and financial focus, all of which it deemed essential for the success of its acquisitions and their integration.

As part of the acquisition communication plan, Clarica senior management gave presentations to staff that were designed to initiate discussions on how best to structure the two companies. Some of the principles were

- Proceed without delay to shape integration plans.
- Maintain clear accountabilities as the plans move forward.
- Align strategic thinking in the new configuration.
- Provide a forum for productive dialogues, leading to making judicious choices in planning the integration.
- Start the process of combining the two cultures into a vibrant new culture.
- Prepare the two companies for integrating with speed and for exceeding customer expectations.
- Resolve issues as they emerge.
- Learn to work across the two companies with a partnership approach.

Clarica defined the two parts of the acquisition as the *transition process* and the *integration process*. Sun Life and Clarica then created a Transition Council to ensure that integration plans were formulated and ready for implementation at the close of the transaction. The Transition Council formed an Integration Management Office to ensure that all of the elements of the complex integration project were coordinated effectively, with the

Exhibit 6-2

The Governance Structure for Transition

The Transition Council was composed of the members of the Transition Steering Committee, the head of IMO, and the representatives of both companies from each of the business and corporate units, as depicted in this diagram with boxes.

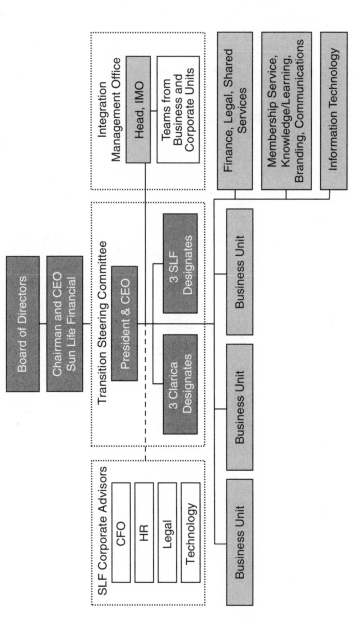

activities placed in the right priority and sequence. A second role for the Integration Management Office was to bring integration issues to the Transition Council.

Clarica and Sun Life developed a set of principles guiding the definition of accountability for the integration process, making sure that clear accountability was a key to the success of the integration. The accountability structure was placed within the context of the governance structure (see Exhibit 6-3).

The accountability principles that guided the integration were:

- The senior managers who were ultimately to assume responsibility for the leadership of business segments were required to take part in the formulation of the integration plans and had to agree to the plans that they were accountable for achieving.
- Decisions and issues that were contained within a business segment were dealt with by the business teams and the head of the Integration Council.
- Decisions and issues that spanned multiple functions or units were elevated to the Transition/Integration Council for discussion and resolution.
- The aggregated integration plans and their progress were reviewed by the Transition/Integration Council.

The Transition Steering Committee had several roles:

- It provided the overall context required for coherence at the business team level.
- It resolved issues that came to its attention in the process of building detailed integration plans.
- It provided guidance on specific decisions based on its knowledge of the context, the history of past decisions, and the emerging company's strategic aspirations.
- It also ensured that the aggregated integration plans corresponded to performance commitments.

Corporate advisors played the role of monitors during the integration process to ensure governance and accountability. They provided advice to the Transition Steering Committee to make sure that the integration plans were aligned with the acquirer's corporate strategies and conformed to its corporate policy. They also provided the business teams with expertise and guidance on specific issues that had implications for corporate direction. Additionally, corporate advisors reviewed the final integration plans and apprised the Transition Steering Committee of any substantive issues.

A third component (as mentioned previously) was an Integration Management Office (IMO), which was charged with coordinating and guiding relationships between Sun Life and Clarica. To accomplish that, the IMO supported the exchange of information among business teams to

Exhibit 6-3

The Accountability Structure in Each Period

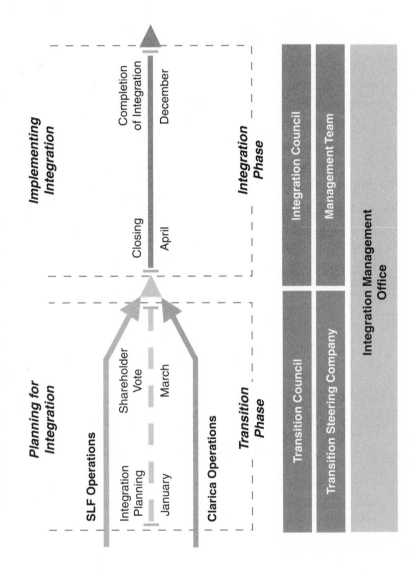

ensure consistency and clarity. The IMO was also responsible for seeing that integration commitments and accountabilities were met, especially budget and timeline requirements. In addition, the IMO worked to see that project priorities were given sufficient attention and resources to meet the objectives and timelines. The IMO was designed to provide consultative support to teams to assist them in managing their interdependencies with the integration teams, ongoing corporate initiatives, and project and related risks. In keeping with its mission, the IMO reached out to manage consultants who were brought in to supplement existing resources. Going back to its communication role, the IMO consolidated a weekly global integration "picture," communicated directional and tactical decisions to teams, and provided timely information for broader distribution across the companies and outside the companies as well.

The Integration Council and the Integration Management Office covered the spectrum of responsibility for the planning and implementation of the integration. There was a difference between the mandates of the two groups. The Transition Council assumed responsibility for the context and content of the integration plans, identifying issues, and putting forward recommendations to the Transition Steering Committee. The Integration Management Office took responsibility for the process of guiding the formulation and implementation of the integration plans, defining the project management framework, and ensuring the effective allocation of time and resources to the specific work involved in the integration.

The membership of these two governing bodies providing direction and guidance to the transition differed. Members of the Transition Council were senior business leaders appointed for the transition period to coordinate the formulation of the integration plans between the two companies. These members worked on a part-time basis while remaining responsible for the management of their respective business areas. In contrast, the head of the IMO was appointed through the completion of the integration project. Members of the IMO were appointed to undertake specific project tasks for a fixed period and on a full-time basis.

The Transition Council formulated detailed integration plans that were aligned with the overall strategy of the new company and that also met commitments to shareholders. It looked outward to assess emerging people and business issues that could affect customers. Internally, it ensured a consistency of approach in both companies, listening to staff to detect and identify issues proactively, setting policy, and making decisions on transition issues. On a strategic level, the Transition Council prepared the two companies to integrate, align, and harmonize as needed.

Another perspective on integration planning is change management. The Transition Council oversaw the implementation of the change management plan and resolved issues that emerged during the integration process as the two legacy companies made the transition from operating as two separate entities and with each migrating its operations into the new company.

Case Example: Dow Chemical Takes Care of the "KIDs"

One of the key learnings for Dow Chemical was to identify its *key implementation drivers*, which Dow's Randy Croyle refers to as "the KIDs." A frequently heard refrain at Dow during integration planning and integration is, "You have to take care of the KIDs." Here's how Croyle describes his company's approach:

> We started that [taking care of the KIDs] as a result of the Union Carbide merger. We reflected upon what [were] the key things that we needed to know at the onset. What is important is that at the very beginning of the Carbide merger, we had an outside consulting firm that came in. At every meeting, there were a thousand and one things that we needed to think about. They wanted to throw more and more people at us because they were into the billable hours mode.
>
> Even after having meetings upon meetings, every issue continued to be difficult to grasp: is this an immediate issue, a large issue, a small issue, etc. We threw out the consultant and said, "Thank you very much." We sat back then and said, "For every merger and acquisition, what are those key implementation drivers? If we can get our arms [around] them and [determine] the answers [to] those key implementation drivers, then we can marshal the appropriate resources and put together the appropriate team to then move forward on the implementation planning." Without that clarity, it is easy to get off the track and spend a lot of time on some of the low-value activities. This made it easier to prioritize amongst our needs. That was one of the key learnings.

Dow identified the following key implementation drivers, or KIDs:

1. The strategic intent of the acquisition.
2. The legal structure, because, for Dow, the legal structure drives a great deal of system activity. Dow is on an SAP R2 system (a software enterprise resource planning system that integrates all of a company's functions, such as accounting, manufacturing processes, supply chain logistics, and human resources), and understanding the legal structure is absolutely critical as it puts together the entire systems integration process. The SAP system has to know how to allocate the costs and revenues associated with different activities,
3. The human resource philosophy. Those involved in framing the integration have to map out early on whether the acquired company's employees are going to be fully integrated into Dow, and to what degree, or whether they are going to be handled with an arm's-length approach.
4. What work processes in Dow will be implemented in the acquisition. Is this acquisition going to be a full integration or a partial integration?

5. Overall communication. Dow develops a very robust communication and change management plan. Dow knows that no matter how good the strategic intent of the acquisition is, people are going to need to know, "What's in it for me?" To portray that clearly and convincingly, there is a need for a very well-thought-out, robust communication plan. Therefore, Dow generates an equally carefully developed plan addressing change management, in tandem with its communication plan.

The lesson here is that every company needs to define and review its own "KIDs" to make sure that they are sufficiently acknowledged and provided for during the acquisition transaction and in the integration phases.

Three Tracks: Implementation Project Management

One useful approach to structuring integration planning is to see the integration as a process supported by a multitrack program. Dow saw three basic tracks:

- Communication and change management
- Synergy
- Work process integration

Here's how Randy Croyle describes these three tracks:

Dow identifies individual tasks or individual projects, and it puts each of those projects in one of these three tracks. That allows the integration team to stay focused.

If you look at an entire implementation plan and you find out you do not have very much in the communication and change management track, then it allows you to sit back and say, "OK, are we doing enough in the way of communicating? Are we doing enough in the way of getting our employees or the acquired employees ready for the big changes that are going to occur?"

Likewise, for things such as synergy. You will know whether you are successful in your integration in the first 100 days. If you have clearly identified projects for capturing synergy, whether it is a cost-reduction or growth synergy, do you have milestones on those projects? Do you know who is accountable for those projects? Do you have a tracking mechanism in place to be able to capture whatever those synergies are? etc.

Finally, the work process integration track makes sure that we are going to be able to service the customer just like he or she has been serviced prior to the acquisition. We really don't want [to give] the customer any reason to go elsewhere. Are we set up for a seamless transition of the work process? The companies that we are acquiring use different processes than Dow has used. As we integrate them into the Dow system, we want to have as smooth a transition as is possible.

One of Dow's capabilities is knowing and being very explicit about all of these major elements.

How Dow Handles Communication and Change Management

Like other companies that are successful in acquisitions, Dow has a well-defined communication plan that reaches out to every major stakeholder—internal and external—over the course of the entire acquisition, from announcement through postintegration. Communication planning is seen as fundamental and is done in concert with the teams at every stage. In a sense, good communication is another face of good leadership.

The title of Dow's communication program was "Communicate the New Dow." That title was so powerful that during integration, people asked whether the new company would be called "The New Dow." Using that title was Dow's way of indicating that the whole company, inside and out, would go through changes—not only the people from the acquired company.

Effective communication creates the channels to keep employees and stakeholders informed about developments in the integration process. An open communications process sets up the conditions for all involved to be open to having a positive perspective on the integration and to collaborate on implementing the changes that are at the heart of the integration initiative.

Track 1: Communication and Change Management

Good communication is critical if your acquisition is to be effective. First, you need to assure your investors that the acquisition is a good financial and strategic move. Second, you need to make sure that your employees are aware of their changing roles and whether they will or will not have a place in the newly emerging company. Transparency, openness, and respect for people's legitimate concerns are key in keeping everyone involved in a positive way during this trying period. If you deal with your employees honestly and directly, you develop their trust, which will help you enormously as you map out their future responsibilities. It is essential that you have a clear plan and communicate information about who will stay and who will not stay as rapidly as possible, in order for your company to implement the changes you want.

Change management has to be an important consideration when you are going through these transitions. Acquisitions and integrations can be extremely novel and volatile experiences for both the acquiree and the acquiring company. When done in accordance with our quantum leap approach, an acquisition is not just a static addition to an existing company but an opportunity to rethink and reframe a large part of your company or even your entire company. This means making almost every dimension of your company eligible for recasting in light of new conditions and new sets of options. It is a time for reappraisal of strategic business goals, major markets, customer targets, core processes, and how your company is structured for making the newly emerging company able to succeed.

Track 2: Synergies

Not every acquisition will have the full-scale effect of a large acquisition, but even smaller acquisitions create experimental zones and merit an effort to grasp and leverage the window of opportunity that the acquisition presents.

For most companies, synergies mean cost savings synergies. The bias is all too often almost entirely toward producing cost synergies. Dow's approach, however, has the potential to identify, capture, and leverage both cost savings synergies and growth synergies. In the way Dow frames its approach, there is the opportunity to detect, name, and assign responsibility for tracking and developing both types of synergy. If you have a specific track for each type of synergy, you will increase people's consciousness so that they will seek to achieve both types and so they will make the effort to capitalize on both types of synergy. When you include this track, there is a record to refer to, or bookmark, both during integration and postintegration, when there may be more time available to seek out growth synergies.

Track 3: Work Process Integration

The work process integration track acknowledges that there are both internal and external stakeholders who need to have their requirements met, regardless of the difficulties encountered during the transition and integration process. There is a difference between efficiency and effectiveness here. An emphasis on *efficiency* during integration tends to focus on *internal* integration actions. In contrast, with an emphasis on the strategic *effectiveness* of the acquisition and on seeking to generate a seamless experience for your customers, the reason for the acquisition and the need for a customer strategy and focus can remain prominent for *everyone* involved in the integration work process.

Conclusion: From Integration Planning to Integration Implementation

Your integration plan should provide for a speedy, comprehensive integration implementation, with the lowest level of costs and the greatest opportunities for both expense and growth synergies.

As mentioned, this plan should take your customers into account so that they experience a seamless transition. In addition, other stakeholders need to know that you are taking their issues into account; these stakeholders include your suppliers, regulators, and the communities in which your company operates. Moreover, the capabilities and readiness that enable your company to have a successful acquisition will be built up each time your company goes through an acquisition, which in turn makes growing through acquisition as well as organically a sound option for your company. Furthermore, your company develops a deserved reputation for being a good "acquirer." As a result, your company is likely to be sought out for future deals as new opportunities present themselves.

The integration plan, along with your business plan, provides a working framework for the company to move forward into implementing the integration and creating the new company. The day the deal closes, the integration plan begins to be tested. This is where the benefits of building a strong, yet flexible integration plan pay dividends. Every day and every action will provide immediate feedback as to how well the integration plan provides footing, vision, and the necessary steps for moving through the broad-ranging implementation process. The ability of the integration plan and the integration team to take in that feedback continuously and adjust the plan appropriately will give the integration plan its life and keep the integration on track to meet its strategic goals.

Success Factors

- Design a framework that is a good fit for enabling the integration implementation.
- Develop a structure of accountability that ensures that those who are carrying out the transition maintain clear accountabilities as they move forward.
- Create a set of integration metrics that allows you to understand how effectively the integration process is operating.
- Maintain continuity of processes and business functions so that your customers experience the integration phase changes as seamless, with no loss in quality of service or significant disruptions.
- Identify key implementation drivers.

Derailing Factors

- Adopting an integration framework without modifying it for the specific requirements of the upcoming integration
- Developing lines of accountability that are either too rigid or too loose to deal with the changing tensions involved in implementing the integration
- Dictating the terms of the integration without involving members of the acquired company as partners
- Concentrating only on financial metrics without giving adequate attention to integration metrics
- Providing insufficient support to be able to carry out the core businesses of the company seamlessly

Questions

- What are the key factors involved in the way you are designing the framework for the integration?
- How are you determining what the lines of accountability are, and how do you plan on adjusting them to take into account the changing conditions and goals as you go through the integration?

- What set of metrics will supply you with the information you need to evaluate the success of the integration? Who will be responsible for those metrics, and how are you planning for the outcomes of those metrics to be shared and used to modify the practices of the integration appropriately?
- How will you plan to ensure that the continuity of core businesses is maintained during the integration phase?
- What are the key implementation drivers to acknowledge in your implementation plan?

Note

The additional material in this chapter comes from the authors' interviews and experiences.

The Integration Team Takes Over: Six Springboards for a Quantum Leap Integration

The first day of your newly combined company is the first day of your integration stage: you've consummated the "deal," and the two independent companies are now under one ownership, so you are facing the challenge of making the promise of the deal become reality. This is when your integration team should take over your integration plan, to implement the integration of the two companies. Your integration planners will have designed a framework and process for integration to jump-start your new company. A major element of the integration plan is determining the key drivers that can open the space of your new company to tackle the array of challenges you face and to seize the opportunities to lead you to quantum leap achievements.

The seeds for breakthrough performance are planted and cultivated as your company goes through each stage of acquisition, and they are framed during integration planning. Your newly emerging company should start with the capabilities it has been developing and then apply all six of these key springboards during integration implementation to transform it into a high-performance, quantum leap company:

1. Customer strategy and branding
2. Company strategy
3. Integrating culture and leadership principles
4. Integrating knowledge insights and business principles
5. People strategy
6. Information technology and systems

Using these springboards effectively provides the thrust to move the integration forward much more rapidly and effectively. Springboards enable you to work through and attack potentially paralyzing issues and areas, while at the same time energizing the people and the emerging structure of your new company.

Planning and then taking action to become a high-performance company strongly contrasts with what most often happens after acquisitions. Instead of moving to a higher level of value creation, too many newly integrated companies end up performing at the lowest common denominator of the two previous companies. In most of these cases, the primary gain is in sheer bulk, in terms of more customers, more distribution channels, more products, and more overall revenue. However, bulking up does not necessarily go hand in hand with achieving high performance. Enhanced bulk may help a company gain a higher market share, but it is another thing to transform a company from one that is simply *bigger* to one that *performs better*. Instead, a frequent outcome is that the increased bulk results in a clumsy, plodding company with a slower response time than it had before it acquired the new company. Let's look at how each springboard can help your company reach a higher level of performance.

Capabilities + Springboards =
Quantum Leap Performance Outcomes

Springboard 1: Identifying the *Customer Strategy* for Your Newly Combined Company

Your new customer strategy should outline how your company will provide value to different segments of your customer base. It should identify the brand experience and the levels of customer relationships that your company is seeking to attain. A good customer strategy examines the new customer franchise that has been brought about by the acquisition and finds new ways of leveraging this franchise as a whole. The key requirement here is for your company to reexamine your previous assumptions as to how to segment and approach your customer franchise. Therefore, when formulating your new customer strategy, consider the essential questions listed in Exhibit 7-1.

An effective customer strategy is geared toward making sure that your new company is focused on your most profitable customers and reinforces the relationships with these customers. Your customer strategy seeks to retain those customers, but also aims to grow a customer base that values your company's updated suite of products and/or services.

Your emerging company should work to define the footprint you seek to occupy in your new market space, given your newly combined capabilities and configuration. This market space is likely to be different from that before the acquisition because your new company will have new products and/or services and possibly new distribution channels to reach customers whom you could not reach previously. In other words, you need to define your market space in terms of

- Who your customers are
- How you segment those customers
- How that corresponds to your company's brand

Branding is central to the development of customer strategy. Companies build strong relationships with customers by leveraging their brand in a consistent manner across all their customer touch points. The brand promise comes from connecting your company's values to the cus-

Exhibit 7-1
_____

Questions to Ask when Formulating Customer Strategy for Your Newly Combined Company

☐ What is the new customer franchise of our newly combined company? How is it different from the customer franchise we had before we acquired this new company? What new opportunities does this present for us?

☐ Is there any merit in keeping the two franchises of our new company separate? If not, how will we segment our new customer franchise?

☐ Given the configuration of our new customer franchise, how can we accelerate its growth with the acquisition of new customers?

☐ What new approach, if any, do we need in order to deal with different customer segments?

☐ How will we structure the portfolio of brands involved in our new company? Are the existing brands best kept separate? Is there any advantage in double branding?

☐ How can we ensure that the combined capabilities of our new company are brought to bear to meet the needs of our customer segments?

☐ What are the most profitable segments of our new combined franchise? Is there any justification for dropping the less-profitable segments?

tomer needs that your company can meet most effectively. The brand promise defines the targeted customer experience. Although it is aspirational in nature, the brand is a manifestation of your company and your products and/or services.

You and other managers in your newly combined company face the challenge of determining how best to leverage the brands of the two legacy companies that have now become one. To meet that challenge,

Case Examples: How Hewlett-Packard, Best Buy, NationsBank, and Norwest Corporation Handled Brand Management

When HP acquired Compaq, it had to determine whether it would keep the Compaq brand. It chose to keep the Compaq brand as a separate identity and market it to different segments of its new customer base.

> *The company has maintained both of its consumer brands by differentiating the lines by giving them different designs and offering different features and price ranges for each. HP Pavilion PCs aim for the high end of the market, competing with companies such as Apple Computer and Sony. Compaq Presarios are designed to compete on price with models from companies like eMachines and Dell Computer. By maintaining both brands, HP enjoys a huge retail presence, regularly claiming the No. 1 PC seller slot, according to research firm NPD Techworld.*[1]

When the retailer Best Buy acquired the Future Shop chain in the Canadian market, it decided to maintain the two brands separately because this gave it access to two different consumer groups, and the dual strategy provided the opportunity for greater potential growth in the Canadian market. Best Buy did extensive research on the different needs of the targeted populations of each brand to find out how each brand could serve its customers best. It also worked to understand what kind of organizational structure and strategy were necessary so that the brands would not be on a collision course. It then developed brand themes that gave each brand a sizable share of the market but also differentiated the brands based on their most distinctive strengths and cultures.

Best Buy went further to see where efficiencies could be realized by acting in common (e.g., through selecting a short list of shared vendors) and where the two brands would be best off working independently. Working the dual brand strategy has not, as some feared, resulted in cannibalization of a shared market, but rather led to a double-digit increases in sales for both brands in 2006 and 2007.[2]

On the other hand, both NationsBank and Norwest Corporation made a strategic choice to adopt the corporate name and identity of their smaller-sized acquisitions, based on the belief that these alternative brands had more powerful national brand recognition than their own. When NationsBank acquired Bank of America, it adopted the Bank of America brand to drop the vestiges of its regional banking past and be more readily perceived as a national banking force. Similarly, when Norwest acquired Wells Fargo and Co., the new company chose to keep the name Wells Fargo to capitalize on the long history of the nationally recognized Wells Fargo name and its trademark stagecoach slogan.

your company needs to rethink its strategy and determine what a new strategy for its brand(s) should be. An integration that does not aspire to a quantum leap will simply erase the brand(s) of the acquired company without an adequate strategic review, in which case your company will simply continue on the course that you had charted prior to acquiring the new company. Brand choices are often unwarrantedly influenced by the ego of the acquiring company. A poor choice does not leverage the opportunity and power of the brands of the company you're acquiring.

A quantum leap integration company asks, "How do we make use of the brands based on our customer strategy?" The new company needs to decide which brands it wants to continue to support. It is more costly to have multiple brands. However, it might be that as part of its customer strategy, the new company finds it useful to have a second brand for some things where that brand is better known or more appealing, or if it gives the company the ability to have a two-tier customer strategy. It could then use the two brands in ways that are more specialized and targeted. Whatever you decide to do with your brands, don't simply let your decision take place by default—in other words, don't let a brand just die off through neglect. If you don't want to continue a brand, that's fine, but you should make that decision with clarity of purpose.

Your customer strategy and brand decisions will determine what new products and/or services your newly combined company will offer. Once you decide who your customers are, you have to determine how to bring together these new products or services and how to gain the most synergy in terms of these products or services. You need to decide which of your products or services are most attractive to your customer segments. You also need to explore whether your company has the capabilities to reshape your products or services in order to obtain a distinctive advantage in your marketplace.

You also need to decide what distribution channel options you will use for any new products or services. You need to review the structure of your combined distribution channels and determine what your new distribution approach will be. The challenge is to look at the two original distribution approaches and strategies and sort out how to optimize them not only in terms of costs, but also in terms of their effectiveness in reaching targeted customer segments.

> **Case Example: How Best Buy Handled Distribution after Acquiring Future Shop**
>
> When Best Buy acquired the Future Shop chain, the two companies had distinctly different approaches to operating their distribution channels. Best Buy stores in Canada were set up to operate on a noncommission sales basis, whereas Future Shop salespeople had operated on commissions. Best Buy decided to keep the Future Shop name and brand because it was a commission-based sales store, and Best Buy did not want to be identified as a commissioned store. It saw that having two different distribution channels gave it two approaches to the marketplace. Moreover, Best Buy has retained the option of opening its Future Shop franchise in other parts of the world where it feels that a commissioned sales force would be a better cultural fit.

Deciding what kind of relationship to have with suppliers is another element to consider when building for a quantum leap performance. As a newly combined company, you should review your supplier base and use your greater size and new configuration to leverage more advantageous terms with your suppliers. Also, not only can your enhanced supplier base lead to a better pricing structure for your customers, but a more actively worked relationship with your network of suppliers can also better leverage any unique capabilities of your suppliers, as well as those suppliers' ideas and insights on market changes. As a newly combined company, you can realign your combined suppliers network to help you bring your customers targeted solutions that were not previously available to them, and you can deliver those solutions more innovatively, rapidly, and cost-competitively than you could before your acquisition.

Springboard 2: Setting the *Company Strategy* for Your Newly Combined Company

The purpose of your company strategy is to make sure that the organizational structure and processes you have put in place can best realize your overall business and customer strategy goals. Specifically, your company strategy ensures that five components of organizational capability are aligned to realize your customer and business strategies:

1. Leadership
2. Strategy making
3. Structure
4. Systems and processes
5. Culture

Organizing Company Functions into a Front Court, Middle Court, and Back Court

A powerful way to look at your company and configure it for integration is to see it through the lens of a front-court/middle-court/back-court model.[3] This framework provides a generic, neutral structure that offers a way to look at any existing company beyond the confusing array of organizational structures. This approach gives your newly combined company a way of deconstructing the functions of the preacquisition companies (which are now being integrated) and then reconstructing their different functions into a new, integrated structure. An advantage of using this framework is that it allows you to consider each function in light of the value it creates for your customers. It is a template for understanding and reconfiguring the structures of any two companies without prescribing, "This is where you have marketing, and so on."

You can then adjust the relationships among all these components as you sense that your customer requirements are changing and as you create new responses to those new requirements:

- The front court is the primary area where your sales force, distribution channel management, and customer touch points are located.
- The middle court is where your company develops and manages solutions based on information you receive from the front court and directly from customers. The middle court is then able to feed necessary information to the back court, where your company's products and/or services are produced.
- The back court can also have customer touch points as part of its customer service activities. These touch points with customers help keep your production elements sensitized to your customers' requirements.

Your company has to determine in what "buckets" the different components of your company strategy fall, and what those components are. Each company needs to define its front-, middle-, and back-court functions to suit its own needs. These definitions will help shape your company's structure, its processes, and the products and/or services that will forge the architecture of your newly combined company. Exhibit 7-2 shows how you might sort out the fundamental functions of your company for review and planning, and Exhibit 7-3 lays out generically what takes place in the different arenas.

The Front Court

The front court concerns itself with anything that pertains directly to interacting with your customers. The front court systematizes these functions so that your company can "do business the way the customer wants to do business."[4] The front court outlines how your company reaches different customer segments through specific distribution channels.

You can optimize your relationships with different customers in different ways. The leadership challenge is to link the different customer segments to the products or services that will best meet their needs. This ensures that customers are able to interact with your new company in the manner that will create the most value for them. A large part of this challenge is for your company to rethink each set of customer segments, sales forces, and geographical coordination systematically so that your company can link your channels and products effectively.

The front court ensures that the company builds the required capability to bring solutions to its customers. This includes:

- Prioritizing markets, identifying what solutions will go where, and determining what blend of distribution channels can best realize targets
- Optimizing the sales channel mix (telesales, direct sales, partners) as part of the "go-to-market" strategy
- Ensuring that optimized solutions are offered to customers in the context of their business needs

Customers can seek an array of relationships. Some may want to buy from the entire line of products, but also want a single contact point or

Exhibit 7-2

Customer Line-of-Sight View of Your Company

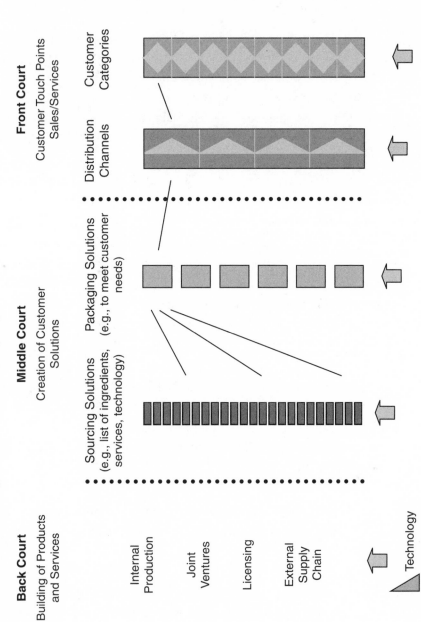

Back Court

Building of Products and Services

Middle Court

Creation of Customer Solutions

Front Court

Customer Touch Points
Sales/Services

Sourcing Solutions
(e.g., list of ingredients, services, technology)

Packaging Solutions
(e.g., to meet customer needs)

Distribution
Channels

Customer
Categories

Internal
Production

Joint
Ventures

Licensing

External
Supply
Chain

Technology

174

sourcing relationship for all products or services. Others want solutions, not components. Then there are those customers who want products and services that are customized to meet their specific needs. For instance, some customers require a highly knowledge-based interaction with their suppliers. Others may not. Your newly combined company has to have the flexibility to engage with customers in the way or ways that work best for them. Therefore, you need to reconsider—and, where necessary, reformulate—your front-end capabilities to offer the distribution channels that best correspond to the way your customers want to interact with you.

The Back Court

The back court is your production function—i.e., where your company "manufactures" products and/or services. For example,

- In financial services, the back court produces insurance policies, actuarial work, or loans.
- In an automobile manufacturing company, the back court makes vehicles, makes after-market items, and provides related financial services.
- In a home and personal products company, the back court manufactures all the items for house and personal cleaning.

The Middle Court

The middle court determines what products/services the back court should produce based on customer needs and also aligns and packages them for specific distribution channels and customer segments. The middle court has to not only resolve how to best satisfy your customers but also work through many contentious internal issues—for example, the middle court needs to do all of the following:

- Translate the company's understanding of customer needs into solutions.
- Define the range of solutions that the company will offer.
- Define and orchestrate the "go-to-market" process, taking solutions from design to development to customer delivery.

Exhibit 7-3

Where Organizational Activities Take Place in the Front, Middle, and Back Courts

Back Court	Middle Court	Front Court
The production function	The set of offerings and how the new company organizes them	Anything that has to do with directly interacting with the customer
Where the offerings of goods and services are produced or sourced	Often understood to be marketing	Everything that interfaces with the customer, systematizing so that the company is able to do business the way the customer wants to do business.
Where the supply chain is located	It has to determine where marketing takes place and who will take on which roles and responsibilities, and establish links between the front and back courts, understanding that "orders are entered in the front and filled in the back and that products are developed in the back and sold by the front."*	Deals with different customer segments and channels that reach different customer segments
	Where research and development takes place	Customers seek different arrays of relationships
		Design the company so that it can serve its customers the way they seek

*Galbraith, *Designing Organizations*, p. 120

- Determine what solutions at what price would represent a superior value proposition.
- Determine how solutions are shaped to fit the particular characteristics of a given distribution channel.
- Determine what components (produced either internally or externally) to use in the shaping of solutions.

Using the Three-Court Framework

You can use this three-court framework to map out the functions of your company and how they meet the needs of different customers, which will provide insights into how you can best structure your newly integrated company. The most effective organization, obviously, is the one that is most conducive to meeting the needs of customers. This framework provides a neutral, more transparent, and less controversial way to define your new structure. Most important, it provides everyone in the organization with a line of sight to the customer.

Because companies that are involved with major acquisitions are typically large firms with offices and customers around the world, these companies also face the challenge of providing an equally high level of performance across an array of both large and small customer segments around the world. Based on these requirements, the strategy for the new company is likely to engage a network of other companies that work in concert with it to respond to customer needs. The front-court/middle-court/back-court model can adjust to all of these changes by establishing a network of partnering relationships that jointly enable it to make solutions available to customers as they want and need them.

The integration team can hold an organizational design workshop to develop a picture of how the front-court/middle-court/back-court model would work in the new company. The integration team reviews the business strategy and from it defines the specific operations that need to take place in each sector. The strategy here is to use the model to frame a future organization toward which the company will evolve. The design team's goal is to set a structure and processes "that fix today's organizational problems and move the company toward tomorrow's desired patterns."[5]

Springboard 3: Establishing the *Culture and Leadership* for Your Newly Combined Company

To integrate the culture of your newly combined company, you need to align the values that underpinned the cultures of the two companies before they combined. To do this most effectively, you need to first understand the values prevalent in the two companies and then draw from them to define a *common* set of values. These reconciled values define the new cultural principles and leadership expectations, in line with the vision of your new company.

When your two companies are integrating, people from both companies will naturally identify with their respective cultures, and this will continue into the postintegration stage. Although you can begin the initial culture work during the integration stage, culture alignment requires significant amounts of time that are not available at that juncture. The integration stage unfolds within a tightly managed time frame so that your company can keep its continuity as far as meeting the needs of its customers is concerned and reach its desired levels of performance as soon as possible. However, you can't completely ignore cultural alignment during this stage, because doing so can impede the emergence of a healthy new culture. To avoid this, here's what you *can* do during the integration phase:

- Recognize and validate differences in cultures and values between the two legacy companies so that communications and interactions are effective in both cultures.
- Maintain an active communications strategy that confirms that you respect the values of both companies.
- Assure employees that a culture realignment process will be a major part of the postintegration phase.

Doing this can avoid actions that contradict cultural norms and impair the speed and process of integrating the new company. Also, respecting the two cultures involved will engender trust and will provide a foundation for the partnering required to build your new company.

Culture is often mentioned as a factor in the success of an integration. The variety of approaches by Dow, Clarica, and Best Buy show how

Case Example: How Clarica Melded Two Companies' Sets of Values

When Clarica acquired the Canadian operations of MetLife, a values survey was carried out with the employees of both companies, and the values identified were combined into one integrated values map. The values of the two companies showed significant differences. Whereas Clarica placed more emphasis on getting work done through *relationships*, MetLife saw it as most important to work through a well-defined set of *processes*. In companies that emphasize process, the steps that get things done are clearly defined and made known to everyone. In contrast, in a relationship-based organization, it is not what but whom you know that counts the most. You need to know only whom to contact to get things done. It is through relationships that you make things happen. The combined set of values reflected what could have been either the basis for a continuous clash or the makings of a complementary orientation of these two cultures. Upon review of the results of the survey, the leadership of the combined company defined the process and relationship orientations and put a great deal of effort into melding them into the definition of the new culture principles.

Clarica's senior-level managers took a leading role in shaping all aspects of integrating the values of both companies. Clarica's managers acknowledged that both companies' values were significant and important to a successful integration, and they communicated that consistently during the integration and afterward. The result was that all employees felt recognized and assured that although they might not agree with everything that Clarica decided or did, they would still be treated fairly. This was confirmed in subsequent employee surveys that showed that the level of trust reported by the employees of the acquired company was the same as that reported by the employees from the acquiring company. This values exercise allowed everyone to understand the difference in cultures through the different priorities given to different values in each of the cultures. The values of the two cultures were then integrated to form one culture. The key is to demonstrate how the values of the acquired company become part of the values of the new combined company. In the case of the integration of MetLife, greater importance was given to more disciplined management through process, instead of relying on relationships to get things done.

culture and values are both challenges and opportunities at the senior leadership level (and all other levels) to take initiatives that highlight both the values of individuals in different organizational contexts and the core values of the two organizations being combined. These efforts are springboards because they enable you to work through contentious issue areas. Not only do they allow your company to resolve those issues, but by

> ### Case Example: How Best Buy and Future Shop Revitalized Their Corporate Culture
>
> When Best Buy acquired Future Shop in Canada, the idea was to have two brands coexisting in Canada. After three years, the managers and employees of the Future Shop brand felt that Best Buy had focused on building the Best Buy brand and hadn't given sufficient attention to continuing to build the Future Shop brand and culture. They felt that their brand and culture were being neglected and were eroding. In the end, this erosion was having a negative impact on the performance of the Future Shop brand.
>
> Senior managers agreed that it was important to Future Shop's ongoing performance to rekindle its culture. Therefore, the company conducted a survey to identify the values that were prevalent at Future Shop. The Future Shop values were to be more aggressive and to go after the customer with zest, placing more emphasis on individual achievement and on competition. These values were then used to redefine and reinterpret the Best Buy core values in terms of the individual values more prevalent in the Future Shop culture. This gave the Future Shop people a sense that their values were being recognized and fully taken into account. It allowed the Future Shop culture to express itself more fully and more genuinely, without the feeling that it had to subjugate itself to the culture of Best Buy as the owner. It gave the Future Shop people a renewed confidence in themselves. This reenergized everyone in the organization and led them to breakthrough levels of performance in the subsequent years.

seeing them as springboards, your new company can also resolve those dilemmas at a higher level, bringing positive energy and experiences to the entire integration process.

Springboard 4: Aligning the *Business Logic* in Your Newly Combined Company

As part of the integration process, it is important that you combine and reshape the best knowledge and best insights of both the acquiring and the acquired companies to form an integrated set of business principles. This is essential for alignment and effective functioning as the two companies

Case Example: How Dow Chemical Lives and Communicates Its Value

Dow has defined its values and communicates them with discipline. Dow leaders talk about those values with the employees of every new company it acquires, spending a lot of time not only communicating these values, but living them as well. As Dow's Randy Croyle put it:

> *If I am moving forward on an integration and I have a Dow leader who is not living those values, I will call him onto the carpet. That is one of my roles.*
>
> *The very first presentation we ever give to the employees of the acquired organization is about our values. For most of the employees of the acquired company, the general feeling is that they want to become part of Dow. I don't think we have had any acquisition that has been viewed as a hostile acquisition by the employees.*

Croyle further said that these values determine how the organization works at Dow:

> *We make sure that people [understand] what our culture is. Dow delayered the organization from twelve to about six layers. One of the reasons for removing the band of layers is [for better] communications. . . . We removed one of those management layers by using our IT, basically our personal computers. . . . Everyone has the same computer worldwide at Dow. We have one network. We have used that as our communications. If there is something that has to be communicated to the organization, we post it on our Dow newsline intranet.*
>
> *During the early days of the Union Carbide integration, as we were explaining how we communicate to our employees, one of the Union Carbide executive leaders said, "I've got a problem with this. Are you telling me that it is entirely possible that either I or my leaders may find out about something after one of our operators on the shop floor has found about it?" Our answer is, "Yes, that is correct. If that operator comes in at 6 a.m. and the newsline is posted at 7 a.m. and you don't come in until 8 a.m., that operator is going to get that information before you do." The Carbide leader said, "I've got a problem with that. Our folks should never have information that I don't know." Our response was, "Well, Joe, you better get used to it. That is the way it is." By the way, that individual did not make the cut.*

become one emerging company. Here again, it is important that you—the acquiring company—acknowledge that your own business logic and principles are not the only ones that apply to your new company.

Every company has a certain sense of the logic of its business. Each has specific insights into the way it approaches the business, the way it configures its strategies, and the way it thinks about how the company needs to operate now and into the future. All managers who are leading the integration process need to be sensitive to the differences in this thinking and actively explore those differences.

For example, consider Newell's 1999 acquisition of Rubbermaid: although both companies' businesses produced household, consumer, and commercial products, the two companies had fundamentally different business logic. The differences could not be swept under the rug here because this $5.8 billion acquisition was 10 times as large as the biggest acquisition Newell had made before. It nearly doubled the size of the company and significantly increased the combined company's portfolio of brands.

> *Rubbermaid competed on the basis of brand strength, whereas Newell competed on the basis of low-cost production. The production processes and costs were different; their value propositions were different. They were actually in very different businesses, and Rubbermaid's strategy wasn't simply going to work in the markets Newell relied upon. . . . Newell attempted to "Newellize" Rubbermaid, and in doing so squeezed out what little talent was left in the upper levels of the acquired company. . . . Newell predicted $300 million in cost savings and $50 million in increased revenues during the two years after the Rubbermaid merger."*[6]

The actual outcome was that when 2001 arrived, Rubbermaid did not contribute any positive revenues to Newell. The cost savings attributed to the acquisition were significantly less than the projected $300 million, and most of those savings were eaten up by increases in the raw materials needed for production. Newell had bought a company that it thought it could align, but it found out that the business logics differed so significantly that there would not be a profitable match-up. Newell shareholders lost 50 percent of their value in the two years following the closing. In 2002, Newell wrote off $500 million in goodwill.

Following the continued financial fallout from the merger, new leadership was appointed in 2006, and the company embraced a consumer-centric focus. The company began focusing on three strategic transformations: building consumer-meaningful brands, restructuring the supply base, and leveraging "One Newell Rubbermaid." It took a complete change in leadership at Newell, a reshaping of its strategy and brand, coupled with extensive organizational restructuring to overcome the differences in business logic and make the new company work.

Reconfiguring the Dominant Business Logic

Reexamining and reconfiguring the business logic of the two companies is central to the ability to take the quantum leap. You need to determine what the best logic is for you to adopt, given what you want to do in your new company.

There are two issues in a dominant business logic:

1. One challenge is that although your dominant logic is actively shaping decisions and behaviors, it is not always articulated, or articulated well.

2. The second problem is that your company can become captive to your own dominant logic to such a degree that you're not even aware of it or you may feel unable to change it. For example, your company may base the way it operates on the idea that only one brand can best serve the company, whereas the reality might be that dual or multiple brands could address a variety of customer segments more effectively. This may be especially important in an acquisition setting where the option of deciding which company brands or product lines to keep has to be dealt with. A company that is captive to its own logic can make decisions that seriously limit its options and not even be aware of the inherent costs involved.

To produce a quantum leap, you need to get a firm grasp of the dominant logic of both companies. You then need to examine what you understand your new company to be about and how you can recast those dominant logics in light of your new circumstances.

During the targeting and due diligence stages, you have the responsibility of making sure that you understand the business logic of your target company. Simultaneously, you have to determine how you want to position your company over time so that you do not acquire the target business and arbitrarily impose your own business logic on it, which can often result in a suboptimal outcome. This is an important test of the fit between the acquiring company and the target company. If that fit is appreciated satisfactorily during the acquisition, due diligence, and integration planning phases, then it can be part of creating the springboard effect during the integration stage.

The issue of conflicting business logic can be a deal breaker. Therefore, the sooner you realize that there is a distinct ill fit between your company and your target, the better. For example, a global professional firm was exploring a possible merger when it discovered that risk management was not an important part of its counterpart's thinking, although it was a major consideration for the other firm.. This difference was too significant for the company to tolerate, and it withdrew from further merger discussions. If the due diligence process had not revealed this difference in the business logic of the two companies, it could have led to substantive conflict and irresolvable disagreements in the combined company. The difference between this example and that of Newell with its Rubbermaid acquisition is that in the case of the global professional business firm, it was decided that the difference in business logic was insurmountable. There are two elements to the decision to proceed despite a gap in business logic. The first element is the nature, extent, and strategic importance of the difference. The second element is whether it is possible to change the business logic of the acquired organization.

Although business logic is *embedded* in a company's culture, it is not the same as culture. The business logic is made up of the assumptions that companies believe will make them successful. It is the sum of what they have learned through experience in the business. It is what your company knows about your business and how you bring that understanding into play to make your business work.

If you integrate knowledge insights and business principles effectively during the integration planning and integration stages of your acquisition, that will reduce the drag effect on your newly combined company as it emerges. At the same time, the cohesion of the business logic and the integration of knowledge insights proves to be a powerful springboard force in moving your company forward along the quantum leap trajectory.

Case Example: How a Manufacturing Company Reconciled Two Approaches to Production

The prevalent business logic at an international maker of water pumps for commercial applications was that each of its products is *mass customized*, based on a computerized configuration. (In mass customization, a company develops a core set of products or services and then allows customers to determine a specific set of features that meets their particular needs. Computerized production allows a producer to incorporate these features to produce the precise product offering that best serves the customer's needs in a way that is highly efficient and at a price similar to that of mass-produced products. In mass customization, each product is a sample of one, whereas in mass production, each product is a replica of one standard design.) The computerized configuration was essential so that any component supplier could readily connect into it from anywhere, at any time, to provide the required parts.

When this company acquired a company that was geared to produce a line of *mass-produced* pumps, it had to reconcile its business logic with that of the company it had just acquired. The acquiring company went through a rigorous examination of the different business logic involved in mass production and mass customization, and the company finally decided to opt for the mass-customization approach.

Although this may seem like a simple choice, the company first had to realize that it *needed to choose* between the two production approaches. The company had tried to carry out its integration for over a year before it realized that it had to reconcile these two business models. It then had to redefine all of the following:

- The products that the newly combined company now made
- Its customer relationships
- Its production processes
- Its brand management
- Its distribution processes

These were not small matters, and it would have been better to have grappled with them *earlier* in the integration process than to rework the practices of the company later on (as this company finally did).

Springboard 5: Defining the *People Strategy* of Your Newly Combined Company

The purpose of the people strategy is to select and retain the best people from the two existing companies for roles in your newly combined company. People play a central role in building a quantum leap performance in an acquisition. (The importance of people should be obvious, but given what actually happens with many M&As, this is not always recognized!)

The people who are brought into the new company through an acquisition may, after all, be the most important source of value after the acquisition. For example, after a series of acquisitions over several years, Tom Jenkins, the chairman of software company Open Text, stated, "More than anything else, what acquisitions gave us were the people that came with these acquisitions."

When you're crafting the strategy for your new company, you need to make sure that your structure, systems and processes, leadership, and culture are all in place so that you can realize your goals in your overarching business plan. Your people strategy then ensures that you have people who are capable of achieving these goals.

Successful integrations are based on understanding who the best people are—in terms of their talent, experience, and potential—from the two companies that are combining. Once you've identified the best people, the challenge is placing them in roles that best correspond to their strengths. In many cases, these people will shape their own emerging jobs.

Recruiting the Best People for Jobs in the Newly Combined Company

The first task of your people strategy is to place people into roles that they will value, a process which has also been called "re-recruitment."[7] Your newly combined company needs to determine whom you will keep and whom you will let go, and how you will handle that. Then you need to harmonize the people policies of both companies into one.

The acquiring company starts by recognizing the people who are potential leaders during due diligence. Although you may obtain information about the people who work for the company you're acquiring (e.g., performance evaluations and other documents), the value of that information is frequently questionable. Our experience has been that the existing documentation of people's performance does not provide a sufficient basis for making recruitment decisions for the new company; in fact, we feel that any written information on people is usually not worth the paper it is written on, and we recommend that the acquiring company start with a clean slate and do its own evaluations.

For larger-scale acquisitions (which are the focus of this book), the approach we advocate when forming a people strategy is that the manager of a function or business unit in the new company should have the main accountability for selecting the members of his or her team. This process is orchestrated so as to ensure that the best people from both companies are selected. In order to have accountability in the structure, each manager has to be the ultimate decision maker, but that manager must also consult horizontally across the two companies as part of the people strategy planning process. This is a tiered decision-making process that will have as many tiers as required, cascading from the top down, through all levels of management.

For example, once you've appointed managers for all functions or business units, you want to make sure that those managers don't limit themselves to the networks they know from the specific company from which they came; in other words, they should consider candidates from *both* the acquired and the acquiring company to get the best person for each job. To ensure that all candidates from both companies are fully considered in the selection process, you should ensure that the management team from one level *above* each role reviews the appointments to those positions. You should build a slate of candidates from pools of qualified individuals from both companies, and you should build these by consulting with managers from both companies. The hiring manager has responsibility for the role being filled, but he or she needs to take into account the discussions that have taken place in that tier horizontally.

You need to maintain a balance between proceeding rapidly to fill all roles and taking time to consult with all appropriate managers and staff members to make sure that you are selecting the best people to fill roles in your newly combined company. Exhibit 7-4 shows how managers typically select their direct reports; in contrast, Exhibit 7-5 shows how a manager

Exhibit 7-4

Typical Staff Selection Process

who is also consulting with peers across company lines ensures that the selection is systematic and comprehensive from both legacy companies.

This type of people strategy selection approach takes time. However, you need to make this investment of time if you want your newly combined company to be a quantum leap company. When it is done well, a well-thought-out and well-executed people strategy is a powerful springboard that will allow your integration to move forward much more effectively and efficiently.

Exhibit 7-5

Staff Selection Process after Acquiring Another Company: Managers Should Consult Their Peers

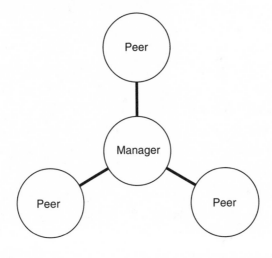

Case Example: How Dow Chemical Developed Its People Strategy

An illustration of the effect of a good people strategy can be seen in the strategy that Dow Chemical arrived at over time. Dow found that it had very limited success when it "parachuted" its own leaders into an acquired company, and even less success when it kept the acquired leaders in place. Therefore, Dow instead brings the leaders from the targeted company into Dow and puts them into different positions in the Dow organization so that they can start learning Dow's culture and systems and the way people work at Dow. This gives them the opportunity to become fully integrated into Dow processes and culture or, alternatively, to find out that Dow is not the best place for them.

Although Dow does place its own people in leadership positions initially, it simultaneously looks at all the top leaders of the acquired company. When Dow acquires a company, the lead people on the Dow integration team sit down with the CEO and the executive management team of the acquired company and ask for their views of the top leaders reporting to them. Members of the Dow integration team then follow up with one-to-one interviews with the leadership, which are mostly "getting to know one another" sessions. Those sessions are followed up with additional one-on-one sessions to get a more fundamental understanding of each individual's capabilities, performance, and related issues.

The role of partnership is very important here. If people in both the acquiring and the acquired companies feel that they are in a partnership seeking a quantum leap outcome, then the opinions they voice about different candidates will be more closely geared to those individuals' true capability. If they do not have a partnership stake, then their allegiance to the people they know may be greater than their sense of accountability to the goals of the new company.

Dow found that every company it acquired had a different culture, and each valued different attributes in its staff. For example, Dow's Randy Croyle commented:

> When we got the performance evaluations for the Union Carbide leaders from their CEO, we went through our one-on-one evaluations, and they did not match up. They had five large manufacturing sites. As they ranked their site leaders, they had one individual who was on the bottom of the list. Yet, through our interview process, etc., we felt that this individual was the best of the lot. When we went through the final selection process, that individual is still with us and is doing an outstanding job, and some of the folks that we did feel were marginal were given a job offer anyway. We have since terminated a lot of those individuals.

> *Each company has its own different persona and [its] own value system. You obviously would like to rely upon the target company's assessment of [its] leadership, but it really boils down to us understanding our values and what we are looking for in a leader, and then going through that type of selection process.*
>
> *Identification of who will be on the leadership team of a particular business or site is a formal process, and something that we spend a lot of time and diligence [doing]. This is because the success or failure of any particular integration is often tied to choosing the right individuals to lead that integration. There have been cases where we have had some doubts on a particular leader, and we said let's give that particular leader a try, and six months later we said, "It's not working. We are going to have to move that person out."*

For Dow, the question of "fit" of staff members into the new company is one that can be determined in a reasonable period of time. Here's how Croyle describes it:

> *They have a choice. They can work for a larger company, but in a different type of role. We don't reduce the compensation, or type of benefits, or anything of that sort. Some people can adapt to that very well, and other people will struggle and within a year have departed. It is either a fit or it is not. People find that out pretty quickly. . . .*
>
> *For those who survive and come with the company, we want them to feel very good, not only that they have come with the company, but that their peers, who perhaps did not get an offer, or who left Dow, also feel good about Dow. We work at making "the survivor thing" a very positive experience for all concerned.*
>
> *The people strategy does not end with the integration. A good integration program will continue to track how leaders from the acquired company progress. The head of the integration team can monitor the performance of these people and keep track of how well they are being retained, who is getting promoted, and who are seeing some new opportunities, etc. These are signs of successful adaptation.*

Forming a Bridge between Companies

Values form a bridge from one company to the other. At Clarica, the values of customer stewardship, learning, knowledge and innovation, and team partnership were very appealing to the employees of a company it acquired and resulted in a 90 percent retention rate for those employees. This was a key accomplishment, because gaining this human capital was a major reason for Clarica's undertaking its acquisition of the reinsurance business of Sun Life. Although a consideration of values may at first seem intangible and idealistic, values are very important to the people involved in acquisitions. Organizational values underpin everything that is going on around them, and they determine if the environment is healthy or toxic. If people are going to fully invest themselves in a new company, they are going to need to know that it is one that works in their interests and one that will meet their needs.

Case Example: British Petroleum's People Strategy

BP has taken a different approach. After acquiring Amoco, BP chose a middle road, deciding to keep the Amoco leadership that was part of Amoco's high-performing units. BP bases its approach on establishing performance contracts with its acquired staff. Its focus is on performance, not heritage. If there was a question of how people from Amoco went about achieving specific levels of performance, BP examined their approach or process. If the process was better than BP's, BP retained it, but not just for that unit. Instead, BP retained that process or approach for the whole of BP.

From a company culture point of view, when Amoco staff members were retained, they saw themselves as "BP staff" after the closing of the acquisition. That singularity of identification was common among all companies examined in our research. Even when there was autonomy of units, there was no question as to who was leading the company and what the company's brand was.

Over time, BP shifted its viewpoint on what makes acquisitions succeed. Organizational leadership played a core role in its people strategy. When BP acquired Amoco, although its integration strategy was still very much focused on hard targets for financial objectives, plant, and equipment, BP became more aware that to achieve its acquisition goals, it needed to pay significantly more attention to its people strategy and related intangibles. Here's how Tony Kuhel, former chief process engineer at BP, described this shift:

> *The targets that people were able to achieve and the capacity to meet those targets was really based on how we could manage the intangibles.*
>
> *There was someone who was driven by the hard targets who had no sensitivity at all to the people targets, even though he was [an] outstanding performer. BP at one point decided that he would be let go. This sent a huge ripple throughout the company. Managing intangible assets, at the highest level, was more important than meeting the hard targets.*

Measures of Effectiveness

A final part of people strategy is measurement. A people strategy measures how that strategy is contributing to the integration and how the company is moving forward toward its strategic goals. These measures evaluate both quantitative and qualitative elements. Surveys, focus groups, and one-to-one discussions provide data on how individuals are adjusting to the integration.

If your company truly implements a people strategy springboard, you can mobilize your employees to reach unprecedented levels of performance. On the other hand, if you neglect the people strategy springboard, you will allow an atmosphere of uncertainty and anxiety to develop. Integration is a difficult time for everyone involved. It is a new set of circumstances, with new leadership heading in new directions. Therefore, the more time and effort you put in formulating a sound people strategy, the greater the opportunity you will have for taking an unstable situation and transforming it into an engine for achieving quantum leap performance gains in your newly combined company.

Case Example: How Clarica Measured the Success of Its People Strategy

Clarica conducted a Web-based survey on values to identify the values of the employees in both the existing and the acquired companies soon after its acquisition of the reinsurance business of Sun Life. The Sun Life employees saw the results of the survey and found how well their own values fit within Clarica's core organizational values. The employees gained a lot of confidence from that exercise, and in a subsequent employee survey showed a higher level of trust toward the company than was found in many parts of Clarica itself. The results of these surveys gave Clarica's leadership a good grasp of how well the integration was unfolding.

Springboard 6: Deciding the *IT Architecture and Systems* for Your Newly Combined Company

The goal in an integration of information technology and supporting systems is to design your new company's information architecture based on what your new company is seeking to achieve. After you establish that, your next step is to determine what systems are best suited to form the technology architecture of your new company.

When the integration begins, the two companies will probably have two different sets of IT systems. Although it is very difficult to make decisions on whether to go with one complex IT system or the other (or some combination of both), there is often a strong conquistador mentality around IT systems—i.e., an overriding attitude that "our company bought your company, and we will use our systems for the new company." Moreover, those running the acquiring company's IT department often say that they are making their decisions "in the interests of speed," but although it is important to move with speed through the integration stage, this arbitrary conquistador attitude can lead to decisions that are less than optimal for your newly combined company.

To make the most advantageous decisions, it is important to identify the key priorities for systems and the criteria for retaining or dropping systems from either of the existing companies. The decisions on these systems are highly interdependent; these systems form an ecology, and therefore they have to function well together, and a decision on one system will affect each of the other related systems. You need to decide what architecture, technologies, and systems are best for your newly combined company, based not on what was best in the past or even what is best in the present, but on the *future* requirements of your new company, while also considering what those requirements will be if you are to achieve quantum leap performance.

That is, your new company needs to redesign your overall architecture and your IT architecture, and then make the following decisions:

- What systems you will shut down
- What systems you will keep
- What systems you will run in parallel for a period of time (and for how long)

Because it takes quite a bit of time to sort out this architecture and decide on appropriate systems, these decisions and their implementations may have a lifespan that goes significantly beyond that of other aspects of your integration.

Also bear in mind that if you don't make these IT decisions, you will find yourself keeping two platforms, one from each company, running over an extended period of time. This is problematic because of what is required to keep these two platforms running; specifically, you will probably need more people (and people with different areas of expertise), and you will probably have other expenditures, all of which will result in your company achieving fewer cost synergies. In other words, you will *increase* your costs instead of reducing them! Choices in IT therefore have a significant effect on how rapidly and successfully your company can carry out your integration business plan.

The task of those involved in the IT selection teams is to operate with both an open mind and extensive rigor to determine the best IT platform to support the forward movement of your new company. IT will be a springboard for integrating the new company when you ensure an attitude that evaluates the qualities of both IT systems fairly, so that your company can make the interim decisions that allow continuity of businesses operations and permit more definitive choices later, when you have a fuller understanding of the promises and limitations of each technology.

The Overall Springboard Effect

Leaders in companies need to understand the six springboard factors described in this chapter singly, but also as a set of interacting forces that the acquiring company needs to bring into play. Any company will have greater strengths on some of these factors, but hardly on all equally, and the significance of these factors may vary considerably from one company to the next. Some companies may find that a customer strategy and brand are central to meeting their strategic goals. Another company may find that at this time, its people strategy or its IT architecture may be the most critical driver for making the leap. Regardless, every company should ensure that each of these six factors is present in the company and in its strategy to develop quantum leap capabilities. Part of the job of the strategy team, the due diligence team, and the integration team is to determine which of these drivers need to be brought into play, to what extent, and how. In essence, the leadership of your emerging company needs to grasp, cultivate, and orchestrate how you bring into play all of these six springboard elements.

Success Factors

- Understand the relationship between organizational capabilities, springboards, and quantum leap performance outcomes.
- Recognize that springboards turbocharge your integration process.
- Rank which springboards are most critical to clearing obstacles and setting the stage for *your* company's integration.
- Systematically understand how the various springboards interact with one another to drive your integration most powerfully.
- Use springboards to forge a path to become a high-performance company.
- Formulate a new customer strategy.
- Use a framework to manage the restructuring of your company, such as the front-court/middle-court/back-court approach.
- Recognize that leadership is the governing force for organizational strategy making, structure, culture, and systems.
- Make sure that you align the key elements of business logic from the acquiring company and the acquired company.
- Use a comprehensive, systematic approach to ensure that you select the best candidates for key positions in your new company.
- Select the elements from each company's information technology systems that will best achieve your current and future strategic goals.

Derailing Factors

- Not using springboards to lay the groundwork for integration
- Being guided by the belief that growth is primarily a product of adding bulk to the company
- Taking a "check the box," procedural approach to integration
- Assuming that past customer strategies do not have to be modified to take the complexities of your new company into account
- Not broadly reviewing how the structure of your company can be revised to best take advantage of the new capabilities of your company
- Believing that you can work through cultural adjustments without active leadership involvement
- Failing to align core differences in the dominant business logic
- Allowing the selection of leadership and staff to be driven by favoritism, with limited exploration to find the most qualified candidates
- Taking the position that the acquirer's technology platform automatically will work best for the new company

Questions

- How are we implementing the six springboards during the integration stage?

    1. How are we implementing a springboard for our customer strategy and brand?

    2. How are we implementing a springboard for our company strategy?

    3. How are we implementing a springboard for the integration of company culture and leadership principles?

    4. How are we implementing a springboard to integrate our knowledge insights and business principles?

    5. How are we implementing a springboard for our people strategy?

    6. How are we implementing a springboard for our information technology and systems decisions?

- Which springboards are the most significant for achieving our strategic goals?
- How do we adjust our customer strategy to take into account the new capabilities that are now available after the acquisition?
  - How do we redefine our portfolio of brands, customer sets, products and/or services, and distribution channels during the integration implementation?
  - What new markets are we now able to penetrate after the acquisition?
  - Does our customer strategy lead to changes in our company structure? If so, what changes are we making, for what goals, and with what effect?
- How are we reorganizing our company structure to support being able to achieve our overall strategic goals?
- What is our process for realigning corporate values and culture in the integration implementation phase?
  - What is the role of leadership in this process?
  - What cultural realignment issues are we facing, and how are we responding to them?
- Are there any significant differences in business logic between the two combining companies?
  - If so, how are we approaching aligning the two business logics?
  - How are we resolving these differences?
  - Are there any remaining business logic issues that we need to reconcile?
- How are we ensuring that we have a people strategy that will select the best people from across both companies for roles in our newly combined company?
  - What is our plan for retaining the people we sought for roles in the new company?
  - How do we make sure that our process for candidate selection is comprehensive and unbiased?

- Do we feel that we need to recruit key leadership and management from outside the company? If so, how do we structure our units so that these people can succeed?
- What evaluation of both companies' technology platforms is being done to determine which (or which elements of each) best supports the strategic goals of our newly combined company?
  - How open is this evaluation process?
  - Is a final selection being made, or is there an interim selection that allows further investigation beyond the integration implementation period?

Notes

1. John C. Spooner, "HP Puts Evo Name Out to Pasture," CNet News.com, March 13, 2003; http://www.news.com/HP-puts-Evo-name-out-to-pasture/2100-1003_3-992518.html?tag=nw.7.
2. TaitSubler Web page; http://www.taitsubler.com/track-record/bestbuy-futureshop.php.
3. Jay R. Galbraith, *Designing Organizations: An Executive Guide to Strategy, Structure and Process*, 2nd ed, (San Francisco: Jossey-Bass, 2001.) We draw from Galbraith's model to provide a simple way to see how an organization actually operates and how proposed changes brought about by a major acquisition can be visualized.
4. Ibid., p. 124.
5. Ibid., p. 174.
6. David Harding and Sam Rovit, *Mastering the Merger: Four Critical Decisions That Make or Break the Deal* (Boston: Harvard Business School Press, 2004), pp. 27–28.
7. Timothy J. Galpin and Mark Herndon, *The Complete Guide to Mergers and Acquisitions: Process Tools to Support M&A Integration at Every Level*, 2nd ed. (San Francisco: Jossey-Bass, 2007), p. 127.

The additional material in this chapter comes from the authors' interviews and experiences.

8

Guiding Your Integration to Success

Activating key springboards prepares the ground for the integration to achieve the new company's strategic goals. The actions of the integration team now need a guidance system to make sure that the integration incorporates key factors and indicators that will keep it on track, on time, appropriately targeted, and yielding the extraordinary gains that will realize the promise of the acquisition.

There are several critical success factors that, when taken together, form a guidance system for the integration—specifically:

- Focus on the primacy of your *customers*.
- Create a strong—but flexible—*business plan*.
- Keep in mind that *speed* is critical to successfully combining two companies.
- *Partner* with the company that you're acquiring.
- Establish clear *accountabilities* for every task involved in the integration.

How well your company attends to these factors will determine whether you achieve a quantum leap in performance and create outstanding value in your newly combined company. The first half of this chapter describes each of these factors in detail; to ensure that you deal with these factors, the second half of the chapter describes four critical actions that your company needs to take:

- Setting time, cost, and performance targets
- Selecting the leaders who will run the new company
- Managing people
- Managing change

Let's begin by looking at the first success factor you need to consider when integrating an acquired company.

Focus on the Primacy of Your Customers

Although many companies say, "The customer is king," that is more often lip service than actual practice. The reality is that as pressures accumulate during the intense work of integration, companies often orient themselves inwardly and focus their energies on internal reorganization. As this happens, customer relationships easily slip into a second tier of importance, and customers frequently experience extended periods of uncertainty about the company and even lack of interest from the new company. Customers may not know who will deal with them, whether they will face significant changes in pricing or products or services, or even if they are going to find themselves without a core supplier.

Therefore, it's critical that you look at your integration from your customers' vantage point. You can do this by actively communicating with them and surveying them to understand their experience, beginning from the time of the closing of the acquisition. For example, many acquirers of a mass-market company (such as a large financial institution) have opted to place ads in major newspapers to assure the customers of the company to be acquired that the quality of the relationship will be not only preserved but enhanced. In addition, these ads typically state that the newly combined company will provide a better array of services and will renew its commitment to serve all of its customers. In some instances, mass-market companies survey their customers to gauge levels of customer satisfaction. During a transition, these surveys will detect issues that need to be addressed during the integration. In the case of a business-to-business relationship, following the closing of the transaction, the acquirer typically makes it a priority to contact each customer at a senior level to emphasize that the relationship will be improved and that greater value will be provided as a result of the acquisition.

Customers need to know that you are making their needs and concerns a priority as you integrate the company you've acquired and that the transition will be as seamless as possible for them. You have to make a special point of doing everything necessary to maintain continuity with your own customers; in addition, you need to reach out to the customers of the company you've just acquired, and you need to determine how you can establish relationships with *potential* customers.

For example, a significant component of the Sun Life–Clarica integration plan, aimed at maintaining healthy customer relationships, was to have a Clarica or Sun Life representative visit each customer during the transition period. The customer representatives were trained in what to communicate to each customer, how to do that, and how to gather feedback from customers on their concerns about the impact of the acquisition. In all of your communications, you need to nurture your ability to inspire confidence that your newly combined company will be better able to serve customers' needs than ever before.

The opposite of this stance is the "scorched-earth" approach, where the pressure to cut costs (i.e., to achieve the expense synergies that too many companies focus on when they acquire another company) leads to both poorer customer service and indiscriminate cost cutting in the acquired company the moment the integration begins. This predatory approach destroys value and the confidence of customers that their requirements and concerns will be taken into account by your newly combined company.

Case Example: How Sprint Nextel Lost Its Customer Focus

Consider this nightmare description of an acquisition gone wrong:

> Since Sprint and Nextel merged three years ago (2005), the deal has turned into something of a fiasco, with the company's stock down 66% since the agreement was struck. Poor service is a central reason. After the merger, unhappy customers defected in droves, and profits evaporated. On Jan. 31 (2008), Sprint Nextel (S) said it would take merger-related charges of as much as $31 billion, wiping out nearly all of the deal's value. In addition, two lawsuits have been filed against the company for allegedly extending customers' service contracts without their consent.[1]

To save the company, Daniel R. Hesse, Sprint Nextel's new CEO, has made restoring customer service a priority. When he came onboard in December 2007, he found that, despite terrible customer ratings, customer service was not even on the agenda. According to Hesse, it is now "the first item discussed at every one of the weekly meetings. . . . [Hesse is] increasing investments in customer care, adding service technicians in retail stores, and reversing many management practices in customer call centers. Hesse is convinced that restoring Sprint's reputation with customers is the key to its future. 'You will see progress,' he says. 'We have the right people in place. We will get it done.'"[2] This late conversion to the "primacy of the customer" is a clear example of why customer focus should be a priority above anything else, including any restructuring.

To understand the "primacy of the customer" perspective, compare these two viewpoints:

1. *From the outside in.* This view starts from your customers' perspective on the effect of *every decision you make* regarding the way your newly combined company will operate. It provides a clear, easy-to-grasp perspective that offers a core set of reference points for planning your integration.

2. *From the inside out.* Here, your customer experience is secondary; your company's dominant attitude is, "If we make it, they will buy it." This "inside-out" view also leads to the acquiring company making statements like, "We acquired you, and we know what is best. Here is what you need to do." This

approach may seem efficient, but in the end, it often results in these problems:

- *Extensive distortion of asset allocation.* Instead of using customer focus to guide the allocation of resources so that you turn out what customers actually want and aspire to have, those resources are directed to resolving internal issues that have little impact on creating value for the customer.
- *Slower and poorer customer service.* Again, the Sprint case is instructive. Sprint made a conscious decision to see its call centers primarily as cost centers and instituted measures that focused on their efficiency "rather than opportunities for strategic advantage. Customer service ended up a secondary priority, say former executives."[3]
- *Lower gains from taking on the acquisition.* As seen in the Sprint Nextel example, all expense synergy gains from the acquisition were lost by allowing poor customer service practices to take root.

Different companies have different ways of cultivating the primacy of the customer attitude, as illustrated in the following case examples.

An outsourcing contract is not, strictly speaking, an acquisition. However, it does involve taking over a component of a client company. It offers an interesting parallel to an acquisition when it comes to the integration of people from the client organization into its own organization. The Siemens case on page 205 offers an excellent example of how to integrate people effectively on that basis.

Making the primacy of the customer a core tenet of a company is a long-term effort. When a company makes this approach part of its way of doing business, carrying that value through during the integration is a logical extension. The increased complexity of an integration makes focusing on the primacy of your customers a far greater challenge. All of the company's networks, including the many elements of how the company connects to its markets, have to be reconsidered, re-created where necessary, and reconnected into a new holistic support system. The acquiring com-

> **Case Example: How Dow Chemical Focused on Its Customers while Integrating a Company It Acquired**
>
> Dow's operating principle is that it wants to at least maintain, if not improve, the level of customer satisfaction and the quality of the relationships that existed before an acquisition as it goes through the transitions involved in the integration implementation phase. That understanding is instilled in everyone in the company. Each employee of Dow starts with the idea that its customers' needs are its priority and that customers will experience their transactions with Dow as seamless, regardless of any changes that may be taking place internally.
>
> Dow carries over this view to the whole range of systems that affect its customers—for example, when its sales task force determines that it will keep a customer's existing sales representative in place so that the customer can continue its existing personal relationship. The same perspective extends to every area in which Dow touches its customers. Dow seeks to know what makes the difference for customers so that it does not eliminate product or service lines that customers might consider important, and it works to keep and expand the ones that customers do value. This viewpoint extends to all aspects of the integration, emphasizing the goal of sustaining the quality of the relationship and retaining the customer.

pany and the acquired company need to work through the extensive turmoil of the organizational change in ways that still maintain customer trust.

If you have not honed your customer relationships skillfully *before* you begin integrating the company you've just acquired, then developing an effective customer relations capability *during* the integration is going to be a particular challenge. Nevertheless, you have to start where you're at. As you begin to shift toward a customer primacy viewpoint, you can enhance the present integration and prepare your company for further acquisition and integration successes.

Create a Strong but Flexible Business Plan

Your company needs to create a business plan for the newly combined company, and it is best to begin planning for this during due diligence and continue it through the integration planning stage. If your company has a clear

Case Example: How Siemens Focused on Its Customers' Needs while Integrating an Outsourcing Contract It Obtained

When Siemens obtained the IT outsourcing contract for the BBC and then proceeded to service the BBC's IT needs, it was aware that the success of the venture depended on its relationship with the BBC as the customer organization. This is a rather common approach for outsourcing of IT, where the company providing the outsourced service has to integrate the people and the technology of the company it contracts to serve. The integration of these people is just as challenging as the integration of any newly acquired company. For example, when Siemens took over the BBC's internal IT group, the BBC was the group's chartered and sole customer. Siemens's task was to make the BBC an even more highly satisfied customer than it had been before the outsourcing contract went into effect, as this would support its 10-year contract to work with the BBC. A part of Siemens Business was charged with transforming BBC IT from an internal services unit of the BBC into a business unit of Siemens that served the BBC. Dirk Ramhorst is the chief knowledge officer and the director of process management of the Business Services division of Siemens, a 36,000-person organization. As Ramhorst put it,

> I am in charge of process management governance in Siemens Business Services. This is one of the 13 divisions that Siemens has. Siemens Business does not offer any product anyone can touch, any real tangible product. In our case, if we took over another business, we are not looking for any product to innovate but what we are looking for is to incorporate the competence of the company. With the BBC, we are looking to build the competence to deal with the whole media industry.

To accomplish this, well before taking over the outsourcing contract, Siemens spent a great deal of time with the BBC Technology Group discussing what its specific needs were. Siemens realigned the new IT organization and provided support so that the customer's needs would be met even more fully than they had been when IT was an internal service. To accomplish this, Siemens took on the challenge of integrating the 1,500 BBC Technology Group people into its knowledge exchange framework so that they could gain the knowledge that Siemens has developed and be able to deliver an enhanced level of capability to the BBC, Siemens's new customer. Ramhorst added,

> We have to be able to utilize the 1,500 people that are in the BBC technologies acquisitions. They have to be brought into the organization so that we can leverage their skills and they can leverage our capabilities. To leverage those 1,500 people is positive, but there is a risk on the other side. To make for a success, we have to provide a very, very strong cultural framework. They have to be willing to acquire the strong value that we bring.

The result was a significantly higher level of performance and customer satisfaction than ever before, even though most of the personnel were the same. Siemens brought in the stronger capabilities of its Innovation and Best Practices Network and instituted informed management practices to create greater value for the customer, that is, more advanced and effective technology solutions at a lower cost.

This integration of the BBC IT unit into Siemens created value not only for the BBC, but for Siemens as well. Success at the BBC has a greater strategic significance because by providing outstanding service to its new customers, Siemens created a strong entry point into a market sector that it sought to penetrate.

strategic intent and if your company's strategic logic is well established, then the people involved at all stages of the acquisition can better focus on the key, fundamental business questions of the acquisition and build a strong, flexible business plan for use during the integration and postintegration periods. The more grounded, well-thought-out, and explicit your business plan is, the more your integration team can use that business plan to map out how to move faster, resolve issues more quickly, and streamline decision making. It is the task of those responsible for the business plan to examine the key issues that can arise in the integration and provide resolutions for those issues as your company launches the integration.

The business plan has value as a guide for the integration as well as having great usefulness as a mental framework for thinking about implementing the integration. In effect, the business plan provides a blueprint and a mental model for the integration. People think as they do. Therefore, as you develop your business plan blueprint, you begin to recognize, anticipate, and work through various issues (e.g., workforce compensation, customer service levels, choosing the best supporting technology, or managing product and service innovation effectively) that may arise during integration, and you will become attuned to the challenges of implementation.

The more issues you can resolve ahead of time while developing your new business plan, the more successful your integration is likely to be, because your integration team will not have to face a sizable backlog of issues that you haven't dealt with or decisions that you haven't yet made! Even so, you should still ensure that the integration team feels free to question and adjust your business plan as the integration proceeds.

The business plan needs to be both strong and flexible because the acquiring company needs to be able to constantly adjust to new conditions and requirements. The moment every business plan is completed, it is obsolete because of the constant change in market conditions. The key to an effective business plan is that it outlines how the organization will deal with issues as it encounters them.

For example, the rapid rise in energy costs seen in 2007–2008 can significantly cut into the chances for the success in meeting the financial goals of one major airline acquisition. But the same conditions can open up new opportunities for other airlines to acquire large but financially distressed carriers. How well the acquiring company's business plan is thought through and how readily the new company can adjust to changing economic realities can determine the degree of success of an acquisition in these volatile business conditions.

The cautionary tale of the Newell Rubbermaid acquisition brings into high relief the need for the acquiring company to ground itself fully in both its own approaches, systems, and processes as well as those of the target company as early in the acquisition process as is possible. Then the acquiring company needs to incorporate all understandings relevant to the acquisition in its business plan. That plan, in turn, has to be open to testing and refining as the acquisition takes place, with the business plan updated and realigned during the integration period as well. The work of providing oversight and regular realignment must be ongoing in a successful acquisition and integration.

Often there is a significant lag between the time when you negotiate the acquisition and the time when the deal is closed and the acquiring company gets to manage the acquired company. During that waiting time, if it is legally allowed, you can start validating your business plans with the leaders and managers of the acquired company, taking a partnership approach to encourage your getting their best inputs. The focus of these conversations is to corroborate that the business plan maps out the strategies, goals, relationships, and principles that are needed to ensure that you can achieve the value proposition of the acquisition.

Keep in Mind that Speed Is Critical when Integrating Two Companies

Speed is frequently a primary issue for companies as they enter an integration. Moving with speed enables all the following benefits:

- It facilitates a seamless transition for customers.
- It promotes framing of your company's new vision.
- It gives momentum to the changes that have to take place.
- It initiates new business strategies.
- It accelerates establishing new brand awareness.

Speed is critical to the success of the integration, but don't just seek speed for speed's sake; you need to do things well while doing them quickly. The best way for an acquiring company to achieve a value-creating type of speed in an integration is by starting with a good business plan, sorting out as many of the issues as possible before the close date, and establishing the principles that will guide decision making and the integration so that your company does not have to go back to basics at every turn. Instead, your business plan ensures that you know what the principles are and the criteria for the decisions you need to make when you are integrating the newly acquired company.

In contrast, if your company takes the attitude of "speed for speed's sake," you risk creating a conquistador type of process, described in Chapter 1 and characterized by a view that says, "We are just going to put in our systems, our people, and our processes, regardless of the quality of the company being integrated, because this will be faster, and we know what to do. We make the decisions, and we don't need to spend the time to understand another company's systems or processes. We can just go in and pave the place over with the way we do things in order to be faster." This distorted approach to speed may yield short-term gains, but it will undermine your ability to create long-term value and quantum leap growth.

The ability to make speed a key element of an integration should be one of the acquiring company's capabilities, but it is one that only a minority of companies have mastered. A 2006 survey by M&A researchers Timothy Galpin and Mark Herndon revealed that "only 33 percent of respondents indicated that their company's integration efforts are typically completed within the first 6 to 12 months after the transaction close; 67 percent of survey respondents indicated that their company has taken from 1 to more than 5 years to fully integrate acquired companies' people, processes and systems."[4] Moving forward rapidly, but not recklessly, gives the new company a chance to implement cost and growth synergies that could save millions of dollars in costs and to invest those savings in creating new value for the company. Extending an integration excessively does the opposite, creating a costly drag effect on the new company, draining energies, and misdirecting resources into efforts that no longer align and often conflict with achieving the strategic goals of the new company.

Case Example: How Clarica Integrated Companies with Speed

Speed was an important element of Clarica's philosophy for acquisitions and integration. To achieve speed in its implementations, Clarica used its predeal time to do extensive preparation as part of its integration planning so that when it got to the point of the actual implementation, it had carried out all of the required discussions. The leadership team had done as much of the decision making as it could possibly do, with the result that when Day One of the implementation came, everything moved forward very rapidly. For instance, 12 weeks after closing, not only was the new structure fully configured, but employees had been selected for the 3,000 positions. At this point in time, each employee affected received a letter stating whether he or she had been hired permanently, would be asked to remain on a temporary basis, or would be released within a certain period of time. This did not leave people in a condition of uncertainty.

Discussions took place with all the employees to let them know what their employment situation would be in a very clear and straightforward manner. As a result, Clarica was seen as an employer that lived up to its commitments.

One reason for focusing on speed is that it cuts down on uncertainty. While it is making decisions with speed, however, the acquiring company needs to make sure that these decisions are well considered. There are a number of instances of acquirers that have let employees go, only to realize later that they needed to rehire them. There are ways to mitigate the risks of decisions. One of these ways it to retain staff on a temporary basis for a period of time; this gives the company an opportunity to bring them back on a full-time basis if the need arises. In case of doubt, err on the side of speed.

If there are a significant number of issues that remain unresolved, stakeholders both inside and outside the company lose confidence in the transition process. An acquiring company wants to cut down on the uncertainty created by the transition by moving decisively through the various steps of the integration process.

Case Example: How Speed Was BP's Number One Concern in Its Amoco Integration

Tony Kuhel describes what BP did:

Speed was the primary driver. As long as it strategically made sense, the focus was on getting this thing going, on getting up to speed, getting the new organization going so that we could get back to work. Our philosophy was, "Get it into action. If it is not perfect, we will make it perfect, quickly." We are better off getting into action/learning than talking about it.

Yet, we had a bipolar focus point. The merger and acquisition was driven by speed, but then the organization itself had a huge focus, with its overall number one priority being its long-term performance. The business performance targets and that sort of thing were very much short term. We had an integration target, but the other part of it was ensuring that the integration would be successful over the long term as well. We had to pay attention to achieving both short and long term goals.

In BP's view, the primacy of the customer and having a strong, flexible business plan were already built into its acquisition and integration approach. It saw them as givens "in the fabric of the organization."

Kuhel raises an important caveat:

Our integration was very quick. Our target was 6 to 9 months—which we met. One of the issues throughout the integration concerned knowledge assets. There was a question of whether the 32-person integration team that oversaw the implementation should continue to be kept in place for up to a year later. One of the problems is that we could be so quick at completing the integration that there were some questions people needed to ask a year to a year and a half later and there was no team to go to.

Case Example: How Dow Chemical Views Speed during Integration

Dow Chemical's Randy Croyle is equally adamant on the role of speed in its integration practices:

Speed is one of the key elements for us. The targeted company's employee base is going to be paralyzed until they know what their status is. In most of our smaller acquisitions, every employee will know their status in the first 90 days. For the Union Carbide acquisition, which involved 12,000 employees, all 12,000 employees knew their status within the first 180 days.

The way we have speed is to have a really robust implementation plan. Also speed is a way of synergy capture. We have got to get costs out of the system as quickly as we can. One, we have a robust plan. We have got individual projects, possibly 1,000 projects, identified for the implementation plan. We have milestones for those projects. We have accountable persons identified for those projects. We have monitoring programs and metrics around each of these projects, etc. We drive the implementation so that we can move as quickly as we can. The example I use is that you cannot move too fast. You will make the same number of mistakes going slow as going fast, so you might as well go fast.

One of the strongest arguments for speed is that any integration is a costly undertaking. It calls for an investment of funds and management time, and allocating those resources to the integration takes away from other important work at the company, such as innovation or other opportunities for organic growth. The integration also has potential costs if it becomes a major disruption for customers, suppliers, and all other stakeholders. From another perspective, when you divert attention and resources to the integration, that can make your company's markets a target for your competitors, who can seek to take advantage of any gaps in the levels of your company's performance or your ability to respond to your customers. Therefore, when you work through the integration expeditiously, you put your company in a much better competitive position. Finally, the ability to move quickly generates other valuable payoffs that appeal to everyone involved, both inside and outside of the company: you can get people to their new jobs, begin a new culture, generate an updated array of products and services, and operate at higher levels of efficiency and quality. This augmented capacity for change serves as fuel for a company's quantum leap performance and for creating value in your new company.

Partner with the Company You're Acquiring

Your business plan will be strengthened by the development of trust between the two management structures. Trust building can start during due diligence, it should be incorporated during the integration planning stage, and it bears its greatest fruit during integration implementation. Partnering can be embedded within the business plan in the course of discussions with both management teams. Partnering requires the capacity for self-initiation, trust, and interdependence. Partnering can take place only between people who are not interacting in a dependent mode. Partners are able to move forward only when the people involved are self-initiating and open to how they can complement one another. If any of the participants is functioning out of a dependency mode, the partnership has a high chance of eventual failure because the partners will reach a point of distrust that will damage the partnership. Partnering also requires a sense of collective ownership, with the individuals involved taking joint responsibility for cocreating the new company's future and recognizing that by doing that, they are creating their own futures.[5]

When trust-based partnering exists, the integration leadership can create a team composed of both management groups to work through any remaining issues that need to be resolved. Other major benefits of engaging with the acquired company's managers are that the integration leadership gets a better idea of the acquired company's strengths and weaknesses and is able to obtain the managers' advice on the items that mattered the most and how to manage them effectively.

Most companies will have put together a business plan by the time they get into the negotiation phase. If the governance restrictions of a particular country allow it, the two companies can begin sharing the details of the business plan at this time. They can participate in discussions, but they cannot take actions or bring any change to the organization being acquired. These conversations with the partners in the acquired company corroborate the different resources, viability, and potentials of the acquired company. The leaders of the acquiring company can say, "This has been our thinking—can you validate that?" Some of the issues that are brought up in these discussions may include the physical location of various groups; the extent to which the new company might downsize here, upsize there, or recalibrate in this or that area; and the type of new customer that the new company can sensibly go after. A good degree of openness at this stage is important for setting the tone of the new company.

Partnering is developed as a capability on an ongoing basis. Companies that understand how they can get the most out of their relationships with other companies work to engage their counterparts to achieve favorable outcomes. Their opposite numbers are not to be regarded as antagonists in an "us-versus-them" stance, but rather as potential collaborators who can be brought into a win-win negotiating and operating framework. Sound partnering tends to start at the more senior levels, but over time, in a quantum leap company, it will be cultivated throughout the entire company.

For example, Clarica had three core values:

1. *Partnering* related to team behaviors that involved building and maintaining high-quality relationships of mutual accountability.
2. *Stewardship* meant acting with integrity and accountability to maximize value and to understand and service the customer.
3. *Innovation* involved sharing information and creating knowledge to constantly find new ways to deliver relevant high-quality solutions.[6]

These core values framed the way the people at Clarica acted and interacted on a daily basis in all areas of their work. When Clarica moved toward acquiring another company (or, in fact, being acquired itself), all Clarica employees keyed their behaviors to those values. In the case of the MetLife acquisition, the fact that Clarica operated from these values had great appeal to and resonance with MetLife staff. Because the MetLife people found the values so attractive, they were much more open to the acquisition and quickly became members of the Clarica organization.

Set Clear Accountabilities for Every Task Required for Integration

Accountability is defined as "who is going to be responsible for what." The integration team has to determine how it divides the responsibilities among the people involved and how those accountabilities are adjusted to take into account the continuous shifting that is part of making the transition to a combined company.

Organization building is fundamental to developing a good accountabilities structure. The integration team needs to be able to build transitional structures as well as the ongoing structure that emerges over time as the new business. It does not have an unlimited amount of time to do so. It must make the first major reorganizations and realignments of the business units from the two companies within 90 to 120 days after the start of the integration. If it does not, it risks a slide into complacency or even inertia—either of which can prove fatal to a successful integration. A significant part of an organization-building capability is being able to assign accountabilities well and to make sure that the integration team can gear the accountabilities to the strategic drivers that are linked to a successful outcome.

The members of the integration team manage the constant tightening up and changing of accountabilities as they go through the process of making the transition from two different companies to the newly emerging one. The integration team manages the shift to the new company and continually aligns accountabilities as that shift progresses.

There is a need for a good understanding of accountabilities by all people involved with the integration, whether they are long-term or short-term participants in the integration process. For example, Randy Croyle at Dow is clear on the need to understand that participation requires being fully engaged as well as putting in the requisite amount of time.

> *There are some interim organizational roles we have because integration is a lot of work. You are trying to run a normal business, but you are also trying to do a major integration at the same time. If the expectation is you are going to do your day job and then you are going to do integration on your afternoon shift, it is not going to work.*

Setting Time, Cost, and Performance Targets

Integrations need to be designed to work through all of the critical issues in a sensible and prudent manner. To manage the integration effectively, the integration team needs to clearly state what the principles of integration are and how the integration team will measure its effectiveness. The integration team can do that by laying out the standards and measures that it will put in place to let all concerned know how well the integration is staying on track and meeting its strategic and tactical goals. When standard parameters are set for the three major criteria—time, cost, and performance—everyone involved can know whether the integration implementation is on course. The members of the integration team and the business team can see if these standards reflect the time and costs required to carry out the implementation and are able to give feedback about any adjustments that may be necessary. The standards do not tell people how they have to carry out their work, but they can stimulate innovative approaches for meeting goals within certain limit conditions. This section examines what is involved in developing and using these three key standards and measures.

There are several types of targets in an integration:

1. The first is the time required for the completion of the overall integration.

2. The second deals with the costs of carrying out value creation synergies. Value creation synergies consist of the combination of cost savings and growth synergies that are the basis for company growth. Capturing and leveraging value creation synergies has a cost in time, money, and other resources needed. For cost-cutting synergies, this relates to determining what costs can be eliminated where and executing what is necessary to achieve those savings over the course of your integration. For growth synergies, it involves the costs required to identify the capabilities that currently exist in both organizations and to map out others that could be developed in the newly combined company. The synergy teams would note how these capabilities could be brought more broadly into play now and what it would take to build the capabilities that would move the new company to achieve substantial gains in the future.

3. The third involves the setting of performance targets. When the company has both defined its sets of performance targets and also clearly articulated its values, principles, and vision, the people in the various businesses can take the initiative on how they will meet those targets, as long as they act in accordance with the guiding principles. Establishing performance targets can greatly reduce the amount of time and effort needed to manage business operations and carry out evaluations. Well

structured oversight and governance can replace more cumbersome micromanagement.

Every organization has to set the time frame it sees as necessary to complete the integration. The time factor is a key driver for every action, behavior, relationship, and decision. All of the work of the integration has to be designed so that it can be carried out within this time parameter.

Case Example: How BP Set Its Targets when It Acquired Amoco

In BP's acquisition of Amoco, the target set for completion of the integration was six to nine months. As Tony Kuhel put it:

Our wrap-up on BP/Amoco was quick. Six to nine months was allocated for these two major corporations coming together. The number one priority was speed.

For BP, [our goal] was very simple: Get through integration as fast as possible. We had huge focus on trust and partnering, so we got everybody into action and got everybody into action/learning mode.

Case Example: How Dow Chemical Set Targets for Its Integration of Union Carbide

Dow had a two-year target period for completing its Union Carbide integration. Because it was able to develop a powerful integration planning approach (in terms of planning both the scope of the integration and cost-saving synergy targets), Dow's integration team completed its work ahead of schedule. According to Randy Croyle:

We had put together a two-year integration plan. We had thought that we identified about $1 billion in (expense) synergies. We were able to do it faster than the two years we had planned for, and we exceeded the $1 billion target. We only announced to the Street [i.e., the major financial institutions] that we would have $500 million in synergy. When all is said and done, we had about $1.3 billion in synergies, and we did it quicker than anybody had ever anticipated. This was given a big boost by having an entire year to put together a robust implementation plan.

Dow carried out its integration and focused on financial savings goals. Seeking expense synergies makes the most sense when it is done as part of an overall integration plan. The areas for savings and the actions needed to achieve them can be identified and implemented with greater acceptance in the integration implementation stage than in almost any other situation. During this time, the integration team also needs to identify and go after all of its opportunities for accessing, nurturing, and leveraging capabilities synergies as well. The integration plan needs to outline the roles and practices of both types of synergy teams, in order to maximize the ability to track and capture these synergies.

Case Example: How BP Set Performance Targets

BP was extremely specific in making performance targets a core part of how it did its business. Tony Kuhel notes:

> *Every business had performance targets. I don't think that we really required anybody to integrate, per se. The business performance part stated that you have to be in the top 10% of the world to stay in the BP portfolio. When Amoco came in, some of their facilities were not at that level. It became incumbent upon them to figure out, "How do I get to that level?" The fact that the business unit had to operate at that level was clearly defined as necessary. If you were not operating at that level, you were going to be "out."*
>
> *One of the problems that kept recurring was when BP had businesses that were given to a business unit leader from the new organization, like Amoco. They had a very tough time because they were not in that culture. To run a major business with hard business targets and not be aware of that, to not actually have lived it, was very difficult.*
>
> *The scale of the BP acquisition of Amoco raised complex issues for BP. Each organization had its background, preferences, and strengths. BP saw itself as more of a trading company and oil exploration company. Amoco's background had more of an oil processing and marketing orientation. That difference made setting targets for integration not a one-time event, but an iterative process.*
>
> *One of the differences in the Amoco case was that the CEO [of BP, John Browne] was more interested in exploration (the upstream businesses) than he was in the downstream businesses [e.g., oil processing]. As a result, things were not always dealt with as abruptly in the downstream businesses as in the upstream ones. Like it or not, the Amoco merger had a huge downstream component, and it probably took longer for that to be dealt with, including developing performance targets, counseling, shared objectives, etc.*

Selecting the Leaders Who Will Run the New Company

Selecting the leaders for the new businesses in your company is a systematic process. It also needs to be an open process, building on the strengths of the two companies to draw on the best people, with the most appropriate sets of skills and talents. If the acquiring company shows any bias or favoritism when selecting the new leaders, the outcome will be corrosive because you may end up appointing less qualified people to leadership positions in your new company and because you may undermine morale.

If your staffing process demonstrates bias, people coming into the new company from the acquired company will not trust the company to have opportunities for them, and as a result, they will limit their level of engagement and commitment. They will not invest their "human capital," and they are more likely to leave if an opportunity comes up. This set of issues could significantly hamper the success of your integration. In contrast, when you select leadership and staff in a way that is transparent, comprehensive, and equitable, your integration can proceed quickly and not leave the dragging effects of contention in its wake.

Case Example: How Sun Life and Clarica Selected Leaders for Their Newly Combined Company

Sun Life Assurance Company of Canada saw great value in Clarica's ability to manage an integration. Based on that perception, Sun Life asked Clarica to lead the integration as part of its deal for acquiring Clarica. The Sun Life–Clarica leadership team used a critical path framework to systematically work through the time frame, actions, and list of candidates involved in selecting the leaders of the integration team and the new business units.

The framework enabled the selection team to choose the people who would be charged with creating the new combined organization. However, the framework was a neutral structure. To ensure that the selection team would choose the best people for these leadership positions, it had to first ground itself in a compelling vision for the new company, including

- What that new company would look like, in terms of its relationships with customers and suppliers, the context for employees, and the culture

- How it would work, as far as the key principles on which the operations of the company were based
- The values based on which it would operate

The newly chosen leadership had to share this vision and how it would be carried out. The people selected for leadership positions did not just need to have specific competencies. They also had to be engaged with and committed to the vision of the new company if the integration was to truly succeed. The integration and the transforming of the business units were based on both the core values of partnership, stewardship, and innovation and the competencies required for the specific role. The extent to which transformation occurred was the extent to which the new company would be able to produce a specific set of strategic benefits for itself and all of its clusters of stakeholders. That included enhanced benefits for Sun Life's customers, its staff members, its independent sales force members, its shareholders, and the local communities in which the new company operated.

Every company has its own methods for leadership selection. However, the commonality in every approach is that each requires a structure, a set of values, and a compelling vision for the new company. The more quickly those elements are developed and articulated, the more effective the integration will be. Clarica drew on its learnings from working through a series of integrations to develop and refine its leadership selection template. Over time, it saw the need to restate its corporate values so that they would resonate with its workforce and support reaching its strategic goals. Additionally, it revisited its vision when conditions for insurance companies in Canada radically changed. A major change in Canadian insurance law in 1999 allowed mutual insurance companies to "demutualize." That meant that they could move from being insurance companies owned by their policyholders to being corporations that would be able to issue company stock and sell it on stock exchanges. The change gave Clarica greater flexibility in how it could raise funds on the open market, have its performance and future earnings reflected in its stock value, and make it significantly easier for it to acquire other companies or seek the best price if it became an acquisition target, which happened in 2002. All of these attributes translated into the higher transaction price that Sun Life agreed to when it acquired Clarica in the C$6.9 billion all-stock transaction. The transaction value of Clarica leadership is implied by Anthony O'Donnell, insurance and technology analyst: "Some even see the deal as a "reverse takeover," with the technologically sophisticated and effective distributor Clarica bolstering Sun Life's disappointing individual sales results. Many plum Canadian management roles are being occupied by Clarica executives. Most notably, Bob Astley, Clarica's president and CEO, is now president of Sun Life's Canadian operations."[7]

The selection framework template provided a guideline for the leadership selection across the new company on a consistent basis, with criteria that reflected what was necessary to realize the vision of the new firm.

Although it is important to have the best possible process for leadership selection, this selection will always involve a certain degree of risk concerning whether individual people will be a good fit and contribute as needed. There must be room for a certain level of risk tolerance in the leadership selection process and an openness to seeing whether choices do in fact stand up to the demands placed upon them.

Leadership selection is a very sensitive and highly visible function. The type of leaders chosen sends powerful messages to stakeholders as to what the new company's values and priorities are. Leadership selection is a judgment call, but the more comprehensive, rigorous, and exploratory the selection process, the greater the chances are that your new set of leaders and managers will be people who have the values, vision, and skills necessary to take your company on the next steps of its journey.

Managing Employee Expectations and Reactions to Change

There is no question but that mergers and acquisitions are disruptive. A sizable acquisition leads to reorganization of companies; a reconfiguration of relationships, roles, and responsibilities; and changes in people's positions. This can be a time of promise if you handle it well, but it also is a time when uncertainty, anxiety, trauma, confusion, and fear are equally at hand.

In an acquisition, the leadership may be replaced, along with coworkers, stated values, operating locations, benefits and salary structures, customers, sales channels, and procedures. Some people are asked to stay with the new company, and others are terminated. People often do not know what to expect in this rapidly changing world and have little say in how it will unfold.

Although an acquisition can open up opportunities for some people, others find that their carefully planned future is gone in an instant. The chances for disruptions may be greater for people from the acquired company, but in many cases the disruption also affects employees of the acquiring company.

The challenge of the acquiring company is to provide a context, a reliable structure and process, and an authentic effort at building a level of trust as the acquisition and integration get underway. When you make a good-faith effort to disclose the rationale for the transaction and when you make provisions for the changes that will invariably occur in people's lives, your employees will feel that you are considering their interests and treating them fairly. If they feel that the changes proposed and being enacted are in their interests and that they are being respected during the change process, they will support those changes. By taking people's interests into account early on, you can incorporate their interests into your business plan and make them part of the principles and practices of your integration. When that happens, the people affected can be systematically informed of what they can expect as the integration begins.

Case Example: How Clarica Managed Employee Expectations and Reactions

This proactive approach became the way of doing business for the Clarica Life Insurance Company. Clarica's senior management team saw that a key reason that it was successful when it acquired MetLife Canada was that it gave a high priority to anticipating the concerns of MetLife Canada's employees. Here's an overview of what Clarica did, which shows how quickly the company acted to reassure employees of MetLife Canada:

- Clarica announced the purchase on March 12, 1998. The same day, the CEO of Clarica and its senior vice president of strategic capabilities met with the top team of MetLife (which included the CEO, the general counsel, the heads of human resources and information technology, and the heads of the different lines of business) and right away started to validate, together, the business integration plans that had been formulated. This was part of the partnership. MetLife managers were fully involved in reviewing these plans and participated in shaping them, and in fact many of the plans were modified accordingly.

- On *the very next day following Clarica's assumption of MetLife's management*, Clarica's president sent a letter to all employees of MetLife Canada. He promised that all employees would know their employment status with the company within seven weeks—and that they would know how the Clarica Group would support their individual situations (i.e., continued employment, a severance package, career transition support, and so on).

Clarica was especially solicitous in its treatment of the MetLife agents: it gave each agent a computer with an information base covering all of that agent's customers. Clarica held regional dinners and two-day meetings at which Clarica talked to the 1,000 MetLife agents about the kind of company it was, its convictions, its aspirations on how to serve customers, and how the agents would be remunerated. And about 97 percent of the agents signed on with Clarica.

In addition, Clarica also went to great efforts to assist MetLife employees who were let go as a result of the acquisition. The leadership of Clarica said:

Clarica's objective is to ensure that 90% of MetLife's employees affected by this transaction will reposition themselves successfully within three months of their end date.

That objective was met. Of the 1,000 people who were not retained or chose to leave for various reasons, 89% were repositioned to their satisfaction by the end of that 90-day period.

Clarica developed a comprehensive set of principles designed to treat people fairly during the transition. It called it the "due process" approach. Treating people with respect and as professionals achieved a number of results. When people who were to be let go as a result of the acquisition, understood the reasons behind the decisions affecting them, they tended to accept those decisions much more readily and even actively participated in the development of the new company during their remaining time with the company. They were much more willing to share knowledge and have a positive view of the new company. People wanted to contribute, and they made their experience available because Clarica provided them with an encouraging environment and proved that it eagerly sought employees' views and experience. Additionally, when the new company sought to retain employees, providing an understanding of the rationale for business choices made for a significantly high retention level. This active and extensional approach served to inoculate the company against the frequent and toxic "survivor syndrome." Survivor syndrome is characterized by people who remain in the company, yet have reduced loyalty to the company, lower trust and increased skepticism, feelings of guilt that they are there but their colleagues are not, lower productivity levels, increased absences, and, eventually, higher turnover.

Clarica listened to its staff and identified issues in a proactive manner, coordinated all of its site visits and established a positive presence, and it made sure that it linked up its transition management group's functional teams. All of this took place to ensure a smooth transition from the end of the old company to the beginning of the new company. It delineated and clearly communicated how Clarica would deal with the employees of the acquired company. Clarica made sure that decisions pertaining to the employment status of individuals were communicated on a one-on-one basis by the appropriate manager. It gave as much advance notice as possible of any decision affecting individuals. Managers saw to it that all individuals received written confirmation of their status, including timing and severance payments. As positions in the new company were identified, individuals from both companies were given equal opportunity to apply for them.

People are not listed as assets in accounting books, but they may well be the most valuable assets of the company. When they are engaged, people create value by sharing knowledge and experience, and they function as representatives of the company in everything they do. People generate innovation, carry out processes, and forge and maintain the links that communicate with customers and other stakeholders. The integration leadership and its teams are responsible not only for meeting financial and operational goals, but also for re-creating the relationships and knowledge flows so that employees can enable the new company to move to higher levels of performance and create value. People's experience during the transaction period and through the integration period is as important to the future of the new company as decisions on plant and production, strategic alliances, and financial market responses. When the company authentically chooses to work through the core people issues with its managers and employees, it provides a strong basis for working through all the potentially difficult issues of multiple labor agreements, downsizings, relocations, and changes in remuneration and benefits. When it does not tackle its people issues, contentious and distracting conflicts continue to resurface, undermining company performance and ending up costing the company far more than they would have had they been dealt with thoughtfully and directly during the integration period.

Managing Change

At its heart, integration is both a change management and a project management endeavor. Both capabilities need to be built into the integration process. Yet, only a small minority of companies bring a well-organized and significant change management process to bear as they implement their integration strategies. A University of Edinburgh Management School/PA Consulting Survey disclosed that, "Companies placed a much higher priority on budgeting and cost control during their integration efforts than they did on change and risk management."[8]

Even if a company has been involved only in smaller acquisitions and has not undertaken a large-scale acquisition before, it has likely gone through significant reorganizations, strategic positioning, and related changes. That being the case, there will be people in the company who have experience in change management because they participated in those earlier change initiatives. They may have worked in operations, engineering, research and development, sales, or finance, but they learned fundamental things about change management in the course of their careers. They may not call what they participated in "change management," but they were working through major shifts in business practices, labor contract negotiations, or technology transfer issues. All of these changes involve achieving stretch goals of one sort or another in revamping structure, people issues, marketing channels, production processes, product innovation, or technology/production process alignment. That is a capacity that the company can capitalize on as it moves into its integration stage.

As Randy Croyle of Dow put it, "I am a chemical engineer by training, but I can't recall the last time I did any chemical engineering. I feel like I am more of a communications person and a change management person than a chemical engineer."

The company can use these talents and capabilities, but it has to make sure that it is operating at the right strategic level, that it has a systematic change management approach, and that it is consistently applying its change management philosophy and practices across all areas of the integration. Major acquisitions may well be the greatest change management effort a company has taken on, and it has to set itself up to be equal to the task. The integration plan may look good on paper, but an effective implementation is far from a certainty.

The change management component has to first "condition the soil." It must aerate the ground and uproot or neutralize beliefs, practices, and structures that can impede the path to integration. It must prepare all of those involved for the types, scope, and depth of changes that will take place in building the new company. That means that change has to be part of the language and character of the integration plan and the core communications to all parties about that plan. Change issues may be organizational system or process issues. They affect those inside both of the combining companies on a daily basis, and time and again they can radically alter both individual and organizational futures. A major acquisition also brings into play all relationships with customers, suppliers, financial reviewers, regulators, and local communities. Each and every stakeholder needs to be addressed in the change management strategy.

For example, Dow makes a clear connection between its change management and communications strategies. Eventually, change management has to exist not as specific acts in a combining company, but as a context and a set of processes that help shape every aspect of the integration and then extend into the postintegration period.

Change management requires buy-in by senior leadership, followed up by similar engagement throughout middle management and then by front-line staff. Senior leaders have to provide leadership in a way that infuses the principles of change management, along with the need for all those in the company to be open to change. Although there may be specific leaders for change management efforts at the top of the company, each and every individual must see that the changes involved in building the new company are in his or her interest and must become an agent for change. The leadership can start engaging people in the change process by clearly laying out the business plan, the changes that are involved in carrying out the business plan, and the benefits that will accrue to all those at all levels in the company. This behavior is central to bringing a change management context into play in a company.

Case Example: An Integration Steering Team Manages the Change Process

One large commodity producer mobilized its leaders in the integration change management effort by incorporating them into its merger steering committee, which initially provided strategic direction and then, as the integration was underway, promoted organizational change. The committee made sure that all of the integration activities were understood within the context of a comprehensive change plan, proactively working with all of the integration task forces to prioritize their activities within that framework.

The steering committee also examined the likely impact of change, and particularly tried to tackle situations where change was being implemented in a way that conflicted with the new operating principles. The managers of the steering committee sought to be a role model of collaborative working and looked for opportunities to promote and support necessary changes in behavior and mindsets.[9]

A change management approach targets all the key areas that must be dealt with and where change has to be worked through. A winning approach pays attention to the personal issues that have to be addressed before people can be expected to personally engage themselves. A good change management approach creates a context in which all levels of the company take on leadership roles that are in their areas of responsibility. Such an approach provides for a continuous flow of information throughout the company. It works to make sure that customers experience minimal disruption during the transition.

At the same time, it makes certain that customers' inputs are sought during the development of the new array of products and services and how those services are provided. It lays the groundwork for making the difficult decisions that are always part of a major change effort, and it keeps the changes that flow from those decisions clearly focused. Finally, it manages expectations and provides for interventions to work through the different types of resistance that can be anticipated.[10]

Case Example: How Dow Chemical Manages Change

Dow has moved to further institutionalize the role of change management in business units that are involved in significant acquisitions. Here's how Dow's Randy Croyle describes this:

We acquired a company. They had a large manufacturing site. We parachuted a team in. That team was basically Dow people. Then we put other people from that site on the leadership team. The new leadership team now had a combination of Dow people plus the acquired company people. One of the very key individuals that we parachute in is a change management leader. I don't know of any other company that does this. Their role is to help guide and counsel the organization through these changes. The position is called change management leader. That change management leader will be there for a couple of years. Eventually, once we are up and running and we feel very good about the integration, that change management leader then moves on to another role.

Change management always has a role in any dynamic company. During an integration, those involved in the change management effort have even greater responsibilities. The intensity involved and the limited time frame for achieving major changes demands a change management framework that is equal to its task. When the company mobilizes its change management component, it is drawing on a capability that is already present to some extent in the company, but it is also building on that to provide an even more powerful capability to support significant change actions in the future.

Conclusion

At this point, the new organization has a plan, an integration team, and a framework for selecting the best people with the right mix of skills for key positions. The guidelines have rooted the new company so that all of its actions are geared to manifest all of the following:

- A prime focus on its customers
- A priority on getting the new business into full operation speedily
- A value on engaging all stakeholders as partners in building the new enterprise
- Well-defined accountabilities for all involved that are linked to achieving the new company's strategic goals

The new company has also defined its time, cost, and performance standards for the integration so that everyone involved will have a sense of urgency and an understanding of priorities as they carry out the work of the integration. Incorporating a change management dimension closes the guidance circle by ensuring both that everyone understands that everything they do is part of and reflects an overall change strategy and that all changes that take place are in accord with the new organization's operating principles and values—in essence, the guiding factors make sure that the integration is not just a step to the new organization, but *is* the new organization in the first phase of realizing its promise.

The next chapter, "Building the Foundations for Quantum Leap Performance," uses these guidance factors to execute all of the actions necessary to combine the two legacy companies into a new company that can reach unprecedented levels of performance and value creation.

Success Factors

- Have your integration team effectively oversee the business management teams that are running both of the legacy businesses while the integration team is building the structure of your newly combined company.
- Manage the use of all your company's resources, both tangible and intangible, effectively during the integration process.
- Recognize and track the success factors that together guide the integration:

  1. Focus on the primacy of your customers.
  3. Develop a strong but flexible business plan.
  4. Keep in mind that speed is critical.
  5. Partner with the company you've acquired.
  6. Set accountabilities for every task involved in the integration.

- Set targets that galvanize the efforts to both capture expense synergies *and* develop capability synergies.
- Have a proactive human capital strategy that takes people's interests into account early on, so that you can incorporate those interests into your business plan and make them part of the principles and practices of your integration.
- Incorporate a change management perspective into all aspects of your integration process.

Derailing Factors

- Targeting cost-saving synergies only and neglecting to identify and pursue growth synergies
- Allowing bias and favoritism to affect your leadership selection process
- Seeing change management as a secondary concern in managing the integration transition

Questions

- How are we focusing on the primacy of the customer?
- How can we create a strong and flexible business plan?
- How are we incorporating speed in the integration implementation process?
- How are we embedding partnering into our approach to integration?
- What is our process for setting:
  - Clear accountabilities?
  - Time, cost, and performance targets?
- How are we addressing the following issues during the integration phase?
  - Our capabilities development
  - Our company structure
  - How we're meeting our customers' needs

- How we manage our people
- How we manage our corporate culture
- How we handle internal and external communication
- How are we selecting the leaders for our new integrated company?
  - To what extent are we taking the leaders of the acquired company into account during our selection process?
  - How are we assessing those leaders?
  - How formal a process is this?
  - Does our leadership selection process play a role in the outcomes of the integration?
- How are we addressing the following issues during the integration phase?
  - How are we managing employee expectations and reactions?
  - How are we managing change?
- Have we put an interim company structure for the integration phase in place?
  - If not, do we believe there should be one?
  - Have we established a multistage organization plan?
  - To what extent have we communicated that plan to our employees?
- What are the key people management issues we have encountered?
  - How are we dealing with these issues?

Notes

1. Spencer E. Ante, "Sprint's Wake-Up Call," *BusinessWeek*, February 21, 2008; http://www.businessweek.com/magazine/content/08_09/b4073054448185.htm?chan=search.
2. Ibid.
3. Ibid.
4. Timothy J. Galpin and Mark Herndon, *The Complete Guide to Mergers and Acquisitions: Process Tools to Support M&A Integration at Every Level*, 2nd ed. (San Francisco: Jossey-Bass, 2007), p. 63.
5. For an extended discussion of partnering, refer to Hubert Saint-Onge and Charles Armstrong, *The Conductive Organization: Building beyond Sustainability* (Burlington, MA: Elsevier, 2004).
6. Ibid., p. 122.
7. Anthony O'Donnell, "Clarica/SunLife Distribution Focus," *Insurance and Technology*, June 27, 2002; http://www.insurancetech.com/resources/fss/showArticle.jhtml?articleID=14705890.
8. Marion Devine, *Successful Mergers: Getting the People Issues Right* (London: Profile Books, 2002), p. 95.
9. Ibid., p. 118.
10. For an extensive discussion of specific issues companies must prepare for in their change management effort, see Timothy J. Galpin and Mark Herndon, "Welcome to the Big Leagues of Change Management," in *The Complete Guide to Mergers and Acquisitions: Process Tools to Support M&A Integration at Every Level* (San Francisco, Jossey-Bass, 2007), pp. 57–71.

The additional material in this chapter comes from the authors' interviews and experiences.

9

Building the Foundations for Quantum Leap Performance

At this point, the preparation work for jump-starting the company on its path to integration is done. A plan and operating principles are fleshed out. Success factors and performance indicators to guide the integration are defined. The stage is set for the implementation to get under way the moment the transaction is closed, and the foundation for optimizing the performance of the newly formed company is in place. Your communications process becomes active as you share your company's preliminary vision and goals with the world. At the same time, you need to define your synergy goals by business area, developing an organizational design for each business unit that is in keeping with those goals. To ensure business continuity, you need to appoint managers and employees within business areas, and you should begin outplacement, severance, and relocation programs. On the program management front, your integration implementation project teams get under way to achieve first-level tasks.

This chapter explores how the leadership and transition teams for the postdeal integration implementation take over from the predeal acquisition team to build your new company. The focus of the integration implementation is to make the transition from the two existing businesses into one ultimate business. This involves how to

- Choose and transfer capabilities from the acquired company to the new company, and begin the process of combining those capabilities into new capability configurations that are unique to the new company.
- Allocate the necessary resources of time, people, and money to enable the teams to reach the target goals of the integration.
- Make the integration plan broadly available to everyone who is involved in implementing the integration.
- Carry out a comprehensive communications strategy to inform all stakeholders of the changes being brought about by the integration.
- Have the leadership steering committee engage in ongoing strategy decisions, making changes so that it can recalibrate the integration as necessary.
- Maintain the flow of necessary knowledge and information so that all parties to the integration are in sync and provide the continuing feedback needed to guide the integration.

A transition structure is put into place to implement this migration. This structure concentrates executive time and talent on how to obtain the strategic synergies of a combination. The major work of this transition structure lasts between three and six months, but its oversight role extends out between one and two years to provide coordination and support during the implementation of all necessary change initiatives.

Transferring Capabilities during Integration Implementation

The transfer of strategic capabilities is at the core of an acquisition. Your company has acquired another company either because it wanted to expand the capabilities that it already had or because it wanted to acquire new capabilities that it did *not* have that would enable it to achieve its strategic goals and position it for competitive advantage. Because the purpose of the acquisition is to build your company's strategic capabilities, you must structure the integration so that you can capture the capabilities of the acquired company and bring them into play in your newly combined company.

A core goal in an integration implementation effort is for your company to accomplish this transfer as effectively as possible without degrading those capabilities. The challenge is to accomplish this transition while the company is moving into a new and tumultuous landscape, simultaneously changing its identity, structures, core processes, and physical facilities, along with its roles, responsibilities, and accountabilities.

There are three types of capability transfer:

- Resource sharing
- Transfer of functional skills
- Transfer of general management skills[1]

Let's look at each of these types in more detail.

Resource Sharing

Resource sharing includes any or all of the following:

- Sharing manufacturing facilities
- Sharing distribution channels
- Combining sales forces

Resource sharing can create extensive organizational stress, even when the capability transfer is fairly straightforward—for example, when you're simply combining assets or coordinating them for joint use by the business units of the two firms forming the new company. One instance of resource sharing is instituting cross-selling between the acquiring company's sales force and that of the acquired company. That can take place with little investment or management cost. Another instance is the adoption of the acquired company's brand as the umbrella brand, with the result that products from the acquiring company are given an increased perceived value through this new association. In instances like this, the benefits of resource transfer are quite evident.

However, resource transfer gains are not always so straightforward. You need to make sure that the benefits derived from these recombinations outweigh the direct and indirect costs. Those costs are a function of how well these changes affect the ability of your new company to create value, but they also depend on how effectively your new company can manage these new configurations.

For example, in one case, two companies combined their sales forces. One sales force was oriented toward marketing a lower-cost, mass-market set of products. The other sales force had specific skills for merchandising and demonstrating high-price-point items. These abilities were not completely interchangeable. Joining the sales forces was economically beneficial, but it had a negative effect in that it decreased the levels of service to customers because the people with the best skill set for each particular product line were not regularly available to customers to explain product functions and provide follow-up service contacts.

Transfer of Functional Skills

Transferring functional skills to your new company may well be your greatest capabilities challenge. What makes a capability strategic and valuable is that it is unique, and that uniqueness is based on the fact that the capability is embedded in the fabric of the company. Capabilities enable a company to approach and carry out its business in a way that competitors cannot imitate easily, if at all. Clarica's high level of full customer-service responsiveness was so interlinked with and supported by its values, its extensive customer service training, and its enabling technology platform that competitors could not readily replicate the company's high level of quality.

The more strategic the skills, the more important it is for the integration teams from the acquiring company to be able to work with the people of the acquired company to learn what those skills are and what is involved in incorporating them into your new company so that those valuable skills can be used and continue to flourish. When the acquiring company can bring in functional skills from the acquired company—such as advanced manufacturing process skills from an appliance manufacturer, the deep knowledge of how to operate complex distribution channels effectively for an oil products firm, or how to develop and customize business models research skills for a financial services group—these skills provide the acquiring firm with the ability to stand apart from its competition.

Transfer of General Management Skills

A third type of capability transfer involves general management skills. These are "broad skills that one company can use to make the other more competitive by improving the range and depth of its general management skills. These skills range from the broad skills needed in setting corporate direction and leadership to more analytically oriented skills and systems,"[2] such as those required for

- Strategy making
- Financial planning
- Process management
- Development and management of human capital
- Acquisition integration

Either or both of the companies you are combining may be more adept and agile in any of these areas, and those skills may enable your new company to achieve new levels of performance in already existing or even new domains.

Although functional skills can be transferred horizontally, general management skills can be transferred both vertically and horizontally. Therefore, your integration implementation team and the leadership of your new company must work diligently to keep communications channels open and trust levels high to enable these skills to be transferred where, and in the ways, they will yield the greatest benefit to your new company.

For example, BP's attitude was that if an acquired company had a better approach, it would not just use that approach in that particular business unit, but would adopt that approach across the whole of BP. Keeping lines of communication open and having the values to support adopting the best approaches, whatever their source, was essential for that type of transfer to be successful at BP.

Although these capabilities are intangible, they can figure quite significantly in the price an acquirer will pay for an acquisition. For example, when Sun Life acquired Clarica, a major incentive for the acquisition was that Clarica had outstanding integration, leadership development, branding, and technology support capabilities. Sun Life paid a significant premium to Clarica shareholders to acquire those capabilities.

In an acquisition, you need to probe all the different types of capabilities. The integration team needs to take a strategic view to prioritize which of these capabilities will provide the greatest benefit to the new company. There are costs incurred in any of these transfers as well as benefits that are derived. The better the integration team can gauge those short- and long-term costs and benefits, the better the choices it will make in allocating its resources to configure the best capability set for the new company.

The Two Dimensions of an Integration Implementation: Strategy Making and Project Management

During the predeal acquisition phase, the integration planning team is made up of members of the acquiring company. In contrast, during the postdeal integration phase, the integration steering committee and the integration team are now composed of a *combined* group from both the acquiring and the acquired companies. When you have members of both legacy companies on your steering committee and your integration team, you will accomplish more than just sharing the tasks of the integration. You will also open opportunities to shape a common understanding of the issues in the integration and a better grasp of how you can approach and resolve those issues. This involves revisiting the strategies and implementation plans developed prior to integration to confirm their validity and to revise them as necessary.

Your company strategy should be embodied in your integration plan. Project management is responsible for taking that strategy in the integration plan and implementing the actions that support it down to its last details as the integration proceeds. Project management handles all of the following:

- Mapping out and monitoring the timelines
- Keeping track of the integration through a consolidated project plan
- Reassessing priorities
- Linking to the rest of the company by informing it of progress made and anticipated issues

Although good project management is essential for the integration, project management teams often tend to emphasize efficiency and seek to minimize any disruptions that might impair an efficient achievement of the integration goals. This attitude can limit the boundaries of the integration too prematurely, for although many aspects of an integration are known and you can carry out the work on them efficiently, the integration is also an exploration of new territory, where potential disruptions are a natural part of the terrain. It can be better to learn what these disruptions are and get to their root causes than to push them out of the way. The disruptions may be symptoms of more significant issues that you will ultimately have to deal with.

In some cases, what you originally see as a disruption can, with some exploration and imagination, turn out to be an area of opportunity. The ability to deal with disruptions can unexpectedly lead to the development of entirely new products or services for your customers. Your steering committee and integration team have to maintain strategic coherence and keep the project management going while having the *option* to shift gears as new market knowledge emerges. They need to have the capacity to revise their responses to deal with emerging problems and opportunities without compromising the need to move rapidly through the integration process.

Keeping the focus on strategy making ensures that the organization is geared to adjust itself to meet market challenges. Strategy making informs the business plan. If market conditions change, then the business plan will need to be adjusted to take those changes into account. The steering committee's job is to make sure that the strategic perspective is maintained in the business plan and in the actions that flow from it. In concert with your integration team, the steering committee selects the leaders and provides oversight for the definition of their accountabilities. These accountabilities are defined as a function of achieving specific outcomes. The integration team needs to ensure that accountabilities are geared to the strategic drivers so that there is the right level of tension between getting the integration done and getting the new company oriented in the right strategic direction.

Tensions exist in every area of a major integration implementation. One such tension involves determining that the efficiencies required for achieving expense-cutting synergies are not carried out at the cost of impairing your key company capabilities or negatively affecting your customer relationships. Another set of tensions stems from the selection of an operational approach from one of the legacy companies versus the other, or choosing an entirely new approach altogether. Resolving these tensions requires a willingness on the part of the leadership to take on the responsibility for making these difficult recalibration decisions.

Some integration activities are part of long-term projects that go well beyond the mandate and time frame of the integration plan. In many cases, the integration team is dismantled after the immediate needs of the integration plan are met, with the management team of the new company taking over responsibility for managing these longer-term projects. Your company needs to develop a second, longer-term strategic view that goes beyond the immediate integration implementation realignments. As we explore in Chapter 10, depending on the complexity of the integration, the new company may need to give substantial attention to these longer-term goals:

- Creating a new identity for your new company
- Aligning the cultures of the legacy companies in your newly combined company
- Shaping and communicating your updated values
- Building on your existing and newly acquired capabilities to form the sets of capabilities that will enable your company to make a quantum leap in performance and in creating value

The Stages of Integration Implementation

The first phase of integration implementation realignment concentrates on systematically integrating the functional departments of the two companies you're combining. During this phase, your integration team focuses on sorting through the functions and processes that both companies have in common and working to achieve a core realignment of your company. As noted earlier, the time frame for completing this reorganization is usually three to six months.

By the time this reorganization has been accomplished, the selections of core staff members will have occurred, and people from the combined companies will be operating in their new roles. Your new company is thus in a position to seek the views of people from both legacy companies for shaping the vision and culture that will support your reaching your strategic goals. A basis for collaboration and trust develops as people from both legacy companies work together to make the transition from their former structures and build new ones.

The senior leadership on your integration steering committee is responsible for ensuring that the integration implementation team combines the two companies efficiently. When integration implementation begins, your steering committee provides a context for evaluating integration plans, sets priorities, and reviews outcomes. Essentially, your steering committee oversees the governance of the integration implementation. One major responsibility of the steering committee is resolving conflicts that may emerge between the activities that are underway and the guiding principles established for the integration implementation.

Your integration steering committee starts by recognizing that the integration plan is a departure point for the actual work of integration implementation. The implementation plan is obsolete the moment it is completed. Conditions change, and the implementation plan must change as well if it is to best serve as the working document for the integration. Building flexibility into the mindset of your steering committee and your integration team gives them the ability to engage in strategy making and make the project management adjustments needed for the integration. As these adjustments are made, your senior leadership and integration team modify accountabilities to keep them in line with the revisions in expectations and responsibilities.

As your integration team works through the first phase of restructuring, it seeks to harmonize and stabilize operations. Harmonization and stabilization address the fact that while there is an extensive amount of restructuring to be done at the start of the integration, there also needs to be significant work to reintegrate the changed structures, staff, and relationships so that the company can continue its business with minimum disruption.

Ensuring a Knowledge-Based Integration

Your integration team has the responsibility to make sure that only relevant, validated information and knowledge flow through your company. It reviews, analyzes, and transforms the constant deluge of information into working knowledge that you can use to create value for your customers and build your emerging company.

The best integrations have a high level of connections linking your company to your customers and your marketplace. Therefore, you should use input from conversations you've had with your company's stakeholders to guide your new company to develop products and services that meet your customers' needs. A good integration builds channels that permit this knowledge to flow into your new company so that you can use it to develop new products and solutions at a pace that meets the rapidly evolving needs of your customers and allows you to outdistance your competitors.

Fostering this flow of knowledge is the responsibility of all those involved with your integration, from your senior leadership levels through your integration project teams. Managing this change transforms your integration from one that works through a set of procedures to one that is a knowledge-based endeavor. When that transformation is underway, people are far less content to operate in an isolated, bureaucratic fashion. They know that they need ready access to good information and knowledge if they are to do their jobs. They also know that they need to make that relevant information available to all integration teams so that everyone can be apprised of how well the integration is proceeding. New insights, problem-solving approaches, and practices can then be deployed quickly across the company. As that happens, your integration begins to operate as an open, interlinked network. A hierarchy manages the complexity of the integration, but there is also openness and a seeking to link horizontally with resources wherever they are to be found to achieve the best integration outcomes.

Getting to Know Strengths and Gaps

At the start of your implementation, your integration teams should be organized by business area and set of projects. Every company has its own unique network of business areas. Each integration project team will have to sort out what the strengths or gaps of each company are and what capabilities each has that can contribute to the new organizational structure.

Although the first several months of your integration implementation will be focused on making rapid changes, this is also a time for discovering the actual capabilities of the new company that is being formed. Now that you have acquired the other company, you need to do a reality check to validate how correct your assumptions were as far as issues of fit and compatibility, gains in the ability to penetrate markets, or meeting other strategic goals are concerned. Many companies have found that even when they and the company they acquired offer the same general line of products or services, expectations that the companies are in the same line of business may be mistaken. Although two companies may both have divisions selling similar products, their approaches and channels to customers may be quite different and difficult to combine.

When the integration project teams realize what the similarities and differences between the two legacy companies are, they need to feed that knowledge back to the integration team. That feedback becomes the basis for evaluating the challenges. Your company then needs to make some decisions to adjust your integration implementation, or possibly even to change the strategy of your new company. In this iterative process, you will gain a fuller understanding of your newly combined company's strengths and gaps over time, which in turn will give you a basis for addressing the organizational issues that you need to take on during the next stage of your company development. Each major business unit and support function will have its own issues that need to be worked through further and resolved. Just a few of these extended issues involve

- *The marketing team*: Determining the new product mix, how to rebrand products, and how to align product lines with customer segments
- *The legal department with collaboration from the human resources department*: Needing to resolve labor union and compensation issues
- *A combined legal, research, and strategy team*: Reviewing the intellectual property portfolio to determine how best to value and leverage these intangible resources—which ones to continue to support, which ones to allow to expire, and which ones to license
- *The IT group*: Evaluating its own and the acquired company's legacy systems, and determining how best to make the transition and upgrade the company's support systems

Synergy Capture

You can judge the value of your acquisition by the extent of the synergies that you capture or develop during your integration implementation.

Expense synergies that are identified during the predeal phase and during the integration yield substantial savings by eliminating redundancies and reorganizing functions. Here are some good things to consider:

- Duplication of positions
- Overlaps in processes
- Multiple supplier lists
- Elimination of items that are no longer necessary in your new company

These changes can produce significant quick wins in a three- to six-month period. Achieving striking expense synergies can provide a great impetus for the whole of your integration implementation effort. As you post your initial quick wins, the expense synergy team can then look into efficiency synergies that take considerably longer to accomplish but may have even greater payoffs—for example, where major processes need to be realigned or legacy information systems integrated.

Growth synergy teams can also be initially chartered during the predeal phase, with the further work of identifying, capturing, and leveraging these "hidden" assets continuing into the integration phase. An incomplete understanding of growth synergies can lead to significant misjudging of possible gains, which is why it is important that you be rigorous and realistic in pursuing this type of synergy. Your integration team should examine your customer base, your market segments, and your competitors. The team seeks to determine how potential synergies can help your new company to reposition itself vis-à-vis changing customer expectations, emerging markets, and emerging technologies.

The growth synergies that will yield the greatest gains will come from tapping into company capabilities in a manner that can be achieved only through collaboration. These strategic conversations take place to analyze any gaps between current capabilities and the set of capabilities needed to produce major gains. If you begin these conversations at the start of your integration, you can gain insights that will produce specific gains in the short term, but your greatest growth synergy gains will occur when you incorporate these capabilities coherently into the longer-term structural, process, and cultural growth strategies of your new company.

Continuously Assess Your Progress

Your integration implementation team needs to carry out structured reviews to know how well your company is achieving your integration implementation goals. A comprehensive review structure serves as a sensing apparatus to adjust responses as the integration implementation continues on its path. A review is an instrument for assessing the progress of the integration and identifying where modifications need to be made. It also provides information needed to understand how well the integration implementation itself is operating. These reviews need to follow a well-defined business cycle, as shown in Exhibit 9-1.

The integration team usually has the responsibility for setting up regular reviews at different levels of your integration implementation:

- At the overall integration implementation level
- At the project team level
- At the subteam level

Each level is responsible for debriefing the integration management office and the integration team on its accomplishments, issues, insights, and recommendations at specific intervals. The integration management office (IMO) is the unit of the company that acts as the custodian, maintaining and developing the company's integration capabilities. Its staff is a resource that any part of the company can draw on to learn how to carry out an integration. It is the repository for all of the company's integration, strategic alliance, and joint venture methodologies and approaches. During an integration, it supports the steering committee and integration team

Exhibit 9-1

Model for Continuing Integration Implementation Appraisal and Recalibration

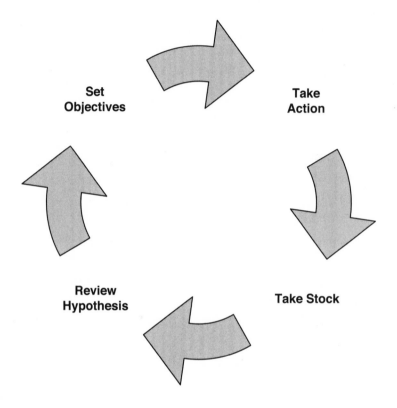

in their decisions, and it advises on how to keep all of the activities of the integration in alignment.

Reviews focus on information from performance and other success indicators, but also explore cultural, technical, or political issues that people have found that could affect the progress and quality of the integration implementation.

Your integration team should assess the harvested information from these reviews and share its findings with your steering committee, along with recommendations for recalibrating the integration plan to adjust for changing perceptions and conditions. When the integration leadership has the goal of making your new company a knowledge-based company, it has to make sure that there is a continuous flow of knowledge that members of the new company can use in their day-to-day actions and decision making.

Here's what these reviews should address:

- *Ongoing prioritization.* This leverages the greatest value from each integration team effort as one set of objectives is accomplished and new objectives need to be defined.
- *Tracking and reporting.* This provides all levels of the integration team (from leadership to subteams) with a current profile of progress, issues, and opportunities. A good tracking and reporting regimen constantly monitors key indicators, setting up a framework for identifying early warning signs and indicators of future performance and permitting sufficient lead time to establish mechanisms for course corrections.
- *Sharing best practices.* This involves sharing learnings across the integration and with business units about best practices that are being developed during the integration as well as ones that have been found to exist in the legacy company.
- *Updating the playbook.* Information gathered from integrations as they happen should be used to update the generic integration template or "playbook." This may include redefining how the integration can best proceed in every functional area of the business (e.g., legal, IT, production, product development, marketing, finance, and safety), recalibrating sets of measures so that the most valuable information is obtained from them, and evaluating the approvals process needed for the integration to move forward. All of these updates ensure that the playbook maintains its currency as a reliable guide for upcoming acquisitions.
- *Maintaining interdependencies.* This ensures that the different projects are coordinated effectively.

- *Maintaining communication and involvement.* This involves making sure that everyone in the company knows that their engagement in implementing the integration is critical for its success.

Participation in the reviews is a chance for everyone involved in the integration (including stakeholders through their feedback on performance) to have input into and be part of guiding the integration implementation process.

Exhibit 9-2 identifies the scope of what needs to be reviewed and aligned during the postdeal integration phases.

Exhibit 9-2
_____

Stages of an Integration Implementation

Deal Phase	Postdeal Phase First-Stage Integration Implementation	Breakthrough Stage
Develop: • **Goals** • **Guiding Principles** • **Desired State**	Project management coordination and integration implementation activities	Revise focus to ensure integration implementation efforts result in real change
Oversee: • **Deal Processes** • **Initiation of Integration Plan**	Coordination and integration implementation activities	Each action understood within the context of a coherent change plan
Provide Context	Evaluate plans and recommendations of integration task force teams	Help task forces prioritize their activities
Define Critical Success Factors	Evaluate project outputs	Tackle changes that are being implemented in a way that conflicts with the new operating principles
	Integration implementation process: recommendations on people	Leaders on the steering committee operate as models in line with the guiding principles.

Managing Internal and External Communications

The challenge of communicating the issues, status, and goals of such a complex undertaking to multiple stakeholder audiences is daunting. However, you want your stakeholders to believe that they have a valued relationship with your new company; therefore, you need to ensure that each and every one of them feels that your company has made an honest effort to apprise them of any significant changes that could be of relevance to them. From the beginning of the integration and onward, you want to show all of these stakeholders that you have a positive story. At the same time, you don't want to overpromise. Therefore, you must be consistent, active in maintaining contact, and authentic in your communications.

In any large, complex acquisition, there will be conflicts of interest among stakeholders. The new company has to anticipate what these arrays of interests are and be prepared to address them starting on Day One:

- Employees are concerned about employment security and advancement opportunities.
- Customers want to know if they have an assured supply of the goods and services, if the service levels will be maintained, and if there will be any differences in pricing or in the products or services offered.
- Suppliers want to know if they will continue to have a relationship with the new company and if there will be any changes in demands or terms.
- Financial analysts want to know if the acquisition will lead to significant cost cutting and higher profit margins.
- Regulators have requirements that they need to have satisfied so they need to know that your new company can meet those requirements.
- The local communities in which your company operates want to know if your company will continue to operate its businesses there, what demands may be placed on them by your new company, or what new prospects might unfold.

Case Example: Sun Life–Clarica's Communications Strategy

The communication strategy developed during the Sun Life–Clarica integration is an example of how one company devised a proactive communication strategy that set the tone for how the new company wanted to be seen and for the kind of relationships it was working to establish. It wanted all of its stakeholders to know that it had an exciting story and future. The best way to use the company's limited communications resources was to design and implement a communication strategy that had a well-defined framework.

The Sun Life–Clarica acquisition and integration implementation had three core principles:

1. Focus on clarity by developing a solid story and using plain language.
2. Provide stakeholders with easy access to key communicators/ spokespeople—focus on direct contact with key communicators wherever possible.
3. Align the communication strategies with HR's employee-retention strategies.

Those principles were tied to communication objectives, which were

- Communicate the deal to key stakeholders with no negative effect on the stock price.
- Retain key employees.
- Convey that the acquisition was a win-win story for both companies and a positive step on a growth path.
- Mitigate any negative perceptions of the new combination.

The next step was to develop a set of key messages. The key message to stakeholders sent out in the Sun Life–Clarica acquisition was that Clarica now had a global insurance resource available to draw on and that the acquisition had moved Clarica from being a niche player into a more solid market position where it could generate additional earnings growth, deepen its talent pool, and leverage its investments.

Sun Life–Clarica targeted nine different stakeholder groups:

1. The media
2. Market analysts
3. Institutional investors
4. Clarica's employees
5. Clarica's independent agents
6. Sun Life employees
7. Existing Sun Life and Clarica customers
8. Rating agencies
9. Regulators

It created a communications plan for each stakeholder audience. The plans consisted of three elements:

- A delineation of specific issues and impacts
- A strategy for mitigating any of these issues
- A strategy for obtaining an optimal reaction

Once the "who" and the "what" of the communication strategy were addressed, the next step was to determine the "how" and develop a timetable for "when" communications would take place. The communications team had to determine the best communication vehicles to employ to deliver particular types of messages to specific stakeholder audiences. In some cases, face-to-face meetings were necessary to communicate the initial changes brought about by the acquisition. In other cases, phone conversations were adequate. In specific instances, a multiprong array of communications was deployed.

On Announcement Day, the communications team issued a joint press release, set up an analyst conference call, and posted the agreement on the company's intranets. In addition, printed materials were packaged for employees, and follow-up meetings were scheduled with specific managers. Internally, meetings with various levels of management were held on a weekly basis to ensure that issues were identified and questions were answered on a timely basis. This was supported by written communications that were made available to all employees.

In the postannouncement period, communication shifted to news releases supporting the "Sun Life–Clarica story" that were sent to targeted investors. Additionally, a road show to major Canadian cities was scheduled so that the Sun Life–Clarica leadership could personally discuss the implications of the new combination with financial analysts and institutional investors. On the internal organization front, senior leaders met with each group of employees to systematically review what the integration implementation could mean for them in terms of any effects on their employment or relocation. This was also an opportunity to share the vision, structure, and plans for the new company. The new combination also made sure that each customer was visited by a representative of the company to inform the customer of what would continue and what new opportunities would become available.

With the communication strategy in place, the next step was to assign communication responsibilities. A communications plan team divided the communications audiences among themselves and designated the specific tasks that each was taking on.

The need for effective communication continued every day for the duration of the integration implementation.

It has repeatedly been said that the secret of success in an integration implementation is that the company cannot communicate too much, too often, and through too many vehicles. If good communication does not take root, poor communication becomes the de facto norm, as was the case during the US Airways, DaimlerChrysler, and Sprint Nextel integrations. Poorly planned and executed communications lead to distrust, undermine collaboration, and result in low levels of performance. Your new company can never afford poor communication, but you especially cannot afford it during the stressful and rapidly changing integration implementation period.

The Emergence of Your New Company

Your integration team is in charge of the integration implementation plan and manages the process of making the transition from two distinct businesses into your new "transformed" business. Your integration team is accountable for a timely implementation that is in line with the targeted outcomes. The exact accountabilities change and tighten as your integration implementation unfolds, up to the point where a new company eventually emerges. At that time, there is no more talk of an integration team; instead, there is a conversation about the management of your new business. With its basic operations reorganized and its business in gear, the new company can shift its attention to fully leveraging the array of capabilities it has identified so that it can fulfill its promise of becoming a breakthrough, quantum leap enterprise with unprecedented levels of performance and continuing value creation as its signature.

Success Factors

- Transfer capabilities from the legacy companies to our newly combined company without degrading those capabilities.
- Allocate time, people, and financial resources based on specific target goals of the integration.
- Encourage adequate exploration for potential capabilities synergies between the two legacy companies.
- Have a strong project management capability that comprehensively implements all the elements in the integration plan.
- Examine disruptions to the integration process to determine their root causes.
- Maintain the right level of tension between goals and accountabilities.
- Support value-adding efforts that go beyond the short-term integration timeline.
- Make sure that the integration implementation teams tie all their actions to the company's overall strategic perspective.
- Hold planning sessions for team leadership to reground them in strategy making.
- Design the integration as a knowledge-based enterprise, with a constant flow of necessary knowledge and information throughout all levels of the integration effort.
- Mandate the use of guiding principles in all integration actions.
- Recognize that speed is a necessity in the integration, and follow the 80/100 rule: when you are 80 percent certain, you should act 100 percent of the time.
- Allocate time during your integration to get to know the strengths and gaps of both legacy companies.
- Recognize that the intangible growth synergies are unique to each company, are embedded in structures and processes, and therefore require extensive partnering efforts to bring them to the surface and leverage them.
- Continuously appraise and recalibrate your integration implementation process.
- Plan and execute a comprehensive communication strategy for all stakeholders at all critical points of your integration process.

Derailing Factors

- Introducing cost-cutting measures that can possibly undermine capabilities
- Permitting expectations of capabilities synergies that are not fully grounded
- Emphasizing efficiency in project management, even at the cost of minimizing flexibility and opportunities for learning

- Allowing the pressing events of the integration to take precedence over strategic concerns
- Restricting the agenda of your integration to the senior steering committee and the integration team
- Operating the integration as a set of standard, uniform procedures
- Assuming that everything significant is known about both combining companies before the integration phase begins
- Operating from the belief that the only synergies that have value are tangible cost-cutting (expense) synergies
- Reviewing your integration process only after you've completed your integration
- Minimizing communications so as not to distract attention from day-to-day activities

Questions

- How are we transferring capabilities from the legacy companies to the new company?
- How are we assessing our progress at different points in the integration process?
- How much are we emphasizing communication following our announcement of the acquisition?
  - To what extent have we sustained communication during the integration implementation phase?
  - Have we formulated an explicit communication strategy to reach our staff, the target company's staff, and other stakeholders?
  - Did we concentrate this strategy at the front end of the integration implementation (e.g., the first couple of months), or did we sustain it throughout our integration implementation effort?
  - To what extent does our communication strategy play a role in the results of our integration implementation?
  - Should we place more importance on communication than we have been doing?
- Have we put in place an interim company structure for the integration implementation phase?
  - If not, should we have one?
  - Do we have a multistage company plan?
  - To what extent have we communicated this plan?
- Have we brought a project management capability into the integration implementation phase?
  - If so, what form is it taking?
- What are the key people management issues that we are encountering?
  - How are we dealing with them?

Notes

1. Philippe C. Haspeslagh and David B. Jemison, *Managing Acquisitions: Creating Value through Corporate Renewal* (New York: Free Press, 1991), pp. 106–110.
2. Ibid., p. 31. Haspeslagh and Jamison provide an excellent discussion of the different types of capability transfers.

The additional material in this chapter comes from the authors' interviews and experiences.

Breakthrough: Moving to Unprecedented Levels of Performance and Value Creation

All the steps in the pre- and postacquisition phases (covered in Chapters 1 through 9) are the stepping-stones to realizing the accelerated growth that can be achieved in the breakthrough phase, which is geared to bringing your new company to a level of performance that no one thought possible before. Breakthrough is not just an extrapolation of the capabilities of the two legacy companies; instead, breakthrough takes the essential core capabilities of the two merging companies and leverages them to bring your newly integrated company to a new level of performance. In this process, you've shed what is no longer relevant to your customers from the original, separate companies, and your new, streamlined company is set to create a new future for itself.

The Engines of Breakthrough

As you complete the initial integration implementation, your transition to the breakthrough phase begins. At this point, you've identified your new company's leadership team, you've streamlined and filled all positions in the new company, and you've defined the principles and initial strategic objectives of your newly combined company. Now you're ready to start the engines for breakthrough:

- Focus on renewal strategies that leverage the core capabilities of the two legacy companies.
- Enlist employees' commitment by creating a vision and engaging them in realizing that vision.
- Create a cohesive culture in which people are driven to collaborate in order to succeed.

When these engines are in place, your company will create the trust-based relationships that are necessary if your company is to engage all employees to mobilize it into breakthrough mode. Let's look at each of these three engines in more detail.

Leveraging Your New Company's Core Capabilities

A major reason for choosing an acquisition path to growth is the belief that new, stronger capabilities are required, and that it will be faster and more efficient to capture the needed capabilities by acquisition rather than through the slower process of organic growth. The breakthrough phase is when all the work of identifying capabilities and harnessing these capabilities in the new organization pay off.

The combination of capabilities from both the acquiring and the acquired company enables your newly combined company to achieve extraordinary performance and create value (as illustrated in Exhibit 10-1). Although you should begin to capture, transfer, and consolidate capabil-

Exhibit 10-1

Capabilities Transfer Model for Breakthrough Phase

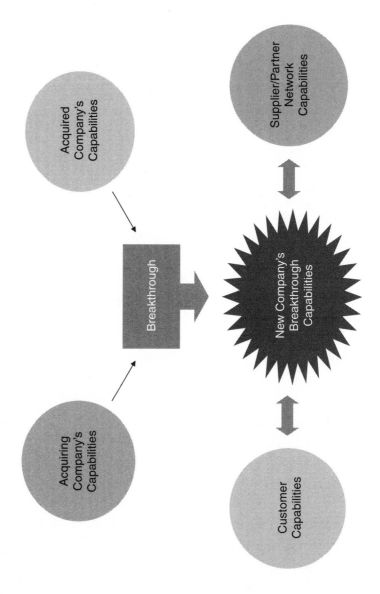

259

ities during the integration implementation phase, you should continue this process even more extensively during the breakthrough phase. These capabilities are then available for your new company to combine, extend, amplify, and modify as you sense opportunities in the market and as your customers require. It is essential that your company interact with your customers, suppliers, and partners to determine what their sets of capabilities are and what capabilities-based solutions you can create to complement their capabilities and add the greatest value to the products and/or services that you offer to your customers.

Engaging Employees' Vision by Having Productive Conversations

Your new company needs to communicate with your newly combined workforce through a series of productive, strategic conversations. What you talk about and how you address the subjects you choose to focus on form the basis for your new company's strategy making and integration implementation. In conversations, people respond to each other as they interact. Conversations do not simply address particular subjects. They also address how those subjects are seen. That is, they can shift the context or perspective of how something is looked at and understood. Conversations can bring new understandings, and the actions that flow from those conversations reflect and embody those new understandings. Whereas conversations are transforming, most communications primarily involve sending messages or information. These communications are useful and necessary. However, while they may transmit important messages, they essentially move information in one direction, from one source to a receiver, and thus they tend not to be effective vehicles for change.

A productive conversation is not a chance or casual occurrence. It flows from an understanding of background goals and principles and addresses the foreground issues and requirements. New understandings of the market and of customers are shaped in productive conversations. It takes commitment, effective interaction skills, and a lot of practice to engage in productive conversations.

People have conversations about the things that matter to them. When people in the company feel free to discuss the issues that they see as making a difference, their personal knowledge and experience flow without constraint, both throughout the company and in interactions with external stakeholders. The role of leaders is to frame the context in which these strategic conversations take place. Based on our extensive experience in this type of work, we have come to believe that organizations function at the level of performance that the quality of their conversations allows them to reach. An inability to have productive conversations leaves piles of unresolved issues that stand in the way of greater coherence and productivity.

Conversations work better when the values of all parties are understood. If a shared set of values exists, there is a good basis for listening and responding to what the other party is communicating. Shared values are the medium for establishing trust, which is at the core of high-quality conversations. When participants share common values, they can

---

Case Example: Bristol-Myers Squibb and DuPont Knowledge Sharing

For example, the Bristol-Myers Squibb knowledge management team (described in Chapter 5) arranged for a large number of conversations between its research scientists and the research scientists of DuPont Pharmaceuticals. Research scientists have similar backgrounds, education, and values. They are a natural community. Within that natural community, the research scientists from both companies saw themselves as engaging in collegial conversations. Because they shared common ethics and a common mindset, they saw little need to hold back on knowledge flow and exchange.

This peer-to-peer knowledge sharing was enormously successful in bringing to light the highly valuable explicit knowledge of what was in the pharmaceutical pipeline, as well as the tacit knowledge of what capabilities had been needed to develop those drugs to that point and what would be necessary to carry the development work through successive stages, culminating in FDA approval. BMS could now recycle that knowledge and move the pharmaceutical process along without a major break. Without those conversations, this valuable and irreplaceable knowledge would have slipped through BMS's fingers, hampering its pharmaceutical development process considerably.

exchange points of view more easily, and they can connect in a manner that allows them to feel confident that they are being heard. At that point, people will be more open to sharing their knowledge and to investing themselves in building the new company. If the company reflects their values, they will be more willing to invest in building it because it means something to them. Trust-based conversations are very intimate experiences for the participants in those conversations. Open sharing is conditional, and your new company will need to earn the trust required; you can't mandate it or simply assume that your employees will trust their new managers and leaders.

Case Example: Sprint and Nextel—The Costs of Holding Conflicting Core Values

A difficult integration at the major telecommunications company Sprint Nextel demonstrates both the missed opportunities and disastrous results that can occur when a company fails to establish shared values and productive conversations. Sprint and Nextel were brought together in a $35 billion merger in 2005, creating the third-largest wireless company in the United States. Yet, instead of becoming a merger of equals, a clash of cultures has led to chronic discord. Until the company deals with the underlying differences in the core values of the two legacy companies, it won't be able to resolve the surface conflicts that have arisen in every area from leadership selection to billing systems.

On paper, the Sprint-Nextel merger made a great deal of sense. The companies had very different but complementary assets. Sprint was a company with a 100-year history as a long-distance and local phone company, and it wanted to bring some of Nextel's feistier, innovative outlook into its business model. Nextel, for its part, wanted access to Sprint's larger customer base. Here's how the aftermath of this "merger" was described in the media two years later, by Kim Hart of the *Washington Post*:

> But it didn't take long for friction to surface, employees at both companies said. At the heart of the tension was a sense of mistrust on both sides, they said. Some Nextel employees say they feel the aggressive, entrepreneurial style that spurred its early growth has been stamped out by Sprint's more bureaucratic approach. Some of the Sprint folks say they feel deceived by Nextel's deteriorating network, the source of the company's deepest customer losses.

As longtime Nextel employees with the expertise to repair the network took lucrative exit packages, Sprint workers said they felt abandoned and blamed the ailing network for the company's financial woes. Nextel employees, meanwhile, felt their brand and technology had been unfairly dismantled.[1]

Executives from both Sprint and Nextel did not work effectively to bridge the differences in their core values through a productive conversation, but instead focused on operational and strategy issues. Without getting the core differences out on the table, the question was whether either side could hear or respond to the other, or even if they wanted to do so:

Nextel employees typically proposed acting quickly and recall becoming frustrated when their ideas were shot down by their Sprint counterparts. It wasn't that they didn't like their ideas, Sprint people said at the time. They just needed to consult their superiors before agreeing on a plan.

Many such meetings ended with Nextel employees storming out, leaving the Sprint side baffled. Sprint people thought Nextel made reckless decisions and spent money impulsively. Nextel people felt stifled by Sprint's process-oriented pace.[2]

This type of clash is not uncommon. A similar culture clash happened at AOL Time Warner, with a similar outcome: a decline in the company's stock value and a loss of customers and of market share. In the AOL Time Warner integration, AOL's executives took key positions. Its aggressive managers actively gave orders to their Time Warner counterparts, who did not always take orders well. The Time Warner managers were much more conservative, on the one hand, and had a long history of operating their Time Warner business units with little questioning, on the other.[3] "Mutual dislike or contempt of key executives was the result, and made it difficult to integrate the media giant's platforms—online, movies, television, radio, and print."[4]

Were these negative outcomes necessary? The answer is no. Is it simple to find a common ground between legacy companies and to build your new company on the strength of their combined capabilities? No, it is not easy, but there is no alternative to success in this matter, as the failures that have come at great cost show.

It may be simple to point fingers at these companies, but every major merger or acquisition is faced with a variation of this dilemma. When your company grasps the significance of both differences and compatibilities from the beginning of the process, your leadership can begin establishing a productive conversation that threads through all the acquisition stages and into the integration itself. Instead of focusing on antagonistic communications, the people in the company can learn how to look for value in each other's perspectives. Productive conversation is not a fast or a one-time fix. It is a carefully managed process, with leadership in the vanguard and full engagement at all levels throughout the integrating companies. Your new company must make it a priority to create an atmosphere in which values-based conversations take place. If you do not, you risk repeating the value-destroying behaviors that have put mergers like Sprint Nextel in serious jeopardy.

As seen in the strategic conversations that BMS organized with the research scientists from DuPont Pharmaceuticals, the benefits of the productive conversation approach are

- The free flow of critical information on a timely basis
- The ability to capitalize on this information in order to discern potential areas for capabilities and expense synergies, and particularly how you can capture those synergies in your new company
- The ability to conduct high-quality interactions, both internally and externally with networks of stakeholders
- An intelligence network that brings forward information that your company needs if it is to best respond to your customers and to chart your business strategies

Company capabilities are determined and confirmed in conversations that take place within integration teams and in the day-to-day work of your newly formed company. Your leaders have to emphasize that conversations about capabilities are key to your new company's efforts to identify, evaluate, and capitalize on short- and long-term synergies. These conversations start during integration implementation but are carried on throughout the entire life of your new company. In these conversations, people at all different levels of your company should delve ever more deeply into the layers of both legacy companies to grasp what these capabilities are, where they reside, how they were developed, who has been involved in nurturing them, and what potentials they may have for your new company. These capabilities are the hidden wealth of your new company. By their nature, they are embedded in the fabric of companies, and you need to patiently explore their various strands in a partnering atmosphere.

Aligning the Values of the Legacy Companies into a Single Company

Your emerging company's underlying values will either support or disrupt your effectiveness in achieving your goals. Working in a single company where the leadership acts on the basis of one set of values, the middle management acts on the basis of another, and the line workers act on the basis of a third set of values is difficult enough. This dissonance is compounded during a large-scale acquisition where multiple value sets coexist after two major, complex companies combine. If you don't manage this situation well, these conflicting sets of values will undermine the best-intentioned and best-financed acquisition. The extent to which the core values align and are commonly held in an emerging company will play a key role in determining whether that company will achieve the necessary level of employee engagement and commitment. Shared values create a trusting environment where knowledge is not seen as a source for personal power, but rather as a common resource.

Managers and leaders often overlook and underappreciate the role of values in knowledge generation and transfer, yet it's not difficult to identify the values that drive individual and organizational behavior. Those values support, or disrupt, the company as it moves forward toward quantum value gains.

One way to gauge core values is to carry out a values survey. A values survey is best performed once you have finalized the selection of employees for your new company and those employees have taken on their new areas of responsibility. You can find various survey instruments online. The surveys ask employees multiple questions offering a matrix of values possibilities, with people choosing what their highest-priority values are. This sets up a values profile that can be analyzed for commonalities and differences among such variables as levels within a company, types of work done, and geographical locales.

Case Example: How Clarica Determined Its Core Values

The Clarica insurance company carried out this type of survey. It analyzed the outcomes and determined that employees strongly identified with three core values, which then became the themes guiding the management practices of the company: *stewardship, innovation,* and *partnership.*

Having a clearly articulated set of core values made a significant difference when Clarica was engaged in acquisitions of other companies. Not only did these values provide clear guide points that helped the company go through the steps of the acquisition process more quickly, but they made Clarica an attractive employer for the type of critical employees Clarica was seeking to retain. (See the discussion of Clarica's core values of stewardship, innovation, and partnership in the Chapter 8 discussion of partnering.) When the employees of a newly acquired company were surveyed for their individual values and the results were integrated into the overall compilation of Clarica values, the employees saw where their values were positioned within the larger framework of the overall Clarica values. When these values were placed in the context of Clarica's core values, the new employees readily identified with them. The core values then contributed to retaining more than 90 percent of the employees that came with the acquisition of a significant reinsurance business.

Clarica saw that it could best achieve outstanding performance when every employee developed his or her capabilities in ways that were aligned with the strategic goals of the company. It worked to gradually realign the values of the company's employees to be more in accord with the corporate values. In Clarica's view, people could engage in partnering, stewardship, and innovation only if they were not in a dependent mode, but rather in a self-initiation way of operating. People in the insurance industry had traditionally accepted the more entitlement-prone context of a benevolent bureaucracy. The integration of successive acquisitions served as an opportunity for Clarica to shift the culture to one of self-initiation, where everyone takes charge of their respective accountabilities while working collaboratively across organizational boundaries. This change in orientation resulted from the consistent application of leadership and culture principles that reinforced the company's core values. Those values were the living, breathing force that guided the behaviors of everyone in the company, from senior leadership, to employees at call centers, to front-line representatives in the field.

Clarica's efforts resulted in building high levels of employee commitment and customer satisfaction. Clarica succeeded in bringing its organizational values to life on a day-to-day basis. These values supported an innovative way of doing business, which, in turn, brought about a growth of revenues and an expanding customer base. These success factors were major incentives making Clarica a sought-after acquisition target. More important to Clarica, however, was that its values reflected its nature inwardly to its employees and outwardly to its customers and to the marketplace. Its values were the basis for its high performance and aspirations.

In addition to surveys, a company can build a core set of values that supports its strategic goals by simply listening to its own workforce. In one company, a group of employees conducted 400 interviews with other workforce members, collecting stories of the great moments when the company did amazing things. The group then analyzed those stories and found the company's "best values" embedded in those stories. The values that were repeatedly revealed in those stories became the basis for the value set that the company adopted as its core organizational values.

For example, one such landmark story was when a delivery person took the initiative, when a road was blocked by a landslide, to deliver a parcel promised to a customer. The delivery person rented a helicopter and made the delivery within the promised time frame. When the company learned of the exceptional effort, instead of upbraiding the person for unauthorized spending, it rewarded him for taking the initiative and living out the company's core value of extraordinary customer service.

A variation of this approach involves asking customers about their experiences with the two legacy companies. Patterns will emerge that your new company can use to identify what customers feel is the value proposition that made them choose the legacy company as their supplier. The values practiced inside that company become the values promise, or "brand promise," made to customers and to the marketplace.

In our rapidly changing world, command-and-control leadership is losing its ability to mobilize for rapid response to the wide variety of complex demands that a company faces. Values-based organizational networks, coupled with a set of compatible partners, are more able to provide viable responses to customers. This difference is especially important in a world where diverse global customers have come to expect high performance regardless of their location, their needs, and when they require a response.

This does not mean that companies can take a shortcut by establishing a hard-and-fast set of rigid, uniform values. What may be considered to be a core value in one company may not be valued in the same way in another company, or even in a different part of the same company that is operating in another culture or another part of the world. The goal of alignment is to create the capability to leverage the diversity of positive values of the two legacy companies in your newly emerging company, not to drive everyone to march in a lockstep fashion or to have cookie-cutter sameness. Diversity has to be seen as an opportunity to get beyond a too-limited viewpoint, not something to be squelched for efficiency's sake. What is needed is to find a core group of values that are among the overlapping values between one legacy company and the other. If this core group includes such values as integrity, respect, and responsiveness, then the other particular values can be seen as complementary. What is key is to have a minimum set of commonly held values that will serve as the foundation for collaboration and interdependence across the new organization. Beyond these few values that must be held in common, all other values can be held in the full diversity that is needed to serve a wide base of very different customers.

For example, an Asian company may acquire a North American company. A certain set of core values may resonate with both, but the Asian company may place considerably more emphasis on team performance than on individual performance and place greater emphasis on working through relationships than the North American company, which may focus on its business processes. If each company respects the other's values, the two companies can establish a network of value clusters where different behaviors and attitudes are recognized as being effective in different settings, but where a core set of values threads through all their actions. This creates a larger umbrella of values with which they both can operate and find ways for collaboration.

Understanding the Emotional Context of an Acquisition

Some companies have also used surveys to deal with the potentially negative effect of an acquisition on the climate of the company.

Case Example: What One Company Learned from an Employee Survey

One instance of the effective use of such a survey took place after a global company acquired a large commodities company with strong roots in its community. The employees of the commodities company felt that the acquisition threatened the more progressive character of their company and their close connection to their community. A survey was carried out to assess the "cause-and-effect" chain that was at the root of the distrust and emotional turmoil that was affecting the workforce.[5] The company found that there was substantial and widespread anxiety that the new ownership would dismantle what had been a very successful and innovative workplace environment. This anxiety was in large part related to a feeling of insecurity about the need to cope with a different organizational environment and the ability to retain employment in what they saw as a great place to work. The reasons for the prevalent insecurity proved to be different at different levels of the company.

The company was concerned that two qualities that made it successful were in jeopardy:

- Its skilled and highly motivated workforce's commitment to providing the highest level of product quality and customer service
- Its leadership position within its industry

With a better understanding of the source of the insecurity, the leaders of the acquiring company were in a position to communicate with the workforce more effectively. In fact, the candid conversation of the survey results allowed the senior managers to openly discuss questions that, until then, had not been brought out into the open. Once business leaders were able to acknowledge what the members of the company were feeling, they were able to more effectively communicate to the workforce that what they had valued in the company would be preserved, regardless of the change in ownership.

Articulating a New Vision

Surveys of CEOs show that "engaging employees in the vision" is a key management and marketplace issue.[6] Although values are at the core of a company, the vision fulfills the need to shape and articulate the company's aspirations in a way that allows all its members to see the role they have in realizing this desired future. Having employees participate in exercises articulating the vision allows the employees to write themselves into the story and brings the level of commitment and ownership that will ensure its realization.

Vision has a special significance in a new company that is emerging from an integration. It galvanizes your new company by inspiring people to a higher level. It leads people to commit to a compelling strategic direction. It also shows that your new company is moving in an uncompromising way toward a significant and promising future. Your vision needs to be convincing to everyone in the new company, from the leadership to the front line. It is equally critical that you actively communicate your vision to your customers, your marketplace, and the local communities in which your company operates. Your stakeholders can then assess how your company's vision fits with their own goals and provides a supportive environment.

The time when your new company is forming is one of intensive change. A vision is especially important at this point to keep everyone's attention directed toward the possibilities of your new company. A clearly articulated overarching vision serves as an antidote to the chaos and often unsettling nature of the change process. People are concerned about their future. The development of a shared vision allows them to participate in developing a joint future with your newly combined company.

Articulating a vision is much more than a vision statement. It is a collaborative process. An attractive, catchy vision that does not resonate with the whole of the company will fall short of its mobilizing role. The vision must be lived by the company's leadership and validated by the company's actual achievements. In a quantum leap company, the company's strategy and practices are part of its effort to fulfill its vision. In that way, the vision generates stretch goals that are measurable.

The process of forging a vision begins when new possibilities are explored during the acquisition process. It becomes more fully delineated during the integration planning stage to become a vision that can be communicated the day your new company comes into existence. The process is carried still further as your integration team gets a better grasp of what is possible for your new company. When you select the leaders of your new company, senior management takes that vision to the next stage with the involvement of every member of the company.

The new leadership team generates a working draft of the company vision, as well as the major strategic thrusts related to that vision and a core set of objectives that flow from those strategies. This draft version of the vision will have the major elements of what your new company aims to achieve. The leadership group can then refine its strategic package over the ensuing months, involving employees and getting feedback from different levels of the company as well as from external stakeholders. It is key that the leadership initiate the process, recognizing that the vision will evolve over time with broader organizational participation.

Fashioning a vision is a challenge for leaders, which again can be a mindset issue. According to Mark Lipton, who has worked extensively in this area, CEOs and executive groups have a difficult time stretching their thinking into the future:

> They are very "grounded," realistic people. They are drawn toward missions, which describe what an organization does now, rather than vision, which describes why an organization engages in these kinds of activities. Visions, therefore, must describe the long-term future of the organization—a future that is typically not quite attainable, but not so fantastic as to seem like a ridiculous pipedream.
>
> The vision development process is therefore a balancing act. It requires imagination, a mental capacity for synthesis, and a trust for intuition.
>
> Visions need to challenge people, evoke a feeling that draws people toward wanting to be a part of something quite special.

When a vision is framed as something that is achievable within a set number of years, then it falls into the terrain of a strategic plan. [A challenging vision will] reach out to the future and serve as a beacon for corporate direction . . . we are now also quite clear that strategic plans have a much higher probability of not being achieved if there is no over-arching vision informing them."[7]

A stumbling block for the development of visions is that strong leaders tend to create visions that are within their comfort zones, not stretch visions. Although the vision may begin with the senior leadership team, when it is cascaded through the company for comment and input, it becomes more of an open statement that more broadly reflects wider and deeper inputs. Ideally, the vision will be owned by everyone in the company.

A vision is a living entity. It is always out there in front of the company, pointing to greater achievements. As the company moves forward, the vision is enriched, amplified, and perhaps even morphed in light of changing aspirations and conditions. On the other hand, the organizational values from which the vision stems are the nonnegotiable ground on which the vision stands.

Being a customer-focused, values-based company is an aspiration that can be incorporated into the vision. Establishing a collaborative, team-based environment could also be an important element of the vision. Companies are increasingly including their relationship to the communities in which they operate and to the environment in their vision as well. Each of these dimensions will affect the organizational strategy, how it is structured, and how it will operate.

In a sense, vision is quite simple. It answers basic questions for the company, such as the questions listed in Exhibit 10-2.

Exhibit 10-2
___

Questions to Help You Articulate Your Company's Vision

☐ What is our reason for being?

☐ How will we achieve that?

☐ What are the nonnegotiable values that support us from day to day and from year to year in pursuit of becoming more of what we are and in our strategies for getting there?

Build an Operating Model

Having built a shared commitment to values, vision, and strategy, along with an environment that is conducive to high-performing teams, an important challenge for the leadership team is to bring the operating model of your new integrated company to life. The operating model outlines how your new company can function to create value for your customers. Core elements are its guiding principles, decision-making processes, and accountabilities. Once your new company emerges from the integration of the two legacy companies, it is essential that you define clearly how this new company will work, make decisions, and allocate resources. As part of the integration "workout," the new operating model includes renegotiating relationships with suppliers and partners to determine the best working arrangements for reaching higher levels of performance and for creating greater value.

Your new company has the initial set of guiding principles that you developed during your integration planning stage and that you restated and expanded on during the integration implementation phase. These guiding principles serve as the "constitution" for your new company. Your new company's leadership team should reevaluate them, share them broadly for comment, and then finalize them. If the guiding principles are to be credible, they need to be coauthored, with inputs from all members of your leadership team and linked management teams. The guiding principles articulate the core of what your new company is about, guiding its shape and direction.

Your guiding principles inform your policies for decision making. For example, if your guiding principles say that the success of your company is based on "long-lasting relationships based on trust, collaboration, and mutual understanding," your company's decision-making processes must specifically reflect that, regardless of the type or scale of the decisions involved. The key is that the basis for decisions is grounded in and reflects the core principles.

Decision making is a multivariable process. It is both an art and a science. Decisions are made and validated on the basis of the foundation provided by the values, vision, and strategy. The validity of the multiplicity of decisions made at all levels of your company will rest to a large extent on the clarity of the framework that is in place. Without this framework, decisions will continue to be made on the basis of the ground rules from the legacy companies, which are no longer pertinent to the aspirations and the strategies of your new company. Even if a decision turns out not to be the best choice or even to be a bad one, if your company and its teams are resilient, you can make course corrections and apply new learning, with a sharper understanding of your new organizational framework. The cumulative effect of placing all company decisions in the context of an explicit framework allows your company to move along its development curve to higher levels of performance and renewal.

Beyond Capabilities: Synergies

Once your new company has eliminated redundant costs and other unnecessary baggage from the legacy companies, you can tackle your new growth possibilities more freely. Discovering your company's embedded "hidden" capabilities is a first step in preparing your company for breakthrough levels of performance.

As you identify the full array of your new capabilities, you can explore potential synergies arising from combining these capabilities in various ways. You can look at these new sets of capabilities as an unlimited spawning ground for new products, services, and relationships. Your new company can blend capabilities to find new and innovative ways of doing things and create new elements for its offerings to customers. In addition, you can even find new markets in which to compete.

Experimenting to Learn How to Operate in the New Company

All of these changes require a tolerance for experimentation. To learn how to leverage your company's new capabilities, all areas of your company need to be willing to experiment. This is especially important during the formation phase of your new company, when people are coming together for the first time, without necessarily having any experience with the new possibilities of the integrated company.

One way to gain that experience is to have access to "practice fields" to try out these new ways of working together to create additional value. Like someone who is trying to ride a horse for the first time, people need to learn how to get on, stay on, and work with the horse. As they do this, they start to be successful and to enjoy the ride. Sometimes they make mistakes, or the ride gets a little rough and they fall off the horse. When that happens, they need to be encouraged to get back on right away and ride again. Like learning to riding a horse, operating in a new structure may be considerably different from the way business was done at their old companies. People need chances for trial and error to gauge what they are now able to do in your new company. Your new values and norms must be tried out in many ways and in many and varied conditions. Engaging people from all levels and areas in values, vision, and strategy-making reviews starts new thinking and can stimulate new actions.

Building Your New Culture

The cumulative experiences that experimental teams share feed into the building of your new company culture. The new culture is created both from the outside in and from the inside out. Your new company's strategies and structure shape employee expectations and are conducive to a certain range of thinking and practices. They are designed so that performance standards are built into the processes of your new company. At the same time, as employees carry out their experiments, they have new experiences and outcomes. These create positive and dynamic feedback within your company. The outcome is a new way of doing business that honors the values and vision, but renames them continually in light of continuous learning and action.

Simply growing by acquisition does not automatically generate a quantum leap, but going through a major acquisition is a high-powered opportunity to leverage the capabilities of two companies and their network partners and move upward along a quantum leap value creation path. The move to institutionalize the elements of the quantum leap differentiates those companies that are primarily able to be good at making effective acquisitions from those that are able to take the next steps to excel at integration and build a postintegration breakthrough company.

A Custodial Capability

As mentioned in Chapter 1, a major element involved in the building of your new company is institutionalizing a custodial capability for acquisitions and integrations. A quantum leap company will use any combination of organic and acquisition growth to reach and eventually surpass its strategic goals. For example, Dow and other companies have set up custodial centers to serve as a catalyst for capturing and leveraging the knowledge, experience, networks, and tools required to plan, implement, and integrate acquisitions, joint ventures, strategic alliances, and licensing.

A breakthrough company will operate such a resource center for know-how, maintaining and developing the perspectives, processes, and tools necessary for taking the initiatives from the predeal acquisition phase through the integration implementation phase and beyond. It supplies the "been there, done that" factor for business unit leaders and their teams who have not had significant experience with sizable acquisitions, and it acts as a link to senior management. Institutionalizing this type of capability establishes the kind of resources and commitment necessary to sustain a quantum leap company.

Such a center has to be a full partner with company leadership, able to propose courses of action as well as carry them out, not just a supporting staff function. It has to be involved from the very beginning of strategic considerations through the postintegration phases to ensure that all potential expense and growth synergies are adequately and consistently explored, prioritized, and implemented. Elevating the custodian's work to a strategic level makes the difference because it moves it from being a support function to being an action-based catalytic function. Its role matures to become one of seeing that all the elements of the quantum leap are in place and operating in every acquisition and integration project.

Exhibit 10-3 identifies major areas of expertise that the custodial resource has to make available to ensure successful integrations and postintegration success.

Exhibit 10-3

After-the-Deal Custodial Capabilities

These are the links in the postdeal success chain. More important than having these elements perfectly in place is having them under development as fully as possible. The quantum leap process is always a work in progress. Every company will have varying strengths of its capabilities at different points and in different areas. Some capabilities will have greater strength and others will be considerably less well developed. What every company does need, however, is to begin the process of capability development, have a framework that encompasses the major elements necessary for success, and start to gain action-based experience that can be used to move the company further and further along an upward spiral of capability strength.

Bringing It Together

Establishing an organizational breakthrough capability requires a substantial investment of time and energy by everyone from the leadership to the front line, as well as across company boundaries, but the returns are more than worth the effort. Breakthrough requires imagination and the ability to think strategically, communicate effectively, engage everyone involved, and execute well. There is nothing magical about it. A variety of companies have carried out many of the elements of breakthrough. The point is to work to develop all the elements of breakthrough systematically, from the time you first conceive the idea of the acquisition through integration and into building your new company.

There is no place or time to stop and be self-congratulatory. Even if you achieve major gains by consolidating and realizing expense synergies, your company must go to the next step: finding and leveraging potential capabilities in both of the legacy companies, as well as in your supplier network and among your customers. Because our world is characterized by rapid change and shifting boundaries, the strategic capabilities must be examined, thought through, and reconfigured to keep the new company at the cutting edge of innovation in its offerings to new and potential customers and how it will deliver them.

A major acquisition is an opportunity to reexamine and recalibrate your overall company to position it for a future of continuous renewal. When this is done well, it brings to bear all the resources of the companies involved and gives them a reality test that is unequaled in any other situation. Feedback is quick and reveals where the strengths and flaws are. When conflicts and structural weaknesses are not dealt with, they will cause a drag effect from Day One. The main capabilities for achieving breakthrough are rooted in systematic and long-term practice. They consist of an active orientation, the ability to cope with risk, a growing set of skills, the capability to develop structure, an institutionalization of learning and knowledge, and a hunger for creating the best company that can be. When those elements are present, an acquisition is an opportunity that provides the potential for growth and high levels of performance that are without limit.

Success Factors

- Carry out capabilities audits regularly.
- Systematically frame and support productive conversations.
- Actively bridge cultures and build trust.
- Implement an enterprise breakthrough model.
- Take the time to plan for aligning values, creating a vision, and engaging in strategy making.
- Cascade your values, vision, and strategies throughout the company for input from and engagement of your workforce.
- Deploy a network of high-performance teams to attack organizational issues and execute organizational breakthrough strategies.
- Set up a framework for accountabilities, both internally in your company and externally with your suppliers and partners.
- Institute a custodial capability group to serve as a resource, guide, and repository for the knowledge, experience, and tools that will enable facilitating the full range of combinations: strategic alliances, joint ventures, acquisitions, and mergers.

Derailing Factors

- Assuming that estimates of capabilities by themselves are adequate
- Believing that all trust and relationship issues will be overcome by a good operational plan

- Using past management models without modifying them for current challenges and conditions
- Thinking that your leadership team will get to new strategies, vision, and values after the tumult of getting the company off the ground has subsided
- Enacting the new values, vision, and strategies unilaterally
- Assigning ad hoc groups to deal with the various organizational issues and goals
- Assuming that everyone inside and outside your company will automatically fulfill accountability requirements
- Relating to each acquisition or combination activity as a separate and unique undertaking

Questions

- How are we working through the issues involved in consolidating the two legacy companies and repositioning our new company in the following areas?
  - How are we gathering the loose ends?
  - How are we tightening up our vision?
  - How are we optimizing our expense and capabilities synergies?
  - How are we reinforcing the culture of our new company so as to integrate the culture of the new entity based on the two legacy cultures?
- How are we building the capability to integrate other companies that we might combine with in the future?
- Have we made a purposeful effort to capture knowledge and build an integration implementation capability while this project was unfolding?

Notes

1. Kim Hart, "Sprint Nextel a Divided Company: Separate Cultures Causing Tensions among Employees,"*Washington Post*, November 25, 2007, p. D01.
2. Ibid.
3. Sharon Walsh, "Do You, Time Warner, Take AOL to Be Your— Company Business and Marketing," *Industry Standard*, October 30, 2000; http://findarticles.com/p/articles/mi_m0HWW/is_44_3/ai_66678887/pg_4.
4. Tim Weber, "Analysis, AOL Tough Challenges," *BBC Online News*, business, January 30, 2003; http://news.bbc.co.uk/2/hi/business/2708965.stm.
5. The survey was offered by www.emotionmining.com.
6. Margaret Lagace, HBS Working Knowledge, February 24, 2003; hbswk.hbs.edu/archive/3342.htmp, p. 1.
7. Ibid., p. 3.

The additional material in this chapter comes from the authors' interviews and experiences.

Epilogue

The Evolution of the Role of Acquisitions

The thinking surrounding acquisitions has been dominated for a long time by financial strategy. It has now become apparent to many people that making successful acquisitions will require a substantial change in the manner in which these acquisitions are undertaken, planned, and realized. A company's need to develop and renew its capabilities will be at the heart of this new perspective. This perspective has gained currency in the last decade, but a great deal needs to be done to realize the promise that it holds. To gain the full value from this perspective, we will need to continue actively experimenting.

Eventually, all organizations reach their limits, even if they are quantum leap organizations. Any particular competitive edge is susceptible to erosion. It is only a matter of time before the next generation of revolutionary technologies or business models will come into play. However, in this world of rapid and exponential change, it will be those organizations that are cultivating their readiness and recasting their generative capabilities that will have the best chance of surmounting these challenges.

A powerful acquisition and integration capability gives an organization the foundation for going to its next level of possibilities. It enables a quantum leap organization to go beyond the possibilities of organic growth by taking advantage of the opportunities for strategically acquiring other organizations and then imaginatively integrating their hidden wealth into the new organization that emerges from the integration implementation process. Organizations will need the capabilities to excel at organic growth and, if they have these capabilities, will be able to complement this work with selective, strategic acquisitions that can be integrated to boost their growth. If an organization does not have the inherent capabilities to realize organic growth, it is unlikely that it will be successful at using an acquisition to bring about a sustainable quantum leap in its level of performance.

There is little doubt that major acquisitions will grow in significance over the next decades. A vast arena for acquisitions is emerging in the increasingly globalized economy. The lowering of legal barriers to cross-border acquisitions all around the world, the development of massive enterprises in China and India, extensive capital accumulations in oil-producing countries, and changes in the valuations of currencies are some key factors creating an unprecedented potential for large-scale acquisitions. Chinese and Indian firms have begun to acquire major stakes in North American and European companies. Major infusions of capital into American companies from the oil-producing states in the Persian Gulf are the start of what is coming to be a much more open acquisition environment. The fluctuating values of the dollar, yen, yuan, rupee, and euro make different acquisitions affordable at different times. These trends will only increase in size and scope. The result is that major acquisitions will continue to play a significant part in capital realignments that would not have been conceivable even a decade ago.

A related dimension is that capabilities and intangible assets have also become global and are often a combination of systems, technologies, and people. For example, IBM developed what it calls the Professional Marketplace, a database that lists the capabilities of 170,000 employees around the world (already, close to one-third of IBM's workforce is based in India). That database is continually updated by employees and their managers as employees gain skills and experience. Project managers use the information on skills, pay rates, and availability to rapidly assemble teams with the right capabilities at the least cost component; this has already saved IBM $500 million. "By sifting through several personnel databases with sophisticated software, IBM's top managers can quantify the skills they have on hand worldwide and compare them with projections of what people they'll need in six to nine months. When they spot a coming shortfall, managers coordinate with colleagues in other countries to recruit or train people. In one case, IBM managers in Phoenix wanted to build a team in Brazil to test software for a large U.S. corporate client. After they put a request on Professional Marketplace, a manager in Brazil assembled a team in a week."[1] This is the kind of sophisticated capability that organizations have to be ready and able to value in a potential acquisition.

This development brings us back to the core themes of this book: readiness and generative value creation. *Readiness* involves cultivating a core group of capabilities. *Generative value creation* comes from identifying the expense synergies and growth synergies of both organizations, and linking the capture of expense synergies with the leveraging of growth synergies to produce unprecedented gains in performance and value creation.

The success of large-scale acquisitions and other combinations is not solely linked to project management skills, as important as they are. These skills are essential but not sufficient for acquisition and ultimately integration success. What will drive success is the kind of leadership that shapes and guides an operating context. It sets the direction and tone for the organization through its work in shaping the vision, values, and strategies for the new entity that emerges from the integration. It is the leadership's role to see that the organization is developing the capability to create opportunities for acquisitions and other growth combinations and to take advantage of those that are brought to the organization. To do this, the leaders' strategic vision has to be shared by everyone who is involved with the organization in its supporting or partnering network. This type of leadership cannot be passively delegated or assumed to exist at other layers or in other areas of a company. However, it can be cultivated and manifested at all levels of the organization. This is of great importance, because every level of an organization is involved in a major acquisition, and each level has to take a leadership role in its area of responsibility.

If the leadership does not keep its organization nimble and responsive as it goes through acquisitions and integrations, the organization is likely to grow in *size* more than in capability, value, and profitability. It is important to note that in some cases, even companies with the best integration capabilities have made only marginal gains in financial and general performance when growth synergies have not been fully pursued. The challenge that must be overcome is to integrate acquisitions in a manner that will continually renew the organization and its capability to perform and grow in a fast-changing business context.

Just as a set of springboards is key to the success of integrations, integrations have to be seen as springboards for the new organization. With this approach, the setting of stretch goals calls for a rethinking of every aspect of how the organization sees its goals and how it operates.

For example, in the case of SAIC, a new CEO set a stretch goal of doubling the company's revenue in a three-year period. To achieve this goal, business unit leaders had to reconsider everything they knew. Standard operating procedures would no longer work. The leaders had to look into options that they had never seriously considered, including an aggressive acquisition model. They had to see new possibilities, learn new skills, work with people inside and outside the organization in new ways, and achieve tangible success. At the corporate level, an infrastructure was created to engage with them to develop the acquisition capabilities to accomplish that audacious goal. In this way, an acquisition/integration approach became an outgrowth of the overall strategy and, at the same time, created the opportunity for the organization to renew itself.

Going "beyond the deal" means making an ongoing series of choices on how to approach and carry out acquisitions and integrations. The first is to look at the organization's business strategy and determine whether pursuing acquisitions is the best choice for growing the organization. If it is, then the organization has to create a structure and set of processes for going through all the predeal stages that culminate in the acquisition. The predeal work is the preparation for the emergence of the new organization. The postdeal stages bring the acquired organization and its hidden wealth into the new organization.

This book provides a strategic framework for taking acquisitions beyond the deal into an effective integration that is geared to bring the new entity to a breakthrough level of performance that could not be achieved with the two organizations as standalone entities. To a large extent, this book is an invitation to others to get engaged in this worthwhile conversation. Organizations will continue to merge, with significant implications for the human beings who build them. Our dedication to this inquiry stems from the belief that we collectively carry the responsibility of ensuring that the legacy of all those who have contributed to building these organization not only is respected but becomes the foundation for a renewal leading to the evolution of better, more fulfilling organizations. This challenge will require leadership conviction and strength to an extent that has rarely been tested in a context of organic growth. This once again confirms the need for high-integrity, visionary leadership as an essential element for sustaining organizational performance and success over time.

Notes

1. Steve Hamm, "International Isn't Just IBM's First Name," *BusinessWeek*, http://www.businessweek.com/magazine/content/ 08_04/b4068036075566_page_2.htm

Appendix A

Is Acquisition Always the Answer?

The acquisition option is often the answer to a company's strategic requirements, but not always. There is a range of combination options that a company can use to achieve its strategic goals, each with its own benefits and limitations:

- Licensing
- Strategic alliances or partnerships
- Joint ventures
- Mergers and acquisitions

Each option can be the best fit for a specific purpose and be part of an overall combination strategy. Having the full range of options available enables a company to evaluate the alternatives and pursue the best course of action to achieve its goals. When deciding which option is best for your company, you need to evaluate and balance the costs, the level of effort required to carry out the option, and the degree of management that will be necessary against what you think you will achieve. You might even consider this as a mathematical equation:

Moving from Simpler to Greater Degrees of Complexity and Higher Levels of Effort
Licensing > Strategic Alliances > Joint Ventures > Mergers/Acquisitions

Here's a brief definition and comparison of each option:

Licensing. This is the simplest way of obtaining a product, service, or trademark. It may be appropriate when a company has very clearly defined requirements and a limited need to have control over what is licensed and how it can be exploited.

Strategic alliances or partnerships. These are cooperative efforts in which two or more companies agree to pursue common activities and interests for specific strategic advantages. On the positive side, strategic alliances are flexible arrangements that may appear to be relatively more easily arranged and do not require as great an investment of financial capital as an acquisition would. There can even be partnerships in which companies collaborate in certain areas but compete in others. Strategic alliances are also advantageous in countries where there are restrictions on acquisition activity or where the risk of ownership is too high. On the other hand, managing strategic alliances and allocating the resulting gains may be difficult.

Joint ventures. These are a more structured option because each company remains a separate, formal organization with its own policies, rules of governance, and methods of operation. Although a joint venture is typically comprehensive and rigorous, each company may still face the challenge of maintaining its desired levels of control and alignment and of allocating specific outcomes on an ongoing basis.

Mergers and acquisitions. These require the most investment and effort, as they involve targeting, planning, and integrating another company; however, complete ownership provides the greatest opportunities for recombining and realigning resources to accomplish quantum leap gains. For the most part, the capital costs are significantly higher, but the ability to generate substantial rewards can also be higher.

Appendix B

Beyond the Deal
Question Set

The following is a compilation of questions that explore a set of issues that need to be worked through to achieve quantum leap (M&A) goals. The answers to these questions that you develop will contribute to your understanding of how you can best proceed through the phases of an M&A, from predeal acquisition and beyond the deal to integration implementation and breakthrough.

Think of this question set as a practice field for assessing your readiness and as a set of capabilities for taking on such a major challenge. Use these questions as a starting point for a conversation on how to prepare to use the M&A and integration as a quantum leap springboard for taking your organization to sustainable breakthrough performance and value creation.

Getting Started

- What do we think the key issues will be that we will face in an acquisition and integration?
- How open is our company to systematically looking into growth option synergies as well as expense synergies?
- What unprecedented gains could our company achieve through a major acquisition as far as performance and value creation are concerned?
- What could block us from achieving those gains?
- What could enable us to achieve those gains?

Lessons Learned from Previous Mergers and Acquisitions

- Are there any stories from the merger (or mergers) we have been involved in that especially evoke the achievements and problems we encountered?
- What were the key issues we experienced during *previous* M&A and integration processes?
- What are the key issues we need to address in *future* M&A and integration processes?
- What lessons have we learned from previous M&A processes?
  - Have we incorporated those lessons into the way our company approaches mergers and acquisitions?
  - Looking back, would we have done things any differently to make more of a quantum leap in performance enabled by the M&A?

The Link between Acquisitions and the Strategic Intent of the Organization

- How does our approach to M&As relate to the way our company is carrying out our strategic intent and enhancing our company's strategic position?

- To what extent have the M&As our company has previously undertaken been driven by our company's business strategy— i.e., pertaining to our customers, the products or solutions our company offers, and the organization required to deliver on these dimensions?
- What key motivations, strategic factors, or circumstances have prompted our M&A initiatives over the past 5 to 10 years?
- To what extent have our company's acquisitions realized the strategic intent that drove those acquisitions in the first place?
  - To what extent has each acquisition enhanced our company's strategic positioning in the marketplace?
  - Do we believe that each acquisition has accelerated or retarded the evolution of our company toward the realization of our strategic goals?
- How are we managing the three basic types of risk in an acquisition and integration?
- How do we take into account the possibility that we may not anticipate particular problems that can arise during the course of the acquisition and integration?
- How are our leaders meeting the challenge of keeping their mindset open and flexible?
- How are we preparing to develop a partnering relationship between the two legacy companies?

The Goals of the M&A(s)

- What were the goals of our M&As?
  - To what extent were those goals met?
  - How did we measure success?
  - What financial synergies did our company achieve?
  - What growth synergies did our company achieve?
- Were our company's acquisitions driven by the need to create greater value for our customers? Or were other concerns more of a factor?

- What roles did the different drivers play when our company decided to initiate an acquisition and when our company planned and implemented the M&A process?
- How does our company approach mergers and acquisitions?
  - Why does our company choose to pursue M&As, rather than strategic alliances, licensing, or other relationships?
  - How do we select potential target companies?
  - How did our leadership guide these decisions?
- When acquiring another company, what emphasis does our company place on intangible assets?
  - How have we taken into account the value of a target company's intangible assets (i.e., its structural capital, human capital, and customer capital)?
- Does our company have a knowledge strategy? If so, how does it relate to how we carry out our M&As?

The Preacquisition Phase

- How did we prepare our company for the M&A?
- How did we initiate the M&A?
  - How did we approach our target company?
  - Who was involved, and in what ways?
  - What was the response from the target company?
- Were we able to balance our due diligence investigations holistically between financial assets, tangible assets, and intangible assets?
  - How did this work and what was the outcome?
- How did we organize our due diligence process?
  - Who was involved?
  - What did our teams focus on?
  - What areas did they cover?
  - How did they communicate what they learned?
  - How was that new knowledge communicated to the leadership of the due diligence effort?

- Did we engage in any knowledge, culture, or human capital audits during the due diligence phase?

The Negotiation/Acquisition Phase

- How did we incorporate what we learned during due diligence into the negotiation phase?
  - Who was involved in the negotiations?
  - How well did the negotiations go?
  - Were there any surprises?
- Were any mistakes made in the context of the negotiations that had an impact on the performance of the integration?
- How could we have avoided these problems or issues?

The Integration Phase—Developing the Integration Plan

- Can we use our past experience and templates to build an integration playbook?
- What was the importance given to speed in the context of our most recent integration?
  - If it was seen as important, what steps did we take to accelerate the pace of the integration?
  - How did we work to have the change take place rapidly and expeditiously?
- Who was involved in the development and implementation of the business plan?
  - During the preselection phase?
  - During the due diligence phase?
  - During the integration phase?
- What areas did our business plan cover?
  - How did our business plan change over the course of the M&A process?
- How did we involve managers and others from the M&A target company during the due diligence and integration phases?

- How much importance did we place on building trust and partnering with the acquired company?
- How successful were those efforts?
- What could we have done better in this regard?
- How broadly and deeply did integration activities reach into the two companies?

Getting the Integration Structure Right

- What are the key factors involved in the way we are designing the framework for the integration?
- How are we determining what the lines of accountability are, and how do we plan on adjusting them to take into account the changing conditions and goals as we go through the integration?
- What set of metrics will supply us with the information we need to evaluate the success of the integration? Who will be responsible for those metrics, and how are we planning for the outcomes of those metrics to be shared and used to modify the practices of the integration appropriately?
- How will we plan to ensure that the continuity of core businesses is maintained during the integration phase?
- What are the key implementation drivers to acknowledge in our implementation plan?

The Integration Phase: Activating Key Springboards

- How are we implementing the six springboards during the integration stage?

  1. How are we implementing a springboard for our customer strategy and brand?
  2. How are we implementing a springboard for our company strategy?

3. How are we implementing a springboard for the integration of company culture and leadership principles?
4. How are we implementing a springboard to integrate our knowledge insights and business principles?
5. How are we implementing a springboard for our people strategy?
6. How are we implementing a springboard for our information technology and systems decisions?

- Which springboards are the most significant for achieving our strategic goals?
- How do we adjust our customer strategy to take into account the new capabilities that are now available after the acquisition?
  - How do we redefine our portfolio of brands, customer sets, products and/or services, and distribution channels during the integration implementation?
  - What new markets are we now able to penetrate after the acquisition?
  - Does our customer strategy lead to changes in our company structure? If so, what changes are we making, for what goals, and with what effect?
- How are we reorganizing our company structure to support being able to achieve our overall strategic goals?
- What is our process for realigning corporate values and culture in the integration implementation phase?
  - What is the role of leadership in this process?
  - What cultural realignment issues are we facing, and how are we responding to them?
- Are there any significant differences in business logic between the two combining companies?
  - If so, how are we approaching aligning the two business logics?
  - How are we resolving these differences?
  - Are there any remaining business logic issues that we need to reconcile?

- How are we ensuring that we have a people strategy that will select the best people from across both companies for roles in our newly combined company?
  - What is our plan for retaining the people we sought for roles in the new company?
  - How do we make sure that our process for candidate selection is comprehensive and unbiased?
  - Do we feel that we need to recruit key leadership and management from outside the company? If so, how do we structure our units so that these people can succeed?
- What evaluation of both companies' technology platforms is being done to determine which (or which elements of each) best supports the strategic goals of our newly combined company?
  - How open is this evaluation process?
  - Is a final selection being made, or is there an interim selection that allows further investigation beyond the integration implementation period?

Organizing for the Integration: Guiding Your Integration to Success

- How are we focusing on the primacy of the customer?
- How can we create a strong and flexible business plan?
- How are we incorporating speed in the integration implementation process?
- How are we embedding partnering into our approach to integration?
- What is our process for setting:
  - Clear accountabilities?
  - Time, cost, and performance targets?
- How are we selecting the leaders for our new integrated company?
- To what extent are we taking the leaders of the acquired company into account during our selection process?

- How are we assessing those leaders?
- How formal a process is this?
- Does our leadership selection process play a role in the outcomes of the integration?
- How are we addressing the following issues during the integration phase?
    - How are we managing employee expectations and reactions?
    - How are we managing change?

Building the Foundations for a Quantum Leap

- How are we transferring capabilities from the two legacy companies to the newly emerging company?
- How are we assessing our progress?
- How much are we emphasizing communication following our announcement of the acquisition?
    - To what extent have we sustained communication during the integration implementation phase?
    - Have we formulated an explicit communication strategy to reach our staff, the target company's staff, and other stakeholders?
    - Did we concentrate this strategy at the front end of the integration implementation (e.g., the first couple of months), or did we sustain it throughout our integration implementation effort?
    - To what extent does our communication strategy play a role in the results of our integration implementation?
    - Should we place more importance on communication than we have been doing?
- Have we put in place an interim company structure for the integration implementation phase?
    - If not, should we have one?
    - Do we have a multistage company plan?
    - To what extent have we communicated this plan?

- Have we brought a project management capability into the integration implementation phase?
  - If so, what form is it taking?
- What are the key people management issues that we are encountering?
  - How are we dealing with them?

Moving to Breakthrough

- How are we working through the issues involved in consolidating the two legacy companies and repositioning our new company in the following areas?
  - How are we gathering the loose ends?
  - How are we tightening up our vision?
  - How are we optimizing our expense and capabilities synergies?
  - How are we reinforcing the culture of our new company so as to integrate the culture of the new entity based on the two legacy cultures?
- How are we building the capability to integrate other companies that we might combine with in the future?
- Have we made a purposeful effort to capture knowledge and build an integration implementation capability while this project was unfolding?

Partnering Questions from the Viewpoint of the Acquirer and Acquiree

- If you are from the *acquiring company* of the M&A:
  - What do you think of how the acquiree is being treated?
  - Do you think the value of the various elements of the newly acquired organization is being taken into account, especially the intangible resources that it brings?
  - Do you approach the acquirees in a way that allows them to bring forward their views?

- • Do you consult with them during the integration process?
  - • To what extent do you believe that an element of trust is developed with them?
- • If you are from the *acquiree company* of the M&A:
  - • How are the members of the acquired organization being treated?
  - • To what extent do you think the acquirer is leveraging all of the intangible assets, including the brand and other such elements from your organization?
  - • To what extent do you believe the acquirer is destroying intangible assets?
  - • Is the acquiring company making a thorough, comprehensive, and open effort in the selection of people for roles in the new organization?
  - • Is the acquiring company partnering with you sufficiently to understand how to get the greatest yield from the acquired organization?

Appendix C

Auditing Strategic Capabilities in the Context of the Deal Exercise

This is a strategic capabilities audit process that each of the organizations in a merger or acquisition can undertake to identify what capabilities are present in each organization. The acquisition and integration teams can use this audit to determine similarities and differences in capabilities. Those capabilities are the basis for complementarities that can come together in the new combination and act as the drivers enabling the new organization to achieve its strategic intent.

Both the acquiring and the acquired organizations need to *determine how capabilities are accessed, shared, and used, and with what effect, and also note who is involved in activating and mobilizing these capabilities.*

1. Senior leadership lists the top three to five core organizational capabilities that enable the organization to meet its strategic goals and differentiate it from its competition.
2. Each business unit manager and his or her subunit managers list the top three to five core capabilities that enable that unit

to meet its strategic goals and differentiate it from its competition.

3. Senior leadership and the business unit managers and submanagers from both organizations compare the two sets of capabilities and discuss how they can be accessed and leveraged, and who would be involved in creating greater value and higher performance in the new organization.

4. Chart out a list of projects that the new organization can undertake to mobilize these capabilities for specific outcomes, noting the investment of time, people, and funds required to achieve these outcomes.

5. Evaluate the potential costs and gains from the work of leveraging these capabilities.

Two additional steps in this exercise are:

1. Map out the value creation path for the organization and each of its business and subbusiness units, and determine what capabilities are used to create new value at each major point on that path. Again, the leaders and managers from both the acquiring and the acquired company would then compare what those capabilities are, how they can be shared and leveraged for specific effect, and with what investment costs.

2. Compare the sets of capabilities found in each of the exercises with the capabilities of key competitors. Carry out a gap analysis to determine where the new organization has advantages and where it has gaps. Develop a plan to build the specific configurations necessary to achieve strategic goals and create a sustainable competitive advantage over the competitors.

Bibliography

Book Citations and References

Badaracco, Joseph Jr. *The Knowledge Link: How Firms Compete Through Strategic Alliances*. Boston: Harvard Business School Press, 1991.

Chatzkel, Jay. *Intellectual Capital*. Oxford: Capstone Publishing, 2002.

_____. *Knowledge Capital: How Knowledge-Based Enterprises Really Get Built*. New York: Oxford University Press, 2003.

Clemente, Mark N., and David S. Greenspan. *Winning at Mergers and Acquisitions: The Guide to Market-Focused Planning and Integration*. New York: Wiley, 1998.

Collins, James C., and Jerry I. Porras. *Built to Last: Successful Habits of Visionary Companies*. New York, HarperCollins, 1994.

Collins, Jim. *Good to Great: Why Some Companies Make the Leap and Others Don't*. New York: HarperCollins, 2001.

Davenport, Thomas O. *Human Capital: What It Is and Why People Invest It*. San Francisco: Jossey-Bass, 1999.

Devine, Marion. *Successful Mergers: Getting the People Issues Right.* London: Profile Books, 2002.

Galbraith, Jay R. *Designing Organizations: An Executive Guide to Strategy, Structure and Process*, 2nd ed. San Francisco: Jossey-Bass, 2001

_____. *Designing the Customer-Centric Organization: A Guide to Strategy, Structure, and Process.* San Francisco: Jossey-Bass, 2005.

Galpin, Timothy J., and Mark Herndon. *The Complete Guide to Mergers and Acquisitions: Process Tools to Support M&A Integration at Every Level*, 2nd ed. San Francisco: Jossey-Bass, 2007.

Giles, Lionel, trans. "Attack by Stratagem," *Sun Tsu on the Art of War*, chap. 3. Project Gutenberg, 1910; http://www.kimsoft.com/polwar.htm.

Harding, David, and Sam Rovit. *Mastering the Merger: Four Critical Decisions That Make or Break the Deal.* Boston: Harvard Business School Press, 2004.

Haspeslagh, Philippe C., and David B. Jemison. *Managing Acquisitions: Creating Value through Corporate Renewal.* New York: Free Press, 1991.

Katzenbach, Jon R., and Douglas K. Smith. *The Wisdom of Teams: Creating the High Performance Organization.* New York: Harper Business, 1993.

Leonard, Dorothy, and Walter Swap. *Deep Smarts: How to Cultivate and Transfer Enduring Business Wisdom.* Boston: Harvard Business School Press, 2005.

Lipton, Mark. *Guiding Growth: How Vision Keeps Companies on Course.* Boston: Harvard Business School Press, 2003.

Marks, Mitchell Lee, and Phillip H. Mirvis. *Joining Forces: Making One Plus One Equal Three in Mergers, Acquisitions and Alliances.* San Francisco: Jossey-Bass, 1998.

Paulson, Ed. *Inside Cisco: The Real Story of Sustained M&A Growth.* New York: John Wiley & Sons, 2001.

Saint-Onge, Hubert, and Charles Armstrong. *The Conductive Organization: Building beyond Sustainability.* Burlington, MA: Elsevier Butterworth Heinemann, 2004.

Schmidt, Jeffrey A., ed. *Making Mergers Work: The Strategic Importance of People*. Alexandria, VA: SHRM, 2002.

Schwieger, David M. *M&A Integration: A Framework for Executives and Managers*. New York: McGraw-Hill, 2002.

Slywotsky, Adrian J. *The Upside: The 7 Strategies for Turning Big Threats into Growth Breakthroughs*. New York: Crown Publishing, 2007.

Tichy, Noel M., and Warren G. Bennis. *Judgment: How Winning Leaders Make Great Calls*. New York, Penguin Group, 2007.

Zook, Chris. *Unstoppable: Finding Hidden Assets to Renew the Core and Fuel Profitable Growth*. Boston: Harvard Business School Press, 2007.

Internet and Article Citations

Anders, George. "7 Lessons from WaMu's Playbook." *Fast Company*, no. 54 (January 2002), p. 102; http://www.fastcompany.com/magazine/54/chalktalk.html?page=0%2C0.

Ante, Spencer E. "Sprint's Wake-Up Call." *BusinessWeek*, February 21, 2008; http://www.businessweek.com/magazine/content/08_09/b4073054448185.htm?chan=search.

"AOL Time Warner: A Merger Gone Wrong." ICMR; http://www.icmrindia.org/casestudies/catalogue/Business%20Strategy1/AOL%20Time%20Warner%20Merger%20Gone%20Wrong.htm.

BBC News, January 30, 2003; http://news.bbc.co.uk/2/hi/business/2708965.stm.

Beusch, Peter. "A Tentative Model for Management Accounting and Control in the Integration Processes of Mergers and Acquisitions," p. 2; http://www.handels.gu.se/epc/archive/00004170/01/Antwerp,_Belgium_(2005).pdf.

Brembo Web site, April 4, 2006; http://www.brembo.com/ENG/About Brembo/CompanyOverview/CorporateGovernance/Corporate+Governance2Eng.htm.

CNNMoney.com, July 3, 2001; http://money.cnn.com/2001/07/03/europe/ge_eu/.

EmotionMining.com.

Fabrikant, Geraldine, and John Schwartz, "Changing the Guard: The C.E.O., Once Again, on His Terms." *New York Times*, December 6, 2001.

Fisher, Lawrence M. "How Elan Grew by Staying Small: Growing a Business with Shrewd Acquisitions," *Strategy+Business*; http://www.strategy-business.com/press/16635507/19343.

_____. "Symantec's Strategy-Based Transformation." *Strategy+Business*; http://www.strategy-business.com/press/16635507/8424.

Gilbertson, Dawn. "US Airways Names Airline Veteran to Tackle Customer Service Woes." *Arizona Republic*; http://www.usatoday.com/travel/flights/2007-09-07-usairways-new-coo_N.htm.

Girard, John. "Words of Wisdom, an Interview with Melinda Bickerstaff." *KMPro Journal*, www.kmpro.org/journal/KMPro_Vol_3_No1.pdf.

Harding, David, and Sam Rovit. "Writing a Credible Investment Thesis." *Harvard Business School Working Knowledge for Business Leaders*, November 15, 2004; http://hbswk.hbs.edu/archive/4485.html.

Hart, Kim. "Sprint Nextel a Divided Company: Separate Cultures Causing Tensions among Employees." *Washington Post*, November 25, 2007, p. D01.

Hays, Constance L. "J.C. Penney Sells Drugstore Chain for $4.5 Billion." *New York Times*, April 6, 2004; http://query.nytimes.com/gst/fullpage.html?res=9B0DE6D81F39F935A35757C0A9629C8B63.

Heffes, Ellen M., and Phil Livingston. "Reflecting on a Mega Merger." *Financial Executives International*, 2002; FEI Web site: http://www.fei.org/magazine/articles/6-2001_shedlarzInterview.cfm.

"HP's Compaq Acquisition (C) | Business Strategy Case Studies," ICMR; http://www.icmrindia.org/casestudies/catalogue/Business%20Strategy3/BSTA022.htm.

"HP: Merger Could Net $3B in Savings," PC MAG.com, June 4, 2002;

http://consumerist.com/consumer/complaints/boa-buys-mbna-starts-charging-customers-extra-for-not-paying-balances-off-in-full-251283.php.

http://www.consumeraffairs.com/news04/2005/mbnbofa.html.

"International Isn't Just IBM's First Name." *BusinessWeek*, January 17, 2008; http://www.businessweek.com/magazine/content/08_04/b4068036075566_page_2.htm.

Kanter, Larry. "Wells Fargo Works to Reassure, Retain First Interstate Customers—Wells Fargo and Co.; First Interstate Bancorp—Special Report: Banking & Finance." *Los Angeles Business Journal*, May 27, 1996; http://findarticles.com/p/articles/mi_m5072/is_n22_v18/ai_18690455.

Knowledge@Emory. "Lessons from the GE-Honeywell Non-Merger." July 4, 2001; http://knowledge.emory.edu/article.cfm?articleid=366#.

Legace, Margaret. HBS Working Knowledge, February 24, 2003; hbswk.hbs.edu/archive/3342.htmp, p. 1.

O'Donnell, Anthony. "Clarica/SunLife Distribution Focus." *Insurance and Technology*, June 27, 2002; http://www.insurancetech.com/resources/fss/showArticle.jhtml?articleID=14705890.

Prahalad, C. K. "The Blinders of Dominant Logic." *Long Range Planning* 37, no. 2 (April 2004).

Skarzynski, Peter. "When Mega-Mergers Don't Make Sense." *Chief Executive*, June 1, 2000; http://findarticles.com/p/articles/mi_m4070/is_2000_June/ai_63841546/pg_4.

Sorkin, Andrew Ross. "A Rare Miscalculation for Jack Welch." *New York Times*, July 3, 2001; http://www.nytimes.com/2001/07/03/business/03WELC.html?ex=1207108800&en=fdf4dc5bf54d9024&ei=5070#top.

Spooner, John C. "HP Puts Evo Name Out to Pasture." CNet News.com, March 13, 2003; http://www.news.com/HP-puts-Evo-name-out-to-pasture/2100-1003_3-992518.html?tag=nw.7.

TaitSubler Web page; http://www.taitsubler.com/track-record/bestbuy-futureshop.php.

Walsh, Sharon. "Do You, Time Warner, Take AOL to Be Your—Company Business and Marketing." *Industry Standard*, October 30, 2000; http://findarticles.com/p/articles/mi_m0HWW/is_44_3/ai_66678887/pg_4.

Weber, Tim. "Analysis, AOL Tough Challenges." *BBC Online News,* business, January 30, 2003; http://news.bbc.co.uk/2/hi/business/2708965.stm.

Interviews

Ron Bowbridge, formerly director of Project Management Office for Mergers and Acquisitions for Alcatel, currently vice president for research and development for Copiprak, 2004.

Randy Croyle, director of the Dow Merger and Acquisition Technology Center, 2004.

Kent Greenes, formerly chief knowledge officer of Science Applications International Corporation (SAIC) and currently president of Greenes Consulting, and his colleagues Kevin E. (Ed) Murphy, senior vice president, director of mergers & acquisitions of SAIC, and Kevin Werner, formerly senior vice president of strategic initiatives of SAIC, 2004.

Anthony E. Kuhel, formerly core member of BP's Group Knowledge Management Team, program manager for the Olympus Initiative (the U.S. KM initiative), and BP's chief process engineer, and currently managing director of Escalys, 2004.

Mr. Dirk Ramhorst, vice president, Siemens Business Services, 2004.

Index

About the Authors

Hubert Saint-Onge is a leading practitioner of organization strategy, and creator of the Knowledge Assets Framework. He has spent over 25 years as an executive in the oil industry (at Shell) and in financial services (at CIBC and Clarica). He currently heads his own consulting firm, SAINTONGE/ Alliance. He can be contacted at Hubert@saintongealliance.com.

Jay Chatzkel is principal of Progressive Practices, where he assists organizations in transforming themselves into becoming knowledge-based enterprises. He serves on the editorial boards of several publications, including the *Journal of Knowledge Management*, and has written extensively in the field. He can be contacted at jaychatzkel@progressivepractices.com.

Beyond the Deal takes the point of view that a strong integration capability on the part of an acquiring company will determine its success with postmerger integration. Should you be interested in determining the strength of your organization's integration capability, you can access a Web questionnaire at www.saintongealliance.com/beyondthedeal.html that will help you assess the different aspects of this capability. Whether you want to answer the questionnaire yourself or you want to involve other members of your organization in this assessment, the questionnaire will point to areas where you can take action to enhance your company's level of readiness for an acquisition.

Explore how the approaches in *Beyond the Deal* can be specifically useful to you in addressing your merger and acquisition integration-related issues. Participate in the Beyond the Deal Forum at www.beyondthedeal.net, a continuing conversation on the core themes found in the *Beyond the Deal*.